UNDERWATER WORK

The author, wearing one of the famous "Big 99" salvage units. These 3,000 p.s.i. tanks are the world's largest self-contained single diving units. An Aqualung reserve valve and the Cousteau-Gagnan demand regulator complete the unit.

UNDERWATER WORK

A Manual of Scuba Commercial, Salvage
and Construction Operations

Second Edition Revised and Enlarged

By

JOHN E. CAYFORD
Master Scuba Diver

CORNELL MARITIME PRESS, INC.
Cambridge, Maryland

1966

Library of Congress Catalog Card Number: 66-28081
Manufactured in the United States of America

DEDICATION

To My Late Brother

GEORGE E. CAYFORD, SR.

For his early training
to which I owe everything

THE DIVER'S PRAYER

Almighty God, Our Heavenly Father, we, who descend into the depths of the seas, beseech Thee to protect and guide us in Your Aquatic Kingdom. We pray that Thee can find a worth in those who search the waters of the Seven Seas to increase the knowledge of man, to seek and understand the vast mysteries of our past as well as that abundant world which lives below the surface of the water, and to enjoy this new found world and all it has to offer.

As we small people work below, Dear God, watch over us and help us to return safely to our earth-world. But, Heavenly Father, should we perish in this watery-world, we beg that Thee will forgive our earthly sins, cleanse our hearts and souls, and lead us to Thy Celestial Kingdom to serve Thee forever and ever. Amen.

From *Skin Diver Magazine.*

CONTENTS

PREFACE

Since two Frenchmen, Captain Jacques Yves Cousteau and Emile Gagnan, invented the Aqua-Lung less than twenty-six years ago and supplied the key that opened the door to the vast world that lies below the waters, thousands of human beings have entered the blue kingdom for sport, adventure, business, or scientific research.

The breathing apparatus that provides the means of the journey—the Aqua-lung, or an equivalent manufactured by another firm—has the technical name, "self-contained underwater breathing apparatus," and this name is usually abbreviated to "Scuba."

Scuba diving has had an amazing development within the past twenty-one years, and already the literature on the subject is quite extensive, as will become apparent in the acknowledgments.

UNDERWATER WORK: A Manual of Scuba Commercial, Salvage and Construction Operations represents, in the author's judgment, a much needed addition to this literature. While there are a number of books on Scuba diving as a pastime and a sport, there have been none heretofore in the area that this book covers.

The primary purpose of this book is to show self-contained divers and prospective divers the many business opportunities open to those divers who would like to translate their specialized skill and knowledge into a part-time or full-time occupation. However, in the later chapters especially, a secondary purpose emerges—to call attention to the many phases of scientific research that may be pursued with both profit and pleasure by the Scuba diver who has a bent in this direction.

The Scuba diver who makes a business of photographing marine life or collecting specimens for biological laboratories cannot help but become increasingly interested in science and scientific research. If he is a young man still deciding on a career, he may be interested in studying marine science and one or more of its many related fields in a college or university. This and other reasons have prompted the inclusion of a chapter on the fields of scientific research. The science of oceanography is a fairly recent development with promise of rapid growth; already there is a lack of trained personnel to meet the demand.

However, American and world technologists during the past twelve years have been busy designing, building, testing and manufacturing various self-contained underwater breathing units to assist all classes of divers. These units have proven themselves through countless hours of faultless usage. American designed and maufactured Scuba, such as the Dacor, SCUBA, Voit, Sportsways, Hydro-Master, Aqua-Lung, Scubapro and Continental, offer research experts, marine geologists, marine biologists, salvors, constructioneers, blasters, torchers and sportsmen alike the finest in underwater breathing apparatus. American engineers continue their never-ending research and each year the public is offered safer, more durable diving equipment.

Finer equipment allows the wearer to penetrate deeper into the depths of the sea to study, observe, photograph and relate to the earth-world the secrets of life in the watery-world. For those men who have forsaken our earth-world to work in the blue kingdom, it is a comforting knowledge to them that other men are interested in their life's work and safety.

It has been a wonderful experience compiling this book. In doing the research to fill each page, the author has learned so much more about this great field of self-contained diving. If anyone were to ask if the task of compiling this book was a pleasant one, the answer would be yes, but the author would add, it required over 15,000 hours of research and fact-finding.

John E. Cayford, MSD.

ACKNOWLEDGMENTS

The pleasant aspect of all this work was the author's association with such great men in the diving field as Richard J. Bonin, Jr., Director, Pacific Moulded Products, Inc., (formerly with Divemaster-U.A.S. Corp., Chicago), who supplied technical data for Chapter II. Mr. Bonin's naval experience as a military diver and CO of U.D.T. Unit 22, U.S.N., has proved very valuable, not only in this particular area of the diving field but also to the education of Scuba divers the world over. Bill Barada, of Bel-Aqua Water Sports Co., and good buddy, Jim Auxier, Editor, *Skin Diver Magazine,* the best in underwater reading, added their knowledge. Knowing these men and being able to work in cooperation with them has been a great experience.

The author is truly indebted to all those who assisted in this tremendous project. It would have been an impossible task to have undertaken the writing of this book without assistance. No one man possesses all the technical data and knowledge contained herein. Besides diving information from many books and magazines covering all phases of the kingdom below the water, the author is greatly indebted to persons directly concerned with Scuba diving, salvage, demolitions, construction, photography, etc. It is a pleasure to acknowledge this valuable and generously-given assistance.

First, I should like to express my deep appreciation to the staff members of International Undersea Services, who contributed their knowledge, time and assistance to this entire project: Richard Rush Bishop, past Vice-President, I.U.S., and Photography Chief; James Franklin Pearson, Director, I.U.S., and Salvage Chief; Jay G. O'Brien, Demolitions Advisor and Electrical Specialist; R. Paul Ruhlin, Research Technologist; and Benjamin Flagg Bigelow, III, Senior Diving Specialist.

For valuable contributions and suggestions concerning underwater photography, I also wish to thank Paul Cherney of Alfa-American Corp., Capt. Jordon Klein of Underwater Sports, Inc., Jerry Greenberg of Seahawk Products, Dmitri Rebikoff, E. E. Peterson Co., Eastman Kodak Co., and Burleigh Brooks, Inc.

Throughout the field of salvage, I consulted such volumes as: *Shallow Water Diving for Profit and Pleasure,* by Schenck & Kendall;

Ship Salvage, and *How Wrecked and Sunken Ships Are Salved,* by Critchley. Dmitri Rebikoff contributed his knowledge to this section, as did members of I.U.S.

For information, technical data, and diagrams pertaining to underwater blasting, sincere appreciation to The Hon. I. A. MacDonald, Esq., Nobel Division, Imperial Chemical Industries, Ltd., Glasgow, Scotland.

The Hon. I. Miller, Deputy for Legislation and Liaison, Department of the Navy, receives my humble thanks for all the Navy Department's assistance in the underwater cutting and welding chapter.

Many manufacturers rendered their services, and I wish to acknowledge specifically: Rene Bussoz, President, J. Y. Cousteau, Chairman, Board of Directors, and Harry Rice, Sales Director, all of U.S. Divers Corp.; Richard Klein, of Healthways; Ken Frogley, of the Garrett Corp. (Northill); Sam M. Davison, Jr., of Dacor; Robert Brewer, of Scott; and Arthur Brown, of Spearfisherman.

The American Forest Products Industries, Inc., contributed greatly to the underwater logging chapter.

The science and technical chapters have been possible only through the most generous kind of cooperation. Numerous scientific organizations, several departments and agencies of the states and federal government, many university staff personnel, and various businesses contributed material in photographs, technical data, and helpful suggestions. It would be impossible to thank here each person for the assistance rendered. I can only acknowledge the major contributors.

Turtox, the General Biological Supply House, contributed a greater portion of the technical data given in Chapter XII.

To Drs. Hyland and Richards, Botany Department, Plants Science Division, University of Maine, and Mr. Douglas Stafford, Biology Department, Bangor Senior High School, Bangor, Me., I owe many thanks for their help.

Throughout the chapter on marine science, I received technical material, photographs, and information from the following: C. P. Idyll, Dept. of Marine Science, Marine Laboratory, University of Miami; T. S. Perry Griffin, Asst. Personnel Director, Woods Hole Oceanographic Institution; Bryant Putney, Director, Public Relations, Socony-Mobil Oil Co.; Ella P. Glennie, Head, Employment Branch, U.S. Navy Hydrographic Office; Everett H. Woodward, Executive Secretary, Potomac River Naval Command, Naval Research Laboratory; Severin F. Ulmer, Personnel Officer, Fish & Wildlife Service, U.S. Dept. of the Interior; Chief H. J. Lawrence, Dept. of Police, Seattle, Washington; R. L. Dow, Director, Marine Research, Dept. of Sea & Shore Fisheries, State of Maine; and Graham DuShane, Editor, *Science Monthly* and *Science* magazines.

Photomicrography, an extremely technical chapter to write, was lightened considerably by the help of: The American Optical Co., Instrument Division; Central Scientific Co.; E. Leitz, Inc.; Eastman Kodak Co.; Exakta Camera Co.; and the R. Y. Ferner Co.

Chapter IX, "The Underwater Craftsman," contains the work of many staff members of I.U.S., plus other contributors; among them: Mr. George Bell, President, Penobscot Boat Co., for technical assistance in the salvage craft design and construction; Mr. Ronald Atkins, AB, E.E., Univ. of Maine, and Mr. Alan Atkins, AB, AM, Dept. of Physics, Univ. of Maine; Mr. Kenneth Manley, Director, Special Events, Maine Divers Association; Mr. John D. Baker, Jr., Maine Divers Association; and Mr. Edward E. Guernsey, Jr., MSD, Vice-President, I.U.S., and President, International Services, a division of I.U.S.

I wish to express my deep appreciation to: The Hon. Frederick G. Payne, United States Senator from Maine, Committee on Interstate and Foreign Commerce, for the generous help he gave the author in the writing of this book, and to The Hon. Edmund S. Muskie, His Excellency, the Governor of Maine, for his generous assistance.

Thanks are due F. T. Bishop, IV, for the use of his personal and extensive library and Mr. F. M. Reeves, Jr., Manager, Olympic Sporting Goods Co., for loaning items of swim and diving equipment to I.U.S. for testing purposes. And thanks to my good friend, Richard L. Brougham, the transplanted Californian, for his valuable technical assistance throughout the writing of this book.

Mr. L. Felix Ranlett, Head Librarian, and the staff of the Bangor (Maine) Public Library receive my deepest appreciation for their valuable assistance rendered in gathering research material.

The author also wishes to acknowledge here his specific indebtedness to the following books and magazines.

Books: *The Silent World*, J-Y Cousteau; *Self-Contained Diving*, Rene Bussoz; *Shallow Water Diving and Spearfishing*, Schenck & Kendall; *Underwater Photography*, Schenck & Kendall; *A Guide to Underwater Photography*, Rebikoff & Cherney; *Deep Diving and Submarine Operations*, Sir Robert Davis; *On the Bottom*, Admiral Ellsberg; *Underwater Cutting and Welding*, Navy Department; *Boat Carpentry*, H. G. Smith; *The Sea Around Us*, Rachel Carson; *The World Under the Sea*, D. W. Smith; *Diving for Science*, L. Poole; *They Found Gold*, A. H. Verrill; *I Dive for Treasure*, Lt. H. Rieseberg; *Doubloons*, C. Driscoll; *Botany*, Williams; *Zoology*, Elliott; *Diving Manual*, Navy Department; *Photographs Through the Microscope*, Eastman Kodak; *Motion Pictures Through the Microscope*, Eastman Kodak.

Magazines: *Popular Science; Popular Mechanics; National Geographic; Holiday; Skin Diver; Yachting; Recreation; American Mercury; Field and Stream; Argosy; Flying Red Horse; Science; Science Monthly; Water World.*

Trade Journal: *The Southern Lumberman.*

J. E. C.

Chapter I

THE PRINCIPLES OF DIVING

Self-contained diving is an enjoyable sport, but also a serious business. The dangers, which are so evident, keep millions from entering the blue kingdom, either for pleasure or profit. This chapter will cover the principles of self-contained diving and some of the dangers that are involved.

The tank of the standard compressed-air Scuba (Self-contained underwater breathing apparatus) carries a working pressure of 2,150 pounds per square inch or 70 cubic feet of air. This amount allows the diver approximately 100 minutes of steady swimming or moderate work. Breathing from the automatic demand regulator is the same as normal breathing. Almost all Scuba units are equipped with safety devices which serve as a warning to the diver that only a fraction of his air supply remains in the tank and he should return, without haste, to the surface—never faster than 25 feet a minute.

A diver walks around on earth with a force of 14¾ pounds per square inch, or approximately 21 tons, pressing against his body. But, at the same time, there is an equal force pushing from the inside, so the body is not crushed. When a diver descends in the water, he adds an extra half pound to his 3,000 square inches of body surface at each 12 inches. At 33 feet, the pressure exerted against his body is double that of the surface. If descent is not too rapid, the body builds an inward force to counteract this added pressure.

Since a man is buoyant in water, weights are required to allow him to penetrate the depths. The amount of weight required in sea water depends upon the person and his own weight and natural buoyancy, but, for the most part, 2 to 9 pounds is the weight range. In fresh water, the weight requirements range from 1½ to 7 pounds. Each diver must adjust his own weight belt, and the belt should always have a quick-release catch. (As long as self-contained divers continue to misuse their ordinarily safe equipment, writers and manufacturers must continue to stress the safety factors of the equipment and the principles of diving.)

1

YOUR FIRST TRIP DOWN INTO THE BLUE KINGDOM

On your first trip down into the majestic multicolored wonders of the blue kingdom, you behold a new world to explore. But, before trying the sea, you should get a little fresh-water experience.

Let us assume that for your first underwater experience, you and your instructor-partner have decided on a pond with a sandy, gradually-sloping bottom and, after getting a good deal of top-side instruction from your experienced partner and slipping into your gear, you check it with your partner, and you walk to the water's edge together.

Your partner explains how to breathe: to breathe slowly and easily, naturally, to avoid getting rattled, to stay calm and cool. Panic has cost the lives of good divers. You learn about the popping noise in your ears and how to deal with it. The blocking of the Eustachian tubes causes the popping noise and pain.

These tubes, which are small passageways leading from the nasal passages to the inner ear, admit air to the ear cavity in small quantities (see Fig. 1). When water pressure builds on the external portion of the ears, the air pressure to counteract this force travels through the Eustachian tubes. When the first pain or popping noise begins, the diver should swallow hard a few times or force a breath of air through his nose. Most experienced divers, before entering the water, hold tightly to their noses and blow hard. In most cases, the ears will pop and this is a sign that they are clear.

The danger of wearing ear plugs cannot be stressed too strongly. Ear plugs trap a pocket of air between them and the eardrums. The pressure that builds up in the Eustachian tubes will force the delicate eardrums outward, and eventually they will break. Broken eardrums often cause total deafness. Ear plugs are made to keep water out of swimmers' ears. Do *not* wear ear plugs when diving.

You may have heard about a group of people whose livelihood depends upon the abilities of their divers. Throughout most of the men's lives, they swim deep (80–100 feet) into the sea, being able to hold their breath for periods exceeding three minutes.

When a boy of this very small group reaches a certain age, he is taken by two of the best swimmers to a spot where the water reaches a depth of 65 feet. A heavy weight is tied to the boy; the swimmers dive in and the boy is dropped. His descent to the bottom is so swift that is is impossible for the body to build up the pressure to meet the force pressing against the ear cavities. The eardrums burst and the boy blacks out. The swimmers then cut him from the weight and he is returned to the surface. After a month of agonizing pain, the eardrums heal and the boy is ready to dive, but, like his fellow divers, young and old, he is stone deaf.

Your partner then tells you that you and he are going down to about 25 feet and sit on the bottom. This is the best way to get accustomed to the breathing procedure with the demand regulator, and to let you experience pressure, buoyancy, and life under water.

So, standing in water above your waist, you moisten the shatter-proof safety lens of your face mask with saliva (or the juice from a potato cut in half), rinse it thoroughly, set it in place just under the nose and above the upper lip, grip the mouthpiece firmly between your teeth, and push yourself gently forward.

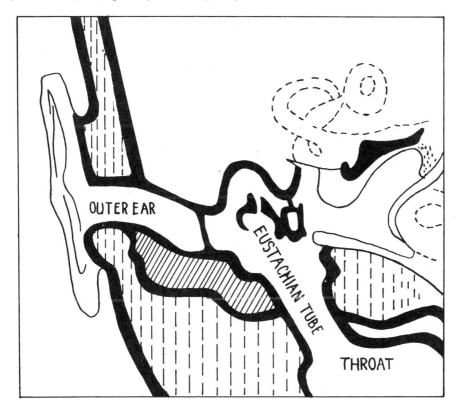

Fig. 1. Drawing of Eustachian tube.

The water rises above your head as you start on your first venture into the blue kingdom. You circle around slowly, going deeper on each wide turn. At 20 feet, your ears pop and you swallow. The noise stops and you know that the Eustachian tubes are clear.

From the corner of your eye, you see your partner motion for you to sit down. You sit easily and breathe smoothly from the demand regulator. You look about you slowly and, for the first time, you fully realize the splendors of the underwater world. Fish, unafraid, swim up to you, peering into your face mask, darting away when the great burst of bubbles is ejected from the exhaust valve of the regulator, and then return for another look at the strange creature who has invaded their domain. With your confidence to live, move about, and breathe under water heightened, you signal your partner that you want to begin to explore the watery world and its wonders.

After half an hour's exploration, you stop and sit again, resting and observing. Then you think about decompression. You remember that between the surface and 40 feet, no decompression stops are necessary for the first 120 minutes. But, what about embolism?

Air embolism is caused by the expansion of air in the lungs during a fast ascent to the surface or from one pressure layer to another of less force. When a diver ascends, he never travels faster than 25 feet per minute, except in extreme emergencies. If a diver holds his breath while ascending, his lungs will burst. When going to the surface, he must continue uninterrupted breathing. The speed of the bubbles coming from the regulator should never be exceeded. Should he run out of air while below and need to use a Res-Q-Pak to bring him to the surface, he must remember to release all the air in his lung during the ascent to the surface, and by the time he reaches the top, his lungs should be empty.

You think about the "bends" and "caisson disease." Nitrogen deposits in the bloodstream cause the "bends." If ascent is too rapid after a sustained dive, nitrogen is released into the bloodstream as bubbles of gas. These bubbles flow along until they come to a joint or muscle, and there they lodge. In the most extreme cases, the nitrogen gas works its way to the heart and ruptures it.

Remembering these few safety precautions, you slide off the rock on which you were sitting and continue on your eventful journey.

Once the initial frightened period of "living" and "breathing" under water passes, nothing can keep you from the blue kingdom and, after a month of daily diving in fresh water lakes and ponds, you tell your partner that you'd like to try the sea.

A FIRST EXPERIENCE IN SEA DIVING

The following weekend you set out, fully dressed in foam-rubber "wet"-type diving dress to keep the cool sea water from draining off too many calories. Your partner gives you a razor-sharp, double-edged knife, and explains why every diver should carry one when diving or working in salt water. Divers can get tangled up in kelp, or a loose rope can wrap about their feet. A diver carries his knife on his diving belt or strapped to a leg, where it is more comfortable and more easily reached in time of need. Your partner explains the reason for the rubber suits. Cold is force which takes the diver's valuable air. When your body is cold, the muscles tighten; this results in excessive oxygen consumption.

You have heard the sea stories told about the shark, barracuda, moray eel and octopus; so you ask about them. Your partner tells you that, for the most part, you will never be bothered by these creatures. You may be afraid of them, but they are twice as afraid of you. He goes on to tell you that there are other dangers much greater, by contrast, that undersea men encounter while diving in salt water.*

Fire coral and sea poison ivy are two chief dangers. The sea urchin, jellyfish, and Portuguese Man-of-War are the other three with which a diver frequently has trouble. The sea urchin has needles much like those of a porcupine. These needles are very brittle and, when stepped on, they pierce the skin and break off. If not treated immediately, they can become infected and very painful.

The other four dangers mentioned are of the stinging variety. If you know what poison ivy can do to you on land, you have a fair idea of what you have let yourself in for by handling or brushing against fire coral, sea poison ivy, jellyfish or the Man-of-War. The sting of the Portuguese Man-of-War can cause a diver's death if it is not treated immediately. Your partner has brought along a first-aid kit which contains a tube of Anti-Histamine Cream to treat mishap if the occasion arises.

Now, you make a final check of your equipment, before you invade Mother Sea's great domain for the first time. The pressure in the tank reads 2,150 psi, a full load. Your weight belt has the proper amount to equalize your buoyancy, and the quick release catch is in perfect working order. The all-important demand regulator is placed on the high-pressure tank valve, and the unit is slipped on. You check the quick release on your Scuba, put on your fins and face mask and have your partner turn on your air. You are already wearing your depth gauge, so you assist your partner into his gear.

With your fins flopping, you both waddle to the water's edge. Slowly, the cool, green water caresses your body. The tingling sensation raises the hair at the nape of your neck and you stand on the bottom, momentarily, when the water reaches just above your waist. Removing your face mask, you moisten the glass with saliva, rinse it and adjust it just over your eyes and nose. Putting the regulator mouthpiece in place, you take a short breath, tap your partner and submerge.

The water rises over your head and a flutter kick of the fins takes you deeper into the great blue kingdom. You wave to your partner for a deeper descent. The sunlight pours through the green water, lending its power to enhance the beauty that is unfolding before your eyes.

At 25 feet, you level off, swimming easily. In front of you is a large mound of coral. The spectrum of light through the water

* For a complete treatise on these underwater dangers, read: *Dangerous Marine Animals that Bite, Sting, and are Poisonous to Eat,* by Bruce W. Halstead, M.D., Cornell Maritime Press.

changes its color at every different angle. Out of the corner of your eye, you see your partner swimming into a school of multi-colored fish. They continue feeding, unmoved by the intrusion of the outsider from the earth world. You pass the hanging tentacles of a giant Portuguese Man-of-War. You steer clear of this fellow; he can do you harm.

Your partner motions you to go deeper and you level off at 38 feet this time. Beneath you, a floral garden of multicolored coral displays magnificent beauties far beyond adequate description. You see great specimens of brain coral, stag-horn coral and others that you cannot identify. In the distance, great sea fans spread their intricate network of lace patterns before your amazed eyes. You cannot possibly look at all the beauties around you; they are too numerous.

Then, the sea suddenly becomes deathly quiet. Hundreds of fish flash by, and then—nothing. You glance back at your partner who is swimming toward you, looking as bewildered as you. Suddenly, a dark shadow crosses in front of you. You reach for your knife and hold it in readiness. A little sweat forms on your forehead, even though you are in 38 feet of water. Your heart is pumping and you know you are a little scared. But, you must keep a cool head, and you know it. Keep cool. Keep calm. Those are the words your instructor has drilled into your head. You know that if you panic, it may cost you your life.

The ugly shadow draws closer.

Lazily, a small sand shark drifts past. With his sleepy eyes, rather drooping head, and sleek brown body, he still appears dangerous. But you know different; so the knives are sheathed and you continue on your exploration of Mother Sea's Treasure House.

A hermit crab scoots across the sandy bottom looking for an empty shell to protect himself from all the creatures that find him to be a tasty meal. A little octopus runs along the coral mounds, changing his skin color to match that of the surrounding area. The fish have returned to their feeding, and you would like to give them your attention.

But you note that your air is nearly gone. You signal to your partner for the ascent upstairs; he nods and you both start up. Going up very slowly, not exceeding 25 feet a minute, you feel the warmer strata of water as you near the surface. On the top, you take the precaution of remaining in the water for a couple of minutes, then paddle to shore.

During the time in which you are changing to your street clothes, you talk about those wonders which you have just experienced. Reluctantly, you wash your gear in the fresh water you brought along—something that is always done after a diver uses his equipment in salt water—and, as you start for the car, you turn back, looking wonderingly at that world which you have just left, thinking about the next and the many more times you will descend into those hidden depths.

Months have passed and daily diving in the sea has given you a great deal of experience. You have felt the pressure changes on your body down to 150 feet; you have gone through the decompression stages, and have not had any trouble with the "bends", air embolism, or the so-called dangerous creatures of the sea. But, like most Scuba divers and women, you have let your curiosity get the better of you, and you have brushed against fire coral and handled jellyfish without gloves. But, fortunately, you have missed sea poison ivy, sea urchins and the Portuguese Man-of-War.

During the months of your venturing into the sea, you have learned a great deal more than you thought you would ever be interested in. You have taken a big interest in the sea and its mysteries, and you have read every piece of literature about the sea, its life, its mysteries, salvage, shipping, and treasure that you could lay your hands on. You have made many notes and, night after night, you study and pore over the typed words in your loose-leaf notebook. You feel that you are about ready to settle down to the running of a business and you would seriously like to make it a diving business.

TYPES AND MAKES OF DIVING UNITS

If you have not already done so, your first important purchase of equipment will be your diving unit.

There are approximately nine different makes of Scuba on the American market. They all employ air as their breathing medium. Other forms of breathable gas compounds have been used in Scuba allowing divers to descend to depths of 1,000 feet. There are several types of rebreather Scuba available on the American market. In some phases of the diving business, the rebreather unit has proven more effective than the compressed air unit. However, compressed air is the most widely used breathing medium for Scuba throughout the world, and the author recommends its usage.

Dacor Corp of Evanston, Illinois, produces the finest two-stage, double-diaphragm, double-hose regulator in the world. This advanced engineering has brought to the diving public the double diaphragm, which provides double protection as well as smoother breathing and operating performance for the user. In the event one diaphragm is rendered inoperable, the other is constructed to function safely while allowing the diver to return to the surface. The "Dial-A-Breath" feature incorporated into the regulator enables the user to select the amount of air desired for ease of breathing.

New England Divers of Beverly, Massachusetts, has entered the manufacturing field. The two-stage, double-hose "Hydro-Master"

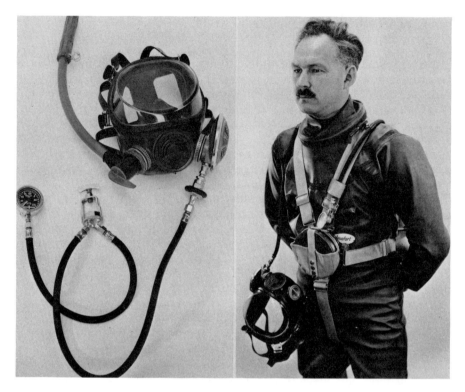

Fig. 1A. (Left) Normalair full-face unit with yoke attachment to fit American Scuba tank valves. (Right) Normalair Scuba with new weight pack and quick-release box.

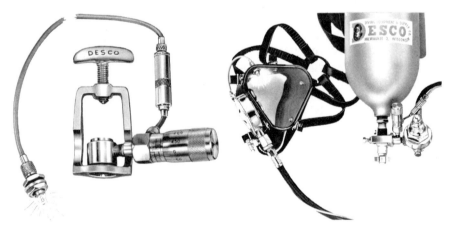

Fig. 1B. (Left) DESCO air tank safety light. (Right) DESCO Scuba with safety light and DESCO full-face mask.

regulator is produced under the strictest engineering principles, and is one of the best the author has tested recently. The "Marvel" line, produced by M & E Marine Supply, Camden, N.J., is ranked with the best as manufactured by Healthways, U.S. Divers, Sportsways, Inc., Voit, Scubapro and DESCO.

The author has tested the British manufactured Normalair Scuba. This unit features some of the most advanced designing in Scuba. The full-face mask has a built-in communications speaker which allows conversation with other underwater personnel. The regulator has a

Fig. 2. Johnson Scoot-R-Top Scuba skiff-boat.

safety feature in the diaphragm, which when manually operated, allows a continuous flow of high pressure air to enter the mask. This action is taken in the event the face lens is broken; the air flow forces out the water, preventing accidental drowning.

Located in the feathered edge of the mask is a full-face seal that is filled with water. Since water is practically incompressible, a tighter seal is provided without the discomforts of facial pressure and squeeze.

The unit incorporates an underwater pressure gauge denoting the amount of air remaining in the cylinder that can be easily read by the diver. The web strapping is of the finest and most pliable nylon, and the quick-release attachment is one of the best to be found on present-day Scuba. The disc-type quick-release unit contains the

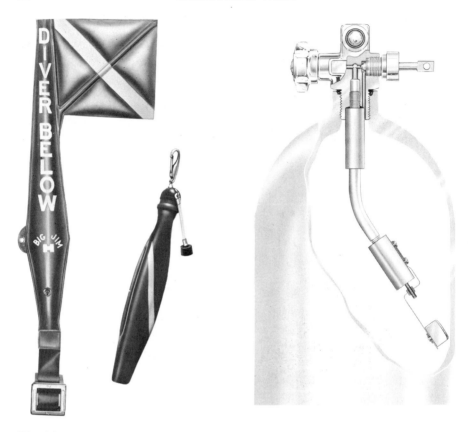

Fig. 2A. (Left) Diver's flag buoy. (Center) Personal marker buoy. (Healthways Co.) (Right) U.S. Divers audio reserve valve.

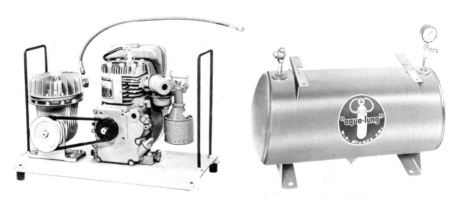

Fig. 3. (Left) Low-pressure compressor for hookah diving. (Right) Hookah air reserve tank.

diver's weights and both harness and/or weights can be jettisoned by snapping levers located on either side of the harness release disc.

An excellent back pack, equipped with stainless steel quick release tank bands, has both inverted and upright cylinder facilities. The author considers this unit to be one of the best developed for commercial Scuba divers. The "Normalair" incorporates the greatest number of safety features and diving comforts of all Scuba tested and used under actual working conditions by the author and members of International Undersea Services.

The Diving Equipment Supply Co., one of America's oldest manufacturers of commercial diving gear, has devised a safety light with an adjustable pressure setting mechanism. The unit can be incorporated into any good face mask. When the air pressure in the cylinder reaches the level as set on the safety pressure mechanism, a light comes on in the mask giving a visual signal to the diver. This outstanding safety device has been incorporated in DESCO's full-face Scuba.

The boat manufacturers have begun production on specialized diving craft. Johnson Motors have a revolutionary boat, the Scoot-R-Top, for Scuba divers. It is a 7 ft. long, 85-pound boat capable of supporting eight hundred pounds. This unusual craft has a depth of nine inches and can also be used as a search and survey craft. The Scoot-R-Top has a seat, motor mount for a 10 hp. outboard, and a folding canopy.

The Healthways "Diver's Flag Buoy" is one of the newest and best safety items produced by a diving equipment manufacturer. The Flag Buoy is made of a durable plastic, inflated when needed, attachable to the diver or a bottom weight, bright and easily seen. All divers should use surface floating marker buoys when under water.

The personal inflatable marker buoy has been carried and used by television's "Sea Hunt" hero, Mike Nelson, played by Lloyd Bridges. The personal marker buoy is small, compact and carried by the diver when under water. It is used to signal surface personnel, mark a search area, or specify the location of a submerged object. The unit is activated by squeezing the trigger mechanism of the gas cylinder located inside the buoy. Divers, sport and commercial, should use the personal marker buoy.

U.S. Divers has added an Audio Reserve Valve in their air cylinders for the diver's safety. This unit is located inside the air tank and is actuated when the air pressure drops to the safety factor. It sets up a continuous rapping against the cylinder wall inside the tank and is clearly heard by the diver signalling him to ascend.

The hookah unit is a valuable tool developed for the commercial Scuba diver. The hookah unit employs low pressure air, sections of hose, a low pressure compressor, air storage tank and special regulator attachment.

Frequently a commercial Scuba diver's work will be in a small, specified area. The job will require many hours to complete, and an

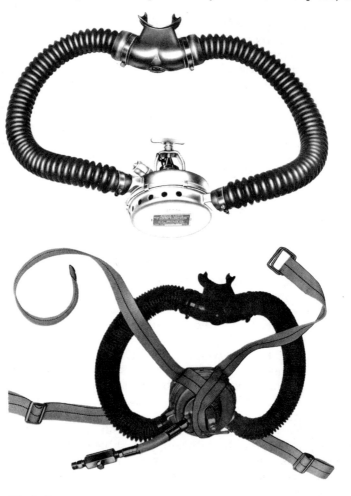

Fig. 3A. (Top) Two-stage, two-hose, aquamaster regulator—Navy approved—has a hookah attachment. (Bottom) Hookah-Master regulator and harness. (U.S. Divers)

excessive amount of air and physical stamina. The hookah unit provides the air necessary for heavy work, eliminates bulky air tanks and the returning to the surface to replace empty air cylinders.

Designer-divers Paul and Ed Connolly of Dedham, Mass., have produced a towed wet submarine with a capacity for two divers and extremely inexpensive to construct.

The "Porpoise I" is towed by a surface craft at a top speed of six knots with a maximum depth of one hundred feet. The unit weighs approximately 150 pounds and has a positive buoyancy of 10 pounds, which means it will float when empty.

Fig. 3B. (Top) Two-man wet-type towed submarine. (Connolly) (Bottom) Wet-type towed submarine with designer Connolly at the wheel. (E. Paradisio)

The construction price depends upon the price paid for the surplus aircraft fuel tank which is the basic component. Total cost should not exceed one hundred dollars for self-propelled units. Electric-powered units would cost more.

Manufacturers and individuals are designing and improving diving equipment daily for the safety and pleasure of all Scuba divers.

Chapter II

DIVING SAFETY

Divers, whether they are deep-sea divers or Scuba divers, can count themselves lucky if they have never suffered a diving accident. Because some simple safety rule has been disobeyed, a diver may suffer serious injury or even forfeit his life while below. When this happens, it reflects on all divers and diving in general. Since divers will continue to overlook the simple safety precautions of diving, the more serious types of diving accidents encountered below are dealt with in this chapter. These include: air embolism, bleeding from the nose and lungs, compressed-air illness, ear pains (bleeding from the ears), and exhaustion.

PHYSICAL REQUIREMENTS FOR DIVERS

The United States Navy has some of the world's finest underwater specialists and their training is most thorough. Men wishing to enter this particular branch of the Naval Service must pass one of the toughest physicals given to any of the Armed Forces personnel. Before deciding on diving as an occupation, you might check yourself against these standards.

Lt. Robert P. Fay, USN, Commanding Officer, U. S. Naval School Underwater Swimmers, has outlined the standard Navy diving physical requirements in the August, 1955, issue of the *Skin Diver:*

1. Excessively overweight persons should not attempt deep diving.

2. Vision should be at least 20/30 bilateral not much lower, correctable to 20/20. Color vision should be normal by standards of the American Optical Company.

3. Teeth should be of high standard oral hygiene. Bridges and dentures should not be such as to interfere with effective gripping of the mouthpiece.

4. Ears should be normal and clear. No acute or chronic disease should be present. Drums should be intact. Eustachian tubes should be freely patent for equalization of pressure changes. Hearing of each ear should be normal.

5. Nose and throat passages should be clear and have adequate ventilation. Chronic diseased tonsils and sinusitis are a hazard, and people with such trouble should not be allowed to dive.

6. The lungs should be clear and normal as determined by a physical and x-ray examinations.

7. The cardiovascular (heart, veins, arteries) system should be without significant abnormality as determined by physical examination. Varicose veins and marked or symptomatic hemorrhoids are a hazard.

8. The gastrointestinal system should be normal. No chronic, acute or recurrent disease or condition should exist.

9. There should be no chronic, acute or recurrent genitourinary disease or conditions present.

10. There should be no active, acute, or chronic disease of the skin.

11. Temperament should be normal. Persons with any abnormal emotional or temperamental condition, epilepsy, personality disorder, neurotic trends, emotional immaturity, instability or associated traits should not be allowed to dive.

12. Ability to equalize pressure. This is checked in a recompression chamber to determine the ability to clear ears effectively and to withstand the effects of pressure otherwise.

13. Oxygen tolerance under pressure. This is very necessary in case treatment is ever needed in a recompression chamber for any of the diving illnesses or injuries.

14. A complete annual physical examination should be given all diving personnel.

There are many swimmers who cannot meet such physical requirements but who use Scuba a great deal with no resultant ill effects. Though some will get by safely, they are defying the law of averages and taking a foolhardy risk. Diving is a strenuous undertaking and for those in good health only. Lieutenant Fay's outline should serve as a guide in the regulation of each diver's personal health qualifications. A medical examination is inexpensive compared with the cost of many doctor bills accrued from long months spent in a hospital because of a diving accident.

SAFETY RULES

The following excellent list of safety rules for Scuba divers was also given in this same article in the *Skin Diver* magazine:

1. Swim with a buddy at all times. Use a buddy line under especially unfavorable conditions.

2. Do not dive if very tired or not feeling well.

3. Make a preliminary check of equipment prior to entering the water.

4. When going out on an underwater task, make complete plans prior to submerging. Incomplete planning for such dives causes most of the hazardous situations in which swimmers find themselves.

5. Know how to use the standard Navy Decompression Tables and stay within the no-decompression limits, unless there is some reasonable necessity for doing otherwise. Use a watch and depth gauge on deep swims.

6. Enter the water feet first.

7. Do not use oxygen in Scuba designed for compressed air.

8. If weights are used, attach them to the Scuba, so that they may be released independently or with the Scuba.

9. Do not use wrenches on valve handles not designed for such usage.

10. If contact is lost with a buddy, it is usually best to surface and look for bubbles. Listening for bubbles is of questionable value, since your hearing underwater is non-directional.

11. Know the location of the nearest recompression chamber.

12. Be proficient in the back pressure arm lift method of artificial respiration.

13. Carry a sharp knife, preferably one which has one sawtooth edge.

14. High pressure air can be hazardous. Do not leave a charged Scuba in the hot sun. Use vigilance during maintenance. Conduct routine hydrostatic tests of high pressure parts.

Table 1. U. S. Navy decompression procedures.

Need for Decompression

A quantity of nitrogen is taken up by the body during every dive. The amount absorbed depends upon the depth of the dive and the exposure (bottom) time. If the quantity of nitrogen dissolved in the body tissues exceeds a certain critical amount, the ascent must be delayed to allow the body tissue to remove the excess nitrogen. Decompression sickness results from failure to delay the ascent and to allow this process of gradual desaturation. A specified time at a specific depth for purposes of desaturation is called a decompression stop.

"No Decompression" Schedules

Dives that are not long or deep enough to require decompression stops are "no decompression" dives. Dives to 33 feet or less do not require decompression stops. As the depth increases, the allowable bottom time for "no decompression" dives decreases. Five minutes at 190 feet is the shortest and deepest "no decompression" schedule. These dives are all listed in the No Decompression Limits and Repetitive Group Designation Table for "No Decompression" Dives, ("No Decompression Table" (table 1-C)) and only require compliance with the 60 feet per minute rate of ascent.

Schedules That Require Decompression Stops

All dives beyond the limits of the "No Decompression Table" require decompression stops. These dives are listed in the Navy Standard Air Decompression Table (table 1-A). Comply exactly with instructions except as modified by surface decompression procedures.

Variations in Rate of Ascent

Ascend from all dives at the rate of 60 feet per minute.
In the event you exceed the 60 feet per minute rate:
(1) If no decompression stops are required, but the bottom time places you within 10 minutes of a schedule that does require decompression; stop at 10 feet for the time that you should have taken in ascent at 60 feet per minute.
(2) If decompression is required; stop 10 feet below the first listed decompression depth for the time that you should have taken in ascent at 60 feet per minute.

In the event you are unable to maintain the 60 feet per minute rate of ascent:
(1) If the delay was within 30 feet of the bottom; add to the bottom time, the additional time used in ascent. Decompress according to the requirements of the total bottom time. This is the safer procedure.
(2) If the delay was above 30 feet from the bottom; increase the first stop by the difference between the time consumed in ascent and the time that should have been consumed at 60 feet per minute.

Table 1. U.S. Navy decompression procedures. (Cont.)

Repetitive Dive Procedure

A dive performed within 12 hours of surfacing from a previous dive is a repetitive dive. The period between dives is the surface interval. Excess nitrogen requires 12 hours to effectively be lost from the body. These tables are designed to protect the diver from the effects of this residual nitrogen. Allow a minimum surface interval of 10 minutes between all dives. Specific instructions are given for the use of each table in the following order:

(1) The "No Decompression Table" or the Navy Standard Air Decompression Table gives the repetitive group designation for all schedules which may preceed a repetitive dive.

(2) The Surface Interval Credit Table gives credit for the desaturation occurring during the surface interval.

(3) The Repetitive Dive Timetable gives the number of minutes or residual nitrogen time to add to the actual bottom time of the repetitive dive in order to obtain decompression for the residual nitrogen.

(4) The "No Decompression Table" or the Navy Standard Air Decompression Table gives the decompression required for the repetitive dive.

U.S. NAVY STANDARD AIR DECOMPRESSION TABLE

INSTRUCTIONS FOR USE

Time of decompression stops in the table is in minutes.

Enter the table at the exact or the next greater depth than the maximum depth attained during the dive. Select the listed bottom time that is exactly equal to or is next greater than the bottom time of the dive. Maintain the diver's chest as close as possible to each decompression depth for the number of minutes listed. The rate of ascent between stops is not critical. Commence timing each stop on arrival at the decompression depth and resume ascent when the specified time has elapsed.

For example – a dive to 82 feet for 36 minutes. To determine the proper decompression procedure: The next greater depth listed in this table is 90 feet. The next greater bottom time listed opposite 90 feet is 40. Stop 7 minutes at 10 feet in accordance with the 90/40 schedule.

For example – a dive to 110 feet for 30 minutes. It is known that the depth did not exceed 110 feet. To determine the proper decompression schedule: The exact depth of 110 feet is listed. The exact bottom time of 30 minutes is listed opposite 110 feet. Decompress according to the 110/30 schedule unless the dive was particularly cold or arduous. In that case, go to the 110/40, the 120/30, or the 120/40 at your own discretion.

(Rev. 1958)

17

Table 1-A. U.S. Navy standard air decompression table.

DEPTH (ft)	BOTTOM TIME (mins)	TIME TO FIRST STOP	DECOMPRESSION STOPS 50	40	30	20	10	TOTAL ASCENT TIME	REPET GROUP
40	200	0.5					0	0.7	*
	210	0.5					2	2.5	N
	230	0.5					7	7.5	N
	250	0.5					11	11.5	O
	270	0.5					15	15.5	O
	300	0.5					19	19.5	Z
50	100	0.7					0	0.8	*
	110	0.7					3	3.7	L
	120	0.7					5	5.7	M
	140	0.7					10	10.7	M
	160	0.7					21	21.7	N
	180	0.7					29	29.7	O
	200	0.7					35	35.7	O
	220	0.7					40	40.7	Z
	240	0.7					47	47.7	Z
60	60	0.8					0	1.0	*
	70	0.8					2	2.8	K
	80	0.8					7	7.8	L
	100	0.8					14	14.8	M
	120	0.8					26	26.8	N
	140	0.8					39	39.8	O
	160	0.8					48	48.8	N
	180	0.8					56	56.8	Z
	200	0.8				1	69	70.8	Z
70	50	1.0					0	1.2	*
	60	1.0					8	9.0	K
	70	1.0					14	15.0	L
	80	1.0					18	19.0	M
	90	1.0					23	24.0	N
	100	1.0					33	34.0	N
	110	0.8					41	43.8	O
	120	0.8				2	47	51.8	O
	130	0.8				4	52	58.8	O
	140	0.8				6	56	64.8	Z
	150	0.8				9	61	70.8	Z
	160	0.8				13	72	85.8	Z
	170	0.8				19	79	98.8	Z

DEPTH (ft)	BOTTOM TIME (mins)	TIME TO FIRST STOP	DECOMPRESSION STOPS 50	40	30	20	10	TOTAL ASCENT TIME	REPET GROUP
120	15	-					0	2.0	*
	20	1.8					2	3.8	H
	25	1.8					6	7.8	I
	30	1.8					14	15.8	J
	40	1.7					25	31.7	L
	50	1.7				5	31	47.7	N
	60	1.5				15	45	70.5	O
	70	1.5			2	22	55	88.5	O
	80	1.5			9	23	63	106.5	Z
	90	1.5			15	27	74	131.5	Z
	100	1.5			23	45	80	149.5	Z
180	10	2.0					0	2.2	*
	15	2.0					1	3.0	F
	20	2.0					4	6.0	H
	25	1.8					10	12.0	J
	30	1.8				3	18	22.8	M
	40	1.7				10	25	36.8	N
	50	1.7			8	21	37	62.7	O
	60	1.7			9	23	52	85.7	Z
	70	1.7		3	16	24	61	102.7	Z
	80	1.5		8	19	35	72	130.5	Z
	90	1.5			19	45	80	153.5	Z
140	10	2.2					0	2.3	*
	15	2.2					2	4.2	G
	20	2.0					6	8.2	I
	25	2.0				2	14	18.0	J
	30	2.0				5	21	26.0	K
	40	1.8			2	16	26	45.8	N
	50	1.8			6	24	44	75.8	O
	60	1.8			16	23	56	96.6	Z
	70	1.7		4	19	32	68	124.7	Z
	80	1.7		10	23	41	79	154.7	Z
	5	-					0	2.5	C
	10	2.3					1	3.3	E
	15	2.3					3	6.3	G
	20	2.2				2	7	11.2	H
	25	2.2				4	17	23.2	K

Top table

150 feet

Bottom time	Time to first stop	50 ft	40 ft	30 ft	20 ft	10 ft	Total ascent time	Repetitive group
30	2.2				8	24	34.2	L
40	2.0			5	19	38	59.0	N
50	2.0		3	12	28	51	88.0	O
60	1.8		11	19	39	62	111.8	N
70	1.8	1	17	19	50	75	145.8	N
80	1.7	1	17	22		84	172.7	N

160 feet

Bottom time	Time to first stop	50 ft	40 ft	30 ft	20 ft	10 ft	Total ascent time	Repetitive group
5							2.7	D
10						1	3.5	F
15	2.5					4	7.3	H
20	2.3				2	11	16.3	J
25	2.3			2	7	25	29.3	K
30	2.3			9	16	39	40.2	M
40	2.2		1	17	23	55	71.2	N
50	2.0	5	18	23	45	69	98.0	N
60	2.0	15	22	37	61	80	132.0	N
70	1.8	17	19	51	74	86	165.8	N

170 feet

Bottom time	Time to first stop	50 ft	40 ft	30 ft	20 ft	10 ft	Total ascent time	Repetitive group
5							2.8	D
10	2.7					2	4.7	F
15	2.5					5	9.5	H
20	2.5				4	15	21.5	J
25	2.3			2	7	23	34.3	L
30	2.3			4	13	26	45.3	M
40	2.2		1	10	23	45	81.2	O
50	2.0	5	18	23	23	61	109.2	N
60	2.0	15	22	19	37	74	152.0	N
70		17	19		51	86	183.0	N

180 feet

Bottom time	Time to first stop	50 ft	40 ft	30 ft	20 ft	10 ft	Total ascent time	Repetitive group
5							3.0	D
10	2.8					3	5.8	F
15	2.7					6	11.7	I
20	2.5				5	17	25.5	K
25	2.5			3	10	24	39.5	L
30	2.5		1	8	17	27	52.5	N
40	2.3	8	14	28	30	50	92.3	O
50	2.2	9	19	19	65		127.2	N
60		16	19		44	81	167.2	N

190 feet

Bottom time	Time to first stop	50 ft	40 ft	30 ft	20 ft	10 ft	Total ascent time	Repetitive group
5							3.2	D
10	2.8					3	6.8	G
15	2.8					4	13.8	I
20	2.7				6	20	30.7	K
25	2.5			1	11	25	43.7	M
30	2.5		8	8	19	32	62.5	N
40	2.3	4	13	23	33	55	102.5	O
50	2.3	10	17	19	72		146.3	N
60					50	84	182.3	N

Bottom table

80 feet

Bottom time	Time to first stop	30 ft	20 ft	10 ft	Total ascent time	Repetitive group
40				0	.0	•
50	1.3			10	1.3	K
60	1.3			17	11.2	L
70	1.3		2	23	18.2	M
80	1.0		7	31	24.2	N
90	1.0		11	39	34.0	N
100	1.0		13	46	47.0	O
110	1.0		17	53	58.0	O
120	1.0		19	56	67.0	N
130	1.0		26	69	*74.0	N
140	1.0	5	32	77	83.0	N
150			36	74	96.0	N
					110.0	

90 feet

Bottom time	Time to first stop	30 ft	20 ft	10 ft	Total ascent time	Repetitive group
30				0	1.5	•
40	1.3			7	8.3	J
50	1.3			18	19.3	L
60	1.3			25	26.3	M
70	1.2	7	30		38.2	N
80	1.2	13	40		54.2	N
90	1.2	18	48		67.2	O
100	1.2	21	54		76.2	Z
110	1.2	24	61		96.2	Z
120	1.0	32	68		101.2	Z
130		5	36	74	116.0	Z

100 feet

Bottom time	Time to first stop	30 ft	20 ft	10 ft	Total ascent time	Repetitive group
25				0	1.7	•
30	1.5			3	4.5	L
40	1.5			15	16.5	K
50	1.3		2	24	27.3	L
60	1.3		9	28	38.3	N
70	1.3		17	39	57.3	O
80	1.3	3	23	48	72.3	O
90	1.3	7	23	57	84.2	Z
100	1.2	10	34	66	97.2	Z
110	1.2	12	41	72	117.2	Z
120		15	37	78	132.2	Z

110 feet

Bottom time	Time to first stop	30 ft	20 ft	10 ft	Total ascent time	Repetitive group
20				0	1.8	•
25	1.7			3	4.7	H
30	1.7			7	3.7	J
40	1.5		2	21	21.5	L
50	1.6		8	26	33.5	L
60	1.5		18	36	55.5	M
70	1.3	1	23	48	73.3	N
80	1.3	7	23	57	83.3	O
90	1.3	12	30	64	107.3	Z
100	1.3	15	37	72	126.3	Z

*See table 1–G for repetitive groups in "no decompression" dives.

(Rev. 1958)

Table 1-B. U.S. Navy standard air decompression table for exceptional exposures.

DEPTH (ft.)	BOTTOM TIME (Min.)	TIME TO FIRST STOP	130	120	110	100	90	80	70	60	50	40	30	20	10	TOTAL ASCENT TIME
40	360	0.5													23	24
	480	0.5													41	43
	720	0.5													69	70
60	240	0.7												2	70	82
	360	0.7												20	119	140
	480	0.7												44	148	193
	720	0.7												76	187	266
80	180	1.0												35	85	121
	240	0.8											6	52	120	179
	360	0.8											29	90	160	280
	480	0.8											59	107	187	354
	720	0.7										17	108	142	187	456
100	180	1.0										1	29	53	118	202
	240	1.0										14	42	84	142	283
	360	0.8									2	42	73	111	187	416
	480	0.8									21	61	91	142	187	502
	720	0.8									55	106	122	142	187	613
120	120	1.3										10	19	47	98	176
	180	1.2									5	27	37	76	137	283
	240	1.2									23	35	60	97	179	396
	360	1.0								18	45	64	93	142	187	550
	480	0.8							3	41	64	93	122	142	187	653
	720	0.8							32	74	100	114	122	142	187	772
140	90	1.5									2	14	18	42	88	166
	120	1.5									12	14	36	56	120	240
	180	1.3								10	26	32	54	94	168	386
	240	1.2							8	28	34	50	78	124	187	511
	360	1.0						9	32	42	64	84	122	142	187	683
	480	1.0						31	44	59	100	114	122	142	187	800
	720	0.8					16	56	88	97	100	114	122	142	187	923
170	90	1.6								12	12	14	34	52	120	232
	120	1.5						2	10	12	18	32	42	83	156	356
	180	1.3					4	10	22	28	34	50	78	120	187	535
	240	1.3					18	24	30	42	50	70	116	142	187	681
	360	1.3				22	34	40	52	60	98	114	122	142	187	873
	480	1.3			14	43	43	60	88	97	100	114	122	142	187	1006
230	5	3.7													2	6
	10	3.3												1	6	13
	15	3.3											3	6	18	31
	20	3.2										2	5	12	26	49
	25	3.2										4	8	22	37	75
	30	3.0									2	8	12	23	51	99
	40	2.8								1	7	15	22	34	74	156
	50	2.8								5	14	16	24	51	59	202
240	5	3.8													2	6
	10	3.5												1	6	14
	15	3.5											3	6	21	35
	20	3.3										3	6	15	26	53
	25	3.2									1	4	9	24	40	82
	30	3.0									4	8	15	22	56	109
	40	2.8								3	7	17	22	39	75	166
	50	2.8							1	8	15	16	29	51	94	217
250	5	3.8													2	7
	10	3.5											1	4	7	16
	15	3.3											4	7	22	38
	20	3.3										4	7	17	27	59
	25	3.2									2	7	10	24	45	92
	30	3.3									6	7	17	23	59	116
	40	3.2								5	9	17	19	45	79	178
	60	2.7					4	10	10	10	12	22	36	64	126	297
	90	2.2				8	10	10	10	28	28	44	68	98	186	513
	120		(SEE EXTREME EXPOSURES BELOW)													
	240															
260	5	4.0												1	2	7
	10	3.8											2	4	9	19
	15	3.7										2	4	10	22	42
	20	3.5									1	4	7	20	31	67
	25	3.5									3	8	11	23	50	99
	30	3.3								2	6	8	19	26	61	125
	40	3.2							1	6	11	16	19	49	84	190
270	5	4.2												1	3	9
	10	4.0											2	5	11	22
	15	3.8										3	4	11	24	46

Table 1-B. (Continued)

Standard / Exceptional Air Decompression (upper tables)

Depth 280 ft

Bottom Time (min)	Time to First Stop	Decompression stops (deepest → 5 ft)
5	3.2	1 … 5
10	3.0	1 4 … 8
15	2.8	1 4 10 … 18
20	2.8	2 7 27 … 40
25	2.8	1 14 25 … 73
30	2.7	2 6 22 37 … 112
40	2.6	2 5 11 23 39 75 … 161
50	2.6	3 5 17 34 61 89 … 199
60	1.8	9 13 17 34 74 134 … 323
120	1.3	1 10 10 18 34 40 64 98 142 187 … 472
180	1.3	6 10 10 10 24 43 64 70 108 142 142 187 … 684
240	1.3	6 24 34 36 43 54 98 98 100 114 122 142 187 … 841
360	1.3	19 29 38 … 142 187 … 1067

Depth 290 ft

Bottom Time (min)	Time to First Stop	Decompression stops
5	3.3	5
10	3.2	2 4 … 10
15	3.0	1 5 13 … 22
20	3.0	4 10 28 … 40
25	2.8	2 7 17 27 … 56
30	2.8	4 9 24 41 … 81
40	2.7	4 9 18 26 63 … 124
50	2.6	1 9 17 18 45 80 … 174

Depth 300 ft

Bottom Time (min)	Time to First Stop	Decompression stops
5	3.5	5
10	3.3	2 5 … 11
15	3.2	5 16 … 27
20	3.0	3 11 24 … 43
25	3.0	1 8 19 33 … 66
30	2.8	1 7 10 23 47 … 91
40	2.7	6 12 22 36 68 … 140
60	—	3 12 17 18 51 86 … 190

Right-hand groups (with Total Ascent Time)

Depth 280

Bottom Time	Time to First Stop	Decompression stops (70 60 50 40 30 20 10)	Total
25	3.2	2 3 8 13 23 53	106
30	3.0	3 6 12 22 27 64	138
40	2.8	5 6 11 17 22 51 88	204

Depth 290

Bottom Time	Time to First Stop	Decompression stops	Total
5	4.3		9
10	4.0	2 2	25
15	3.8	1 2 5 13	49
20	3.8	1 3 4 11 26	81
25	3.7	3 4 8 23 39	113
30	3.5	2 8 7 18 23 56	150
40	3.3	1 3 7 13 22 30 70	218

Depth 300

Bottom Time	Time to First Stop	Decompression stops	Total
5	4.5		10
10	4.2	2 3	30
15	4.0	1 3 5 16	52
20	4.0	1 3 6 12 26	89
25	3.8	3 7 9 23 43	120
30	3.8	3 5 8 17 23 60	162
40	3.7	1 5 6 16 22 36 72	264

(SEE EXTREME EXPOSURES BELOW)

Depth (exceptional)

Bottom Time	Time to First Stop	Decompression stops	Total
5	4.7		11
10	4.3	3 3	32
15	4.2	1 3 6 17	56
20	4.0	2 3 6 15 26	104
25	3.8	2 3 7 10 23 47	128
30	3.8	1 3 6 8 19 26 61	171
40	3.7	2 5 7 17 22 39 75	234
60	3.0	4 6 9 15 17 34 51 90 187	458
90			
120			
180			

(Rev. 1958)

EXTREME EXPOSURES – 250 AND 300 FT.

DEPTH (ft.)	BOTTOM TIME (Min.)	TIME TO FIRST STOP	300	190	180	170	160	150	140	130	120	110	100	90	80	70	60	50	40	30	20	10	TOTAL ASCENT TIME
250	120	1.8								10	10	10	10	16	24	24	36	48	64	94	142	187	682
250	180	1.8						5	8	10	22	22	32	42	44	60	84	114	122	142	187		929
250	240	1.8						9	14	21	22	24	40	42	56	76	98	100	114	122	142	187	1107
300	90	2.3					3	8	8	10	10	16	24	24	34	48	64	90	142	187			691
300	120	2.0					4	8	8	14	24	24	34	42	58	66	102	122	142	187			887
300	180	1.7			3	8	14	20	21	28	40	48	56	82	98	100	114	122	142	187			1165

Table 1-C   U. S. Navy "no decompression" limits and repetitive group designation table for "no decompression" dives.

DEPTH (ft.)	NO DECOMPRESSION LIMITS (Min.)	REPETITIVE GROUPS														
		A	B	C	D	E	F	G	H	I	J	K	L	M	N	O
10	–	60	120	210	300											
15	–	35	70	110	160	225	350									
20	–	25	50	75	100	135	180	240	325							
25	–	20	35	55	75	100	125	160	195	245	315					
30	–	15	30	45	60	75	95	120	145	170	205	250	310			
35	310	5	15	25	40	50	60	80	100	120	140	160	190	220	270	310
40	200	5	15	25	30	40	50	70	80	100	110	130	150	170	200	
50	100	–	10	15	25	30	40	50	60	70	80	90	100			
60	60	–	10	15	20	25	30	40	50	55	60					
70	50	–	5	10	15	20	30	35	40	45	50					
80	40	–	5	10	15	20	25	30	35	40						
90	30	–	5	10	12	15	20	25	30							
100	25	–	5	7	10	15	20	22	25							
110	20	–	–	5	10	13	15	20								
120	15	–	–	5	10	12	15									
130	10	–	–	5	8	10										
140	10	–	–	5	7	10										
150	5	–	–	5												
160	5	–	–	–	5											
170	5	–	–	–	5											
180	5	–	–	–	5											
190	5	–	–	–	5											

(Rev. 1958)

INSTRUCTIONS FOR USE

I. "No decompression" limits

This column shows at various depths greater than 30 feet the allowable diving times (in minutes) which permit surfacing directly at 60 ft. a minute with no decompression stops. Longer exposure times require the use of the Standard Air Decompression Table (Table 1-A).

II. Repetitive group designation table

The tabulated exposure times (or bottom times) are in minutes. The times at the various depths in each vertical column are the maximum exposures during which a diver will remain within the group listed at the head of the column.

To find the repetitive group designation at surfacing for dives involving exposures up to and including the "no decompression limits": Enter the table on the exact or next greater depth than that to which exposed and select the listed exposure time exact or next greater than the actual exposure time. The repetitive group designation is indicated by the letter at the head of the vertical column where the selected exposure time is listed.

For example: A dive was to 32 feet for 45 minutes. Enter the table along the 35 ft. depth line since it is next greater than 32 ft. The table shows that since group "D" is left after 40 minutes exposure and group "E" after 50 minutes, group "E" (at the head of the column where the 50 min. exposure is listed) is the proper selection.

Exposure times for depths less than 40 ft. are listed only up to approximately five hours since this is considered to be beyond field requirements for this table.

Table 1-D. U. S. Navy surface interval credit table.

REPETITIVE GROUP AT THE END OF THE SURFACE INTERVAL

	Z	O	N	M	L	K	J	I	H	G	F	E	D	C	B	A
Z	0:10-0:22	0:34	0:48	1:02	1:18	1:36	1:55	2:17	2:42	3:10	3:45	4:29	5:27	6:56	10:05	12:00*
O		0:10-0:23	0:36	0:51	1:07	1:24	1:43	2:04	2:29	2:59	3:33	4:17	5:16	6:44	9:54	12:00*
N			0:10-0:24	0:39	0:54	1:11	1:30	1:53	2:18	2:47	3:22	4:04	5:03	6:32	9:43	12:00*
M				0:10-0:25	0:42	0:59	1:18	1:39	2:05	2:34	3:08	3:52	4:49	6:18	9:28	12:00*
L					0:10-0:26	0:45	1:04	1:25	1:49	2:19	2:53	3:36	4:35	6:02	9:12	12:00*
K						0:10-0:28	0:49	1:11	1:35	2:03	2:38	3:21	4:19	5:48	8:58	12:00*
J							0:10-0:31	0:54	1:19	1:47	2:20	3:04	4:02	5:40	8:40	12:00*
I								0:10-0:33	0:59	1:29	2:02	2:44	3:43	5:12	8:21	12:00*
H									0:10-0:36	1:06	1:41	2:23	3:20	4:49	7:59	12:00*
G										0:10-0:40	1:15	1:59	2:58	4:25	7:35	12:00*
F											0:10-0:15	1:29	2:28	3:57	7:05	12:00*
E												0:10-0:54	1:57	3:22	6:32	12:00*
D													0:10-1:09	2:38	5:48	12:00*
C														0:10-1:39	2:49	12:00*
B															0:10-2:10	12:00*
A																0:10-12:00*

REPETITIVE GROUP AT THE BEGINNING OF SURFACE INTERVAL (FROM PREVIOUS DIVE)

(Rev. 1958)

INSTRUCTIONS FOR USE

Surface interval time in the table is in hours and minutes ("7:59" means 7 hours and 59 minutes). The surface interval must be at least 10 minutes.

Find the repetitive group designation letter (from the previous dive schedule) on the diagonal slope. Enter the table horizontally to select the listed surface interval time that is exactly or next greater than the actual surface interval time. The repetitive group designation for the end of the surface interval is at the head of the vertical column where the selected surface interval time is listed. For example — a previous dive was to 110 ft. for 30 minutes. The diver remains on the surface 1 hour and 30 minutes and wishes to find the new repetitive group designation: The repetitive group from the last column of the 110/30 schedule in the Standard Air Decompression Tables is "J". Enter the surface interval credit table along the horizontal line labeled "J". The 1 hour and 47 min. listed surface interval time is next greater than the actual 1 hour and 30 minutes surface interval time. Therefore, the diver has lost sufficient inert gas to place him in group "G" (at the head of the vertical column selected).

*NOTE: Dives following surface intervals of more than 12 hours are not considered repetitive dives. Actual bottom times in the Standard Air Decompression Tables may be used in computing decompression for such dives.

Table 1-E. U. S. Navy repetitive dive timetable.

REPET. GROUPS	REPETITIVE DIVE DEPTH (Ft.)															
	40	50	60	70	80	90	100	110	120	130	140	150	160	170	180	190
A	7	6	5	4	4	3	3	3	3	3	2	2	2	2	2	2
B	17	13	11	9	8	7	7	6	6	6	5	5	4	4	4	4
C	25	21	17	15	13	11	10	10	9	8	7	7	6	6	6	6
D	37	29	24	20	18	16	14	13	12	11	10	9	9	8	8	8
E	49	38	30	26	23	20	18	16	15	13	12	12	11	10	10	10
F	61	47	36	31	28	24	22	20	18	16	15	14	13	13	12	11
G	73	56	44	37	32	29	26	24	21	19	18	17	16	15	14	13
H	87	66	52	43	38	33	30	27	25	22	20	19	18	17	16	15
I	101	76	61	50	43	38	34	31	28	25	23	22	20	19	18	17
J	116	87	70	57	48	43	38	34	32	28	26	24	23	22	20	19
K	138	99	79	64	54	47	43	38	35	31	29	27	26	24	22	21
L	161	111	88	72	61	53	48	42	39	35	32	30	28	26	25	24
M	187	124	97	80	68	58	52	47	43	38	35	32	31	29	27	26
N	213	142	107	87	73	64	57	51	46	40	38	35	33	31	29	28
O	241	160	117	96	80	70	62	55	50	44	40	38	36	34	31	30
Z	257	169	122	100	84	73	64	57	52	46	42	40	37	35	32	31

INSTRUCTIONS FOR USE
(Rev. 1958)

The bottom times listed in this table are called "residual nitrogen times" and are the times a diver is to consider he has already spent on bottom when he starts a repetitive dive to a specific depth. They are in minutes.

Enter the table horizontally with the repetitive group designation from the Surface Interval Credit Table. The time in each vertical column is the number of minutes that would be required (at the depth listed at the head of the column) to saturate to the particular group.

For example – the final group designation from the Surface Interval Credit Table, on the basis of a previous dive and surface interval, is "H". To plan a dive to 110 feet, determine the "residual nitrogen time" for this depth required by the repetitive group designation: Enter this table along the horizontal line labeled "H". The table shows that one must start a dive to 110 feet as though he had already been on the bottom for 27 minutes. This information can then be applied to the Standard Air Decompression table or "No Decompression" Table in a number of ways:

(1) Assuming a diver is going to finish a job and take whatever decompression is required, he must add 27 minutes to his actual bottom time and be prepared to take decompression according to the 110 foot schedules for the sum or equivalent single dive time.

(2) Assuming one wishes to make a quick inspection dive for the minimum decompression, he will decompress according to the 110/30 schedule for a dive of 3 minutes or less (27 + 3 = 30). For a dive of over 3 minutes but less than 13, he will decompress according to the 110/40 schedule (27 + 13 = 40).

(3) Assuming that one does not want to exceed the 110/50 schedule and the amount of decompression it requires, he will have to start ascent before 23 minutes of actual bottom time (50 - 27 = 23).

(4) Assuming that a diver has air for approximately 45 minutes bottom time and decompression stops, the possible dives can be computed: A dive of 13 minutes will require 23 minutes of decompression (110/40 schedule), for a total submerged time of 36 minutes. A dive of 13 to 23 minutes will require 34 minutes of decompression (110/50 schedule), for a total submerged time of 47 to 57 minutes. Therefore, to be safe, the diver will have to start ascent before 13 minutes or a standby air source will have to be provided.

15. After initial physical examination, undergo periodic re-examinations.
16. Be able to recognize symptoms of divers' illnesses.
17. Conduct routine maintenance of your equipment.
18. Charge your Scuba only where you know there is good breathing air.
19. Use a Scuba harness with quick-release feature.
20. Do not charge cylinder above rated pressure.
21. Avoid kinks in flexible charging hose.
22. Use safety line when current is requiring near maximum propulsive effort.
23. Never use goggles or ear plugs.
24. Do not rush descent or ascent. Pace yourself at the rate of your exhaust bubbles on ascent, and breathe continuously.
25. Use a life jacket or some floatation device when conditions warrant.
26. Do not continue to dive after reserve device has been actuated.
27. Be able to relieve cramped muscles, both your own and your buddy's.
28. When visibility is poor, ascend with your arm or arms extended above your head, and listen for propeller noises.
29. Do not continue descent if pain in ears and sinus continues.
30. Know your own overall ability and govern your actions by this knowledge.

Observing these safety rules will help to ensure that you will live to re-enter the blue kingdom many times over to work, study, observe and play. These safety rules are compiled for your benefit; so be wise and benefit yourself by paying careful heed to them. Should there be any rule you do not understand clearly, write to the author of this book, and he will be happy to explain in detail.

INJURIES

Air Embolism. Air embolism is perhaps the diver's biggest concern, for it has cost the lives of many divers. It is caused by the entrance of air bubbles into the left side of the heart and arterial circulation as a result of air being forced into the small blood vessels of the lungs.

Why does this happen? Simply because a diver forgets to breathe out while he is coming up to the surface.

While he is submerged, the air in his lungs is under pressure. Then, when he comes to the surface where the pressure is lessened, the air expands and ruptures the delicate tissues of the lungs. Figure 4 will give you an idea of what happens to your lungs when you forget to exhale during an ascent.

Air embolism may be prevented by two different methods. The first, outlined in all diving manuals and stressed in Chapter I, is never to exceed the regulator bubbles during an ascent, or, to make this quite plain, *do not return to the surface faster than 25 feet per minute.* And, *never* hold your breath during an ascent to the surface.

Treatment. The treatment for air embolism is recompression. Now here is an important thing to remember: there are very few civilian-manned recompression chambers and the Navy Department's are scattered. If there is no recompression chamber in the immediate area, the diver should take a fresh tank and go back down below with an assistant. Spare tanks should be ready to be supplied by all stand-by divers. The diver and injured man descend together and there the decompression begins. A full-face mask, such as used on the British Normalair, or the DESCO full-face unit—either shallow water type or Dolphin Scuba, is used on the injured man.

The decompression table is as follows:

171 ft.	75 psi	2 mins.	30 ft.	13-1/2 psi	15 min.
50 ft.	22 psi	5 "	20 ft.	9 psi	20 "
40 ft.	18 psi	6 "	10 ft.	4-1/2 psi	30 "

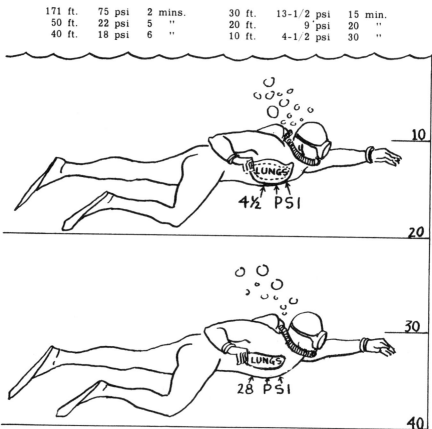

Fig. 4. (Top) Air in lungs, expanded under low pressure. (Bottom) Air in lungs, compressed under high pressure.

When the man has been returned to the surface, he should be taken to the nearest recompression chamber or to a local hospital as fast as possible.

All the stand-by divers should station themselves along the decompression line to either assist or relieve the diver with the injured man. One of the stand-by men should have informed the local office of the State Police and requested assistance and an ambulance.

Air embolism is a serious illness and only prompt action will save a diver's life. The old saying that one ounce of prevention is worth a pound of cure certainly applies in this case.

Bleeding from the Nose and Lungs. Bleeding from the nose usually originates from the middle ear spaces or the nasal sinuses. This condition is often caused by too rapid a descent or by strenuous efforts to clear the ears and sinuses.

Bleeding from the lungs is usually due to the effects of a squeeze or from rupture of the lung tissue incident to air embolism.

Bleeding from the nose and lungs can be avoided if one observes the proper method and rate of descent and avoids taking pressure until the ears and sinuses can be cleared freely. This is the preventative and, by following it to the letter, no divers will experience bleeding from the nose and lungs.

Treatment. Treatment for bleeding from the nose or lungs starts with giving the man medical attention. No recompression is necessary unless the man has been down the length and depth to require it.

Should the man be brought to the surface unconscious, artificial respiration is applied. Cold packs are placed around his head and face. These will serve to stop the bleeding.

Upon arrival of a doctor and ambulance, the doctor should be in-informed, if he does not know it, that 50 cc. of 50% glucose by vein will relieve any headache and allay vomiting so that oxygen may be administered.

Ear Injuries. Pain in the ear usually is experienced when a diver is descending. The pain is caused by a greater amount of pressure being on the outside of the ear drum than on the inside. This is due to the inability of air to flow through the Eustachian tubes into the middle ear. Inflammation and swelling about the opening of the tubes, associated with a head cold, sore throat, etc., will cause this lack of pressure on the middle ear rather than the diver's failure to clear the Eustachian tubes and passages. Only slight pressure is sufficient to cause rupture of the drum with bleeding from the ear or nose.

The prevention is merely a matter of keeping the Eustachian tubes open to allow a sufficient pressure to reach the middle ear to offset the outside water pressure. Divers with colds or ear conditions should not be allowed to dive until this condition has been corrected.

If bleeding occurs or the pain is severe, the diver should report to the doctor immediately.

Exhaustion. Exhaustion occurs to many divers, and usually it is through nobody's fault except the diver's. For the most part, exhaustion is caused by purposeless or ineffective activity.

Exhaustion is prevented by carefully planned and supervised work. Under no circumstances should a diver try doing more than his normal capacity. Underwater work requires good physical stamina and much compressed air from the tanks. Overwork may cause a serious injury.

Treatment. If a diver is brought to the surface unconscious suffering from exhaustion, he should be given oxygen and intravenous fluids. Usually, adequate air supplies, salty fluids and rest are sufficient treatment for divers suffering from exhaustion.

Compressed-air Illness. Compressed-air illness has many other names which divers will recognize: bends, decompression sickness, or caisson disease. It is a condition resulting from an inadequate decompression following exposure to pressure. Bubbles of nitrogen are formed in the tissues and blood stream and, by their mechanical obstruction, cause pain, paralysis, asphyxia and, in severe cases, death.

As the diver works at any depth, nitrogen bubbles form in his blood stream. Should he ascend too fast, not giving these bubbles enough time to dissolve, they will cause symptoms directly in the cells by their pressure on nerve cells or, indirectly, by interfering with the body's circulation. When nitrogen bubbles interfere with the body's circulation, either they unite to make large bubbles which block the blood vessels, or there are so many bubbles that they replace the blood.

The U.S. Navy has found that the compressed-air illness strikes a majority of men within 30 minutes of their return to the surface. Only 1% of the Navy divers had the symptoms delayed over 6 hours.

Compressed-air illnesses are found to occur with the following frequency:

1. Local Pain _____ 89
2. Legs _____ 70
3. Arms _____ 30
4. The Staggers (dizziness) _____ 5.3
5. Paralysis _____ 2.3
6. The Chokes (shortness of breath) _____ 1.6
7. Extreme Fatigue & Pain _____ 1.3
8. Collapse with Unconsciousness _____ .5

A typical case of compressed-air illness may begin with an itching or burning sensation of a local area. The itching and burning may spread and then return to the area of original location. This itching and burning sensation may be accompanied by a tingling or numb feeling. There may be a rash, and the skin can become mottled and blotched.

Pain is usually slight at the start and grows progressively worse until it finally becomes unbearable; it is described as being felt in the bones and in the joints.

Paralysis, asphyxia, collapse, extreme fatigue, and the chokes are easily recognized because of their dramatic onset. These symptoms are rare; but when they occur, they are the final and most serious stages of compressed-air illness.

Whenever there is any doubt as to whether a diver is suffering from compressed-air illness, the diver should be treated without any unnecessary delay. Any delay regarding compressed-air illness is most dangerous.

Compressed-air illness may be prevented by observing a few safety rules.

No man should be allowed in the water when he has overindulged in alcohol. Also, excessive fatigue or a general "run-down" condition is sufficient reason to restrict a diver from going below.

In any diving operation, it is the unrestricted duty of the senior diving officer, operations foreman, or supervisor present, to prohibit any diver from entering the water when it appears that his condition is not satisfactory. Should there be any doubt as to the physical condition of a diver, he should be sent immediately to a qualified doctor for an examination and not be permitted to go below until cleared by the doctor.

The doctor should be informed as to the man's type of work. Upon completion of the examination, the doctor's report should be phoned to the officer who requested it and a written certified copy sent as soon as possible.

The senior diving officer, operations foreman, or supervisor should maintain detailed records of every dive. These records should show the exact time of the dive, the depth of the dive, the duration of the dive. There is no excuse for not keeping records up to date. From such records important diagnosis and treatment can be made.

Decompression should be practiced at all times, allowing for unforeseen accidents to equipment, etc.

If a diver feels he is not well, regardless of the nature of the illness, whether slight or serious, he should report it to the supervisor immediately. Many serious cases of the bends have begun with just a slight itch or pain. Failure to report any such pain may cause permanent injury to the diver or even cost him his life.

Treatment for Compressed-air Illness. The United States Navy has set up Treatment Tables for compressed-air illness. These tables should be strictly adhered to, and the recommended time should not be shortened for reasons of convenience or economy.

Nitrogen Narcosis. Narcosis normally occurs at depths over one hundred feet. The effects are similar to drunkenness. Typical effects are recklessness, loss of ability to perform simple tasks, and other strange behavior. It is almost impossible to prevent nitrogen narcosis when employing compressed air as the breathing medium.

Table 2. Treatment for Compressed-air Illness

Stops

Bends— Pain only

Rate of descent, 25 ft. per min.	Rate of ascent, 1 min. betw. stops	Pain relieved at depths less than 66 ft. Use table B if O_2 is not available	Pain relieved at depths greater than 66 ft. Use table D if O_2 is not available. If pain does not improve within 30 mins. at 165 ft. the case is probably not bends. Decompress on Table C or D.
lbs.	**ft.**	**Table A** **Table B**	**Table C** **Table D**

lbs.	ft.	Table A	Table B	Table C	Table D
73.4	165			30(Air)	30(Air)
62.3	140			12(Air)	12(Air)
53.3	120			12(Air)	12(Air)
44.5	100	30(Air)	30(Air)	12(Air)	12(Air)
35.6	80	12(Air)	12(Air)	12(Air)	12(Air)
26.7	60	30(O_2)	30(Air)	30(O_2)	30(Air)
22.3	50	30(O_2)	30(Air)	30(O_2)	30(Air)
17.8	40	30(O_2)	30(Air)	30(O_2)	30(Air)
13.4	30		60(Air)	60(O_2)	2 hrs. (Air)
8.9	20	5(O_2)	60(Air)		2 hrs. (Air)
4.5	10		2 hrs. (Air)	5(O_2)	4 hrs. (Air)
Surface			1min. (Air)		1 min. (Air)

Table 3

Stops

Serious Symptoms

Rate of descent, 25 ft. per min.	Rate of ascent, 1 min. betw. stops	Symptoms relieved within 30 mins. at 165 ft. Use Table A.	Symptoms not relieved within 30 mins. at 165 ft. Use Table B.
lbs.	**ft.**	**Table A**	**Table B**
73.4	165	30(Air)	30 to 120(Air)
62.3	140	12(Air)	30(Air)
53.4	120	12(Air)	30(Air)
44.5	100	12(Air)	30(Air)
35.6	80	12(Air)	30(Air)
26.7	60	30(Air) or (O_2)	6 hrs. (Air)
22.3	50	30(Air) or (O_2)	6 hrs. (Air)
17.8	40	30(Air) or (O_2)	6 hrs. (Air)
13.4	30	12 hrs. (Air)	First 11 hrs. (Air) Then 1 hr. (O_2) or (Air).
8.9	20	2 hrs. (Air)	First 1 hr. (Air). Then 1 hr. (O_2) or (Air).
4.5	10	2 hrs. (Air)	First 1 hr. (Air). Then 1 hr. (O_2) or (Air).
Surface		1 min. (Air)	1 min. (O_2)

(Time at all stops in minutes unless otherwise indicated.)

If only pain is present, treat in accordance with Tables, A, B, C, or D, as shown in Treatment Table 2.

If serious symptoms occur, treat in accordance with Tables 3A and 3B, as shown. The symptoms requiring this treatment are:

1. Unconsciousness
2. Convulsions
3. Weakness or inability to use arms or legs
4. Visual disturbances
5. Dizziness
6. Loss of speech or hearing
7. Shortness of breath

If dizziness, nausea, muscular twitchings, or blurring of vision occur while breathing oxygen, remove the mask and proceed as follows (in a recompression chamber):

If using Table 2A, complete remaining stops on Table 2B.
If using Table 2C, complete remaining stops on Table 2D.
If using Table 3A, complete remaining stops on Table 3A, breathing air.

At the discretion of the medical officer, oxygen breathing may be resumed at the 40- and 30-foot stops for a total of 90 minutes if using Tables 2A or 3A, and for 150 minutes if using Table 2C.

Should the diver be taken down too fast, he may become temporarily worse. Do not exceed the rate of descent prescribed.

When a diver suffers from a severe case of compressed-air illness, it is advisable to transport him to the nearest recompression chamber without delay.

When dives over one hundred feet are necessary, only the most experienced divers should make the descent. These divers will know the narcotic effects and will control their actions accordingly. Divers descending in Scuba over two hundred feet for work are not capable of effective performance.

Carbon Monoxide Poisoning. This diver's accident occurs when the compressor intake valve is located close to the exhaust from an internal combustion engine. It can also be caused by a flashing of the lubricating oil in the air compressor cylinder.

Prevention. Carbon monoxide poisoning can be prevented by keeping the air intake system of the diver's air compressor away from the fumes of all internal combustion engines or other toxic fumes such as gasoline, paints, etc.

Treatment. Carbon monoxide poisoning can frequently be recognized by pale skin and bright red lips of the victim. Artificial respiration should be given in the presence of apnea. Oxygen should be administered in all cases. A mixture of oxygen and four to seven percent carbon dioxide is preferable. The use of intravenous procaine also has been recommended. Oxygen will accomplish a reconversion of the carboxyhemoglobin in approximately thirty (30) to ninety (90) minutes. Air will require two hours or more for the reconversion. If a coma should persist beyond the above periods of time using either medium, it suggests organic brain damage as a result of anoxia.

Hyperventilation, or Shallow Water Blackout. Skin divers take a series of forced inhalations and exhalations prior to diving. This action reduces the CO_2 content in the blood stream and tissues; if practiced too much, it can cause shallow water blackout.

Prevention. Hyperventilation can be prevented by practicing a moderate use of inhalation and exhalation.

Treatment. Artificial respiration in any prescribed method such as Chest Pressure–Arm Lift; Back Pressure–Arm Lift or Mouth-to-Mouth.

Thousands of divers enter the water each day and return safely without ever feeling the effects of the illnesses listed. It is only the foolhardy who becomes a casualty or a name on a death certificate. Practice safe diving procedure and your diving buddies will never be placed in a position where they will have to practice the illness treatments on you.

Fig. 4A.   Scubapro-Galeazzi recompression chamber. This is a one-man unit, contains all the latest safety equipment, and is low priced. (U. Zancolli)

TREATMENT WITHOUT CHAMBER

Frequently, diving operations are carried on without a recompression chamber being available. Should a diver develop compressed-air illness, the attending personnel may be hard put to administer adequate recompression. If the man is conscious and able to care for himself, he should be put in a suit and recompressed in the water. If he is partially paralyzed, another diver should be put down with him to operate his valve and help him. This is a particularly difficult and dangerous procedure which should not be undertaken unless absolutely necessary.

In certain instances, especially in emergency harbor clearance work, a man may develop compressed-air illness and there will be no chamber available and an insufficient depth of water in which to recompress him in accordance with the treatment tables. In such cases, the diver should be taken to 30 feet and there treated as instructed in Table 3A.

In order that all possible safety precautions may be offered readers of this book, the locations of recompression chambers have been secured from the United States Navy.

Cmdr. M. desGranges, U.S.N., Officer-in-Charge, Experimental Diving Unit, U.S. Naval Gun Factory, Washington, D.C., in supplying this information, wrote that, "while recompression chambers are located as per attached list, it frequently occurs that qualified submarine medical officers are not at hand. Personnel transfers make it impossible to maintain accurate records of this condition. Secondly, a recent decision by the Comptroller of the Navy directed that navy diving facilities who render recompression treatment to civilians would require payment for this service. The exact costs of such treatment are being considered. They would, of course, vary with the type of treatment required and also with the installation performing the service."

MILLIONS IN SALVAGE

Salvage is the biggest underwater business that a Scuba diver can enter. There are millions of ponds, lakes and rivers in the United States, and resting on the bottom of them are billions of dollars in salvagable goods. Our coastal waters are dotted with an untold number of wrecks which are all worth money to the divers possessing the courage, knowledge and desire.

There will be some salvage operations which you will contract to undertake that will be so easy you will wonder why they bothered to call a diver at all. As a general rule, the greater part of your salvage operations will be spent in trying to locate an object that requires only an hour to restore to the surface.

These remarks make salvage sound easy, but don't be misled. Bankruptcy has befallen some of our country's largest salvage organizations in their attempts to raise sunken vessels. Failing to complete the job they undertook, the companies not only lost their money but, in some ventures, good divers and equipment as well. Proper management will save your diving salvage firm from flirting with bankruptcy.

Deep-sea commercial salvage divers have been operating for a long time, and a great part of the knowledge and experience accumulated by these men has been applied with modification to techniques of operation for Scuba salvage divers.

Marine salvage experts have devoted many hours in devising the salvage tables which work successfully in restoring sunken objects to the surface. From the experience of such men as Adm. Edward R. Ellsberg, USN (Ret.), Tom Eadis and Frank Meier, all master salvors, the Scuba salvage methods have been formulated. Earl Cross, Dick Bonin, and Lieut. Bob Fay, USN, have also contributed their knowledge. Dmitri Rebikoff, brilliant French engineering consultant, devised the table for gas-filled lifting balloons. Many others have contributed to make salvage operations for Scuba divers easier.

SALVAGE EQUIPMENT

Equipment is the first necessity in operating any business successfully. Following is a list of the basic tools needed for a salvage diving business.

Scuba Unit. The compressed-air type is the best, although it is not necessary.

Rubber Suit. Either type will do for a starter, but, as business progresses, both should be owned. In the colder waters of the New England Coast, the wet suit is worn as underwear with the dry suit as the outer garment for complete protection.

Grapnels; Drag Hooks. These instruments often make the underwater search a great deal easier.

Air Supply. If the diver does not own his own compressor, it is wise to rent 200 to 300 cu. ft. oxygen tanks from a local concern and have them charged with compressed air to carry along to the job.

Accessories. Ropes, chains, tools, block and tackle, winch, hosing, small portable compressor, lifting devices, etc. The ropes, chain, tools, and block and tackle should always be handy, for their need is inevitable. The compressor, lifting devices, and hosing are inexpensive and serve an essential function in restoring sunken objects to the surface.

The compressor can be purchased at a second-hand dealer's, junk shop, or refrigerator-repair shop. This is used to pump up lifting bags or air drum lifts. A small gasoline engine will suffice for the power supply needed to run the compressor. The lifting devices also run from the air supply of the compressor.

Lifting bags may be purchased from various dealers who will be listed in the manufacturer's index. Air-drum lifts are made from 55-gal. surplus gasoline drums, purchasable at $4.00 from any local garage, junk dealer, etc.

Salvage Craft. A large skiff with high sides is the best for this type of work. Plans for building such a craft can be found in Chapter IX.

This amount of equipment is enough to start and maintain a salvage business. As time progresses, more equipment can be added in accordance with the amount and type of business contracted.

LOCATING AN OBJECT

Before an object can be restored to the surface, it must be located. There are many methods used to locate sunken objects and articles. Some are quite simple; others more complex.

The O-V-O Method. This is perhaps the simplest method, but at the same time one of the most costly. O-V-O is olive oil. When it is poured on the water on a calm day, great distances can be seen by the searcher. Nevertheless, the price of olive oil may well write this simple method off the books.

The Observation Scope. This is a length of tube with a glass at one end, or a box-like wooden structure with glass on the bottom. Observation scopes are commercially manufactured from wood, metal and plexiglass. A home-built model can be constructed with additional pieces, such as lights, buoys, etc., built into it to suit the diver's needs. Incidentally, a good carpenter is an asset in the salvage business.

The Circle-wheel Method. This method of searching employs a large wooden spool weighted with cement, lead, sand, etc., with a long length of rope attached to the spool. The wheel is sunk at the spot designated as the area for the search to begin. A line is nailed to the wheel and runs to the surface, where it is attached to a small float with the International Flag, "Divers Down," or a sign denoting that divers are working below.

The diver descends to the wheel, takes the rope in one hand, and starts his circular search (*see* Fig. 5). As the rope unwinds, the diver thoroughly covers an area the distance of the rope. If the salvors cannot find an old discarded electrical wire spool to use for this purpose, one can be built. A line wrapped about the anchor chain serves the same purpose.

Fig. 5.   The circle-wheel search method.

A similar device is a pole driven into the bottom with a line which has small pieces of cloth tied on it at 20-foot intervals. The line is taken out to its full length by the diver. Circular search begins and, when the cycle has been completed, the diver moves up the line to the next cloth marker and repeats the action. If the diver prefers not to drive a metal pole into the bottom, it can be sunk into a large can filled with cement.

The Field-string Method. This requires the diver to place two weighted lengths of rope parallel, 25 to 50 feet apart. The diver swims back and forth between the ropes, covering all the area. If the object is not there, the farthest rope is moved up.

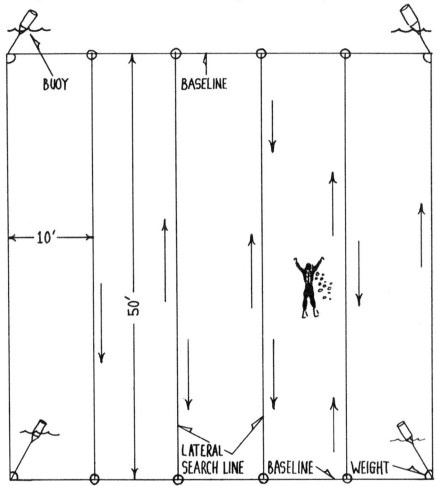

BUOY

BASELINE

←—10'—→

50'

LATERAL
SEARCH LINE BASELINE WEIGHT

Fig. 6.   The jackstay search method.

The Checker-board and Criss-cross Search Pattern. These are similar, inasmuch as the tender directs the operations from the surface by means of a safety line attached to the diver's weight or life belt.

Underwater Metal Detector. The Goldak Model UD-10 Underwater Metal Detector is a portable, self-contained, battery-operated metal detection instrument designed for underwater use.

Completely waterproofed, the UD-10 makes use of an 18″ diameter antenna loop which permits a maximum detection range of 10 feet. As the swimmer carries the instrument over such objects as outboard motors, ship's hulls, anchors, chests, coins and other metallic objects, the lighted meter indicates their presence by swinging "full scale." The meter is read through the main loop disc which is fabricated from ½″ thick lucite sheet. The electronic components are

Fig. 6A. Woman diving-historian locates sunken Spanish wreck. (Voit)

mounted below and sealed by a one-piece molded lucite cover. The detector is weighted so that no effort is expended in swimming with it and yet it will slowly rise to the surface if released. Detection in both salt water as well as fresh water is possible.

Plans for constructing a ferrous-nonferrous metal detector from surplus military electronics parts will be found in Chapter IX.

The Jackstay Search Method. Figure 6 shows this method of locating sunken objects.

SURFACING SUNKEN OBJECTS

After the object has been located, it must be brought to the surface. Following are described some popular methods used by Scuba divers for raising sunken objects.

Manual Labor. This, of course, is by far the cheapest method of restoring objects to the surface, but requires plenty of arm, leg, and back muscles. There will be many times when the "ML System" will be impossible because of the size and weight of the object and other factors, as well.

Block and Tackle. For objects of extreme size and weight, and for some that are covered with mud, seaweed, kelp, or other bottom debris, block and tackle are used. The apparatus is generally worked from the diver's salvage boat on which a brace is set up for the tackle gear to operate efficiently.

The Hoisting Boom and Winch System. This is used only with a salvage draft of the flat-bottom type. The hoisting boom is constructed to set in the middle of the craft and work in all directions without shifting the position of the boat. The winch is operated from a ramp platform built in the bow. If the boom has been constructed properly, all the weight is equally distributed, but extra planking and bracing are needed to insure that, when it is in operation, the weight of the object being lifted will not rip the boom from its mooring or drive the boom shaft through the bottom of the craft.

The winch is secured to a ramp or foredeck platform by bolting and operated from the bow only.

When lifting an object of considerable weight, the after section of the salvage craft should have extra ballast to keep the bow from being pulled under by the object's weight. Many types and models of winches can be employed in salvage work. Those using short multilines have been found to give better service than single, long-line types. Surplus outlets have a wide selection to choose from.

Air-drum Floats. Salvage divers construct these from used gasoline or oil drums of any size. The large 55-gallon drum is capable of lifting up to 500 pounds. Two of these drums welded together can lift objects weighing 1,000 pounds and more.

The air-drum floats are fitted with standard faucets to admit the water for sinking the floats to the work, and to allow the water to escape when air from a top-side compressor is forced into the drums. A needle valve attached to the drum's manifold is used to regulate the drum's buoyancy. Any number of these air-drum floats can be used in raising a sunken object. Plans for fitting the floats are given in Chapter IX.

Lifting Bags. These work on much the same principle as the air-drum floats, although they are a standard manufactured salvage product. These bags are the Scuba salvor's dream, inasmuch as they are easy to handle, inexpensive and do a powerful job. They are made of rubber, canvas, mesh wire and nylon-webbing reinforcement and located on the top of the bag are the inlet valve and throat. The throat serves as an escape route for the expanding air, which increases as the bag lifts toward the surface. The throat also has an optional non-return valve fitted to it.

Dmitri Rebikoff has devised the following table which shows the amount of gas required to fill lifting bags.

Table 4. Gas Requirements for Lifting Devices*

Diameter ins.	Lifting Power	Cu. Ft. to Fill Lifting Bags (90 ft.)	(180 ft.)
20	140 lbs.	4.4	8.8
30	490 "	15.	30.
40	1175 "	41.	82.
60	3930 "	90.	247.
80	9460 "	280.	565.
120	14 tons	989.	1977.
160	33 "	2366.	4731.
200	65 "	4590.	9230.
240	113 "	7985.	15960.
280	180 "	12762.	25423.

* From "Free Diving," Sidgwick and Jackson.

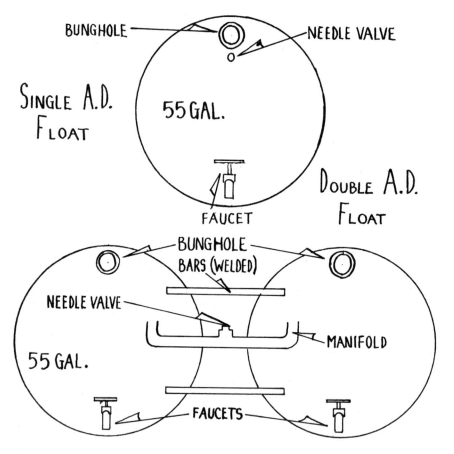

Fig. 7. Air-drum float system. (*Shallow Water Diving and Spearfishing,* Schenck and Kendall, Cornell Maritime Press)

Fig. 7A. Lifting bags being used to raise a sunken compressor. (Hypro Diving Equipment Co.)

Manufacturers have lifting bags of many different styles and types, but they all serve the same purpose. A salvor definitely needs bags such as these in his business, perhaps not at the beginning, but before too many seasons pass.

Plans for making lifting bags will be found in Chapter IX.

Using air to bring an object to the surface is no easy task. The first lesson to be learned in floating an object by air is to keep pressure constant. At the object's depth, *exactly* 2 pounds more of air pressure should be employed in the lifting devices than there is water pressure surrounding the object. When the object rises, the water pressure begins to decrease and the air in the lifting devices expands. Thus, the air in the lifting devices must decrease at the proper rate in accordance with the decreased water pressure. When the object breaks the surface, both air pressure and water pressure must be the same.

If a diver chooses to place his lifting equipment inside the object to be brought up, he must remember to keep a constant check on the air pressure. If air is allowed to enter the lifting devices too fast, the object might blow up just as though a charge of explosives had been used. The art of salvage by air is not easily learned; it requires experimentation and practice. The longer a diver is in the salvage game, the more knowledge about the sea he acquires and he learns a variety of new tricks to be employed in raising a sunken object.

The newer type open end lifting bags do not present the problems of employing the 2-pound air pressure requirement. As the bag ascends toward the surface into lesser pressure, the excess air will be forced out the large opening at the bottom of the bag. Tubular bags have a throat discharge tube on the top of the bag which allows the slow escape of expanding air.

Floating Equipment. The diving-salvor must have some means of transportation to take him to and from underwater jobs. A small salvage boat such as described in Chapter IX can be built in the back yard. This boat may be built to any length up to 22 ft. and 6 ft. wide. It can have a cabin, storage lockers, electronics equipment, and powered by an inboard engine in the 18 ft. to 22 ft. models, and in the smaller models, everything would be scaled down. The smaller models would most likely be powered by outboard motors thereby allowing the diver to utilize all the on-board space for tools of the trade.

If the individual diver or salvage diving group has sufficient funds, the purchase of a surplus military amphibian DUKW (Duck) would be a great asset to the business. The DUKW is a boat placed over a 2½-ton GMC heavy-duty truck chassis. It is capable of traveling over the highways at speeds up to 50 mph and in the water at 6 knots per hour. The DUKW has a large cargo or working compartment, a built-in air compressor capable of sustaining a hookah diver in shallow water, a winch and boom assembly for lifting. The author's company uses amphibian DUKWs and consider them to be the best all-purpose units for a diving company. DUKW can be purchased from surplus dealers or directly by bid from the Federal Surplus Sales Office, The Federal Center, Battle Creek, Michigan. Upon written request, the government will send all necessary forms free to those interested in bidding on federal surplus property. Divers should take advantage of the surplus market; there are hundreds of items available which divers can purchase at military salvage yards at reasonable prices.

In the event a DUKW is not available, the M-29 Weasel can be used. This unit is an amphibian with rubber tracked lags. Since the lags are rubber capped, it is allowable on the highway. The Weasel is small, neither too fast on the road nor on the water, but serviceable in many jobs. It can be converted to do many other land jobs. This unit can also be purchased from surplus dealers or directly through government surplus outlets.

Fig. 7B. (Left) M-29 Weasel. (Right) Amphibian DUKW. (U.S. Army)

WAGES FOR SALVAGE WORK

Salvage, like all underwater occupations, is dangerous and divers doing this work must be well trained and experienced all-around mechanics. The equipment and tools to service the trade are very expensive. Because of the dangers involved and the expense of equipment, the wage scale is high. The following scale has been compiled with the assistance of the Research Division, AFL-CIO Headquarters, Washington, D.C., and the former Navy Salvage Service. Union pay scales and work conditions have been taken from California, Florida, Washington-Maryland, New York, and New England, as a cross comparison of the United States. The figures have been compiled and the general average is given here.

Diver without equipment and tenderman	$65.00
Diver with basic diving equipment	90.00
Diver with equipment and tenderman	145.00
Diver handling explosives (in addition to regular diver's pay)	50.00

Time of personnel starts from date of preparation for service and continues until date of return to home office. Due to varying conditions, the working hours and number of divers to be employed on a specific task shall be under the discretion of the Chief Diver. Prices include an eight (8) hour day or any part thereof in water not in excess of fifty (50) feet in depth, between the hours of 8 A.M. and 5 P.M.

A Senior Scuba Diver must be qualified to handle salvage, recovery, construction, repair, and cutting and welding operations. A Master Scuba Diver is fully qualified for undersea construction, repair, salvage, cutting and welding, demolitions, recovery, inspection and investigation. He is also qualified as an instructor, with the authorization to sign training and work logbooks and diver's papers.

A diver's day is usually 6 hours; but if he is under contract and employed by a construction company where the work is steady and in comparatively shallow water, he may extend the working day to 8 hours. If a diver is required to remain below over the 8-hour period, the hourly pay rate is doubled. From then on, the pay basis is in terms of 4 additional hours:

Hours	Pay Scale (Master Scuba Diver)
0—8	$ 22. 50 per hr.
8—12	45. 00 " "
12—16	100. 00 " "
16—20	250. 00 " "
20—24	500. 00 " "
Over 24	1000. 00 " "

There have been only two Scuba divers who have remained below over 24 hours. The world's foremost undersea photographer, Ed Fisher, has achieved this marvelous feat. More recent is the report that a Canadian also has accomplished the same feat, but with a special tank. The self-contained diver who remains below for more than 12 hours, especially if working, is a rarity. The author strongly advises that divers do not attempt to remain in the water any longer than necessary. Six hours is a long day for a diver. The record feats of self-contained divers have been mentioned merely to prove that self-contained diving equipment is every bit as good as the commercial deep-sea diving gear.

If a diver plans to become an accomplished salvor, he must give up any thoughts of trying to break depth records or time-endurance records. A salvor's business is primarily the raising of objects

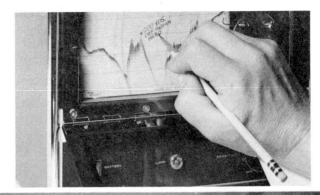

Fig. 7C. (Top) Depthometer used by salvors to check underwater conditions. (Bendix) (Center) Navy Scuba diver instructs deep-sea diver trainee. (Bottom) Navy divers replace a damaged propeller blade. (U.S. Navy)

which have gone below and making money for his work. A diver is well paid for his services, but, since no insurance company in the United States will issue a policy to a diver, except at the cost of a month's salary, and, since work comes infrequently, a diver must receive good pay for his services.

A diver who works for himself and has a small business must set the prices for a job in accordance with the known facts. Two primary factors determine the cost of the job: the approximate depth of the water in which the article was lost and the value of the lost article. Secondary facts which a salvor should know are the size of the object, its weight, possible buoyancy, the accuracy of its known location, the legal ownership, and the bottom conditions of the area of dive and search.

Many divers have found themselves in awkward situations because they neglected to have the customer prove legal ownership of the article in question. In the case of salvage in coastal, federal, or international waters, there is definitely no law concerning original ownership. Objects become the property of the diver when they are found below with no buoy attached.

SALVAGE LAW INFORMATION

What is salvage? It is compensation given or due salvors for their work, time and efforts in saving any or all of a ship's cargo, or the vessel, or the vessel with cargo intact. Material salvaged from a wreck or a derelict is classed as salvage, and so is the saving of a ship and cargo from loss.

Salvage can be performed by anyone capable of doing the work. The right to receive salvage is an absolute legal right. All salvage cases are Cases of Admiralty and come under the maritime jurisdiction. Each salvage case is heard and each is decided on its own merit.

Salvage Returns. The amount of an award by the Court of Admiralty depends upon a number of factors. Prime consideration is given to the amount of property saved, the amounts of work, danger and time spent by the salvors, and the salvors' equipment, professional experience and dangers encountered.

Property which has been designated as a total loss by the owners, insurance companies, etc., and which is safely salvaged and returned to the appropriate parties normally brings the highest awards. Fifty percent (50%) of the property value is the customary award in such cases. However, awards up to and including seven-eighths (7/8) of the value have been given in some total loss cases.

Wrecks. A wreck is anything that has been cast ashore by the sea, or sunk beneath the sea, or that is afloat upon the sea, and having no apparent owner. However, maritime law provides that nothing is ever lost at sea, therefore the phrase "having no apparent owner" would have to be disregarded; everything seems to have an owner. Yet, continuing ownership does not prevent lawful salvage.

Wrecking is the removal, destructon, stealing and/or plundering of cargo, fittings, money, goods and/or other effects from a vessel, within maritime jurisdiction, lost, wrecked, aground or in distress. This act is a crime against the vessel's owners and is punishable in the country where the crime is committed. The crime is compounded when the salvors bring ashore these ill-gotten gains. The illegal landing of such salvaged goods is termed smuggling and this act is a punishable crime in all countries throughout the world.

Vessel and Cargo Ownership. Although a vessel has been completely sunk, or is classed as a derelict, abandoned or aground, the vessel and its cargo remains the property of the owner(s). In some cases, the insurance underwriters will have paid the owners for their loss, in part or in full, and the portion which the underwriters have reimbursed the owners becomes their property.

If a vessel, equipment from a vessel, or the cargo, in part or whole, is salvaged, this property does not automatically become that of the salvors. Admiralty Court *must* be notified of the salvage accompanied by a complete listing of the salvaged items. and a salvage claim must be filed. The award made to the salvors for their efforts will fully compensate them for their efforts, and it will normally amount to more than if the items were illegally sold.

Locating Owners. When a salvage group locates a vessel, and they desire to salvage portions of it or any cargo, they should contact the owners. Large ocean vessels usually have the ship's name on the stern, in the ship's bell, or on a name plate. Boats registered with the U.S. Coast Guard (or a state watercraft bureau) will have a number painted on the hull usually near the bow. Many of these ships will carry a name located across the stern. Small boats operating in coastal waters will also carry numbers. Documented vessels will have an official number stamped on a main strength member, or in a wooden vessel, the number would be carved or burned.

The Bureau of Shipping, Washington, D.C., or Regional District Offices of the U.S. Coast Guard maintain ship records. With the name of a vessel, or the numbers found on the hull or main member, locating the owner should not be a very difficult task.

In the case of small privately-owned pleasure boats, the inboard engine, outboard motor, possible fittings, and even the anchor will have a serial number. The owners can be traced through the manufacturer and the dealer.

Do *not* neglect to contact the owner(s) when property on, under, or in the sea has been found and there is a desire to salvage.

Most diving jobs are contracted on a time basis. When a diver's chance of finding an object is slight, payment by the hour is the general rule. However, it should be the policy of the diver to explain to the customer the slight chance of his locating the object in question and to set a minimum time limit for searching. On a job of this nature, the basic pay is usually $15.00 an hour. When a diver uses a tenderman, an extra $5.00 to $7.50 an hour is added to the diver's fee to pay the tenderman, who is usually essential for a successful operation.

The following information* will be helpful in arriving at bonus fees:

1. Outboard Motors: If motor was properly lubricated, it is worth recovering after 2 or 3 months submersion in sea water but will need a new ignition system and carburetor parts. Cost of parts: about $25. After 6 months to a year, any motor is of doubtful value.

2. Moorings: Chain moorings, ⅓ to ½ the purchase price; Iron mushroom moorings, up to ½ the purchase price, or up to 12¢ a pound.

3. Prop, Shafting and Stems, $10.00 to $20.00 for a complete unit.

4. Anchors, up to $1.00 per pound (patent only, such as Danforth & Northill).

5. Scrap Metals: Lead, 9–14¢ per pound; copper, brass, and bronze, up to 50¢ per pound.

Iron is not worth getting unless there are tons of it lying on the bottom. The lead keel is one of the most valuable parts of a boat and the shafting and props are always worth recovering.

OTHER JOBS FOR DIVERS

Besides the salvage work dealt with in this chapter, there are many other jobs for a Scuba diver. Divers are employed by federal, state, county, and civic agencies, working at such jobs as fisheries science research, cleaning public swimming pools and beaches, recovering drowned victims and inspecting water tanks, bridges, pier pilings and docks. Industries and businesses that have a connection with the water will employ divers to check docks, underwater piping and company vessels. Insurance companies often call upon a diver to locate articles that have gone below and check various items on damaged or wrecked automobiles which have been involved in accidents by going over bridges, docks, or piers. Removing valuable commercial metals and inspecting boat hulls also should be mentioned. When the question of prices arises regarding this last type of job, the diver must know whether it is to be done at a drydock or in a boatyard.

Cleaning and scraping hulls is a job which divers can perform while the vessel remains in the water. This work saves the boat owner from having his vessel tied up in a dry dock for several days. A staging resembling a painter's scaffold is set up from which to work. Two divers can clean a 35 ft. ship's hull in one day. Fee is based on the charges as established by the boatyard for the same work.

---

* From *Shallow Water Diving and Spearfishing*, Schenck and Kendall, Cornell Maritime Press.

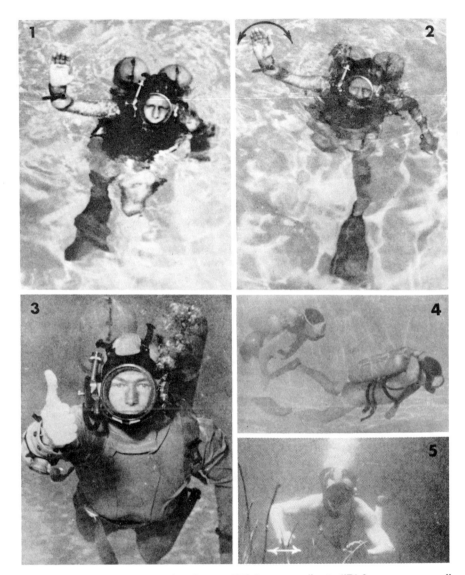

Fig. 8. Underwater hand signals. *1.* "Pick me up." *2.* "Pick me up now." *3.* "Lets go up." *4.* "I am having trouble with my air." (Right hand back to air valve at top of tanks.) (U.S. Navy) *5.* "How deep?" (Right hand back and forth parallel to sea floor.) (H. Braun, *Skin Diver Magazine*)

Propeller replacement is profitable. Check with a boatyard to learn the correct method of removal and replacement. Fee is the same as charges by the boatyard. Always employ safety procedures when working with props. See Fig. 7C (Bottom).

Diving salvage requires the buddy system. If the job below requires only one man, the buddy serves as tender and standby diver. Refer to the National Safety Council's Safety Data Manual, *Diving in Construction Operations,* for safe diving procedures in all underwater work situations.

Scuba divers without communications should use a signal line. The tenderman-standby diver handles the signal line and all the tools used by the diver. The U.S. Navy line signals are universally used.

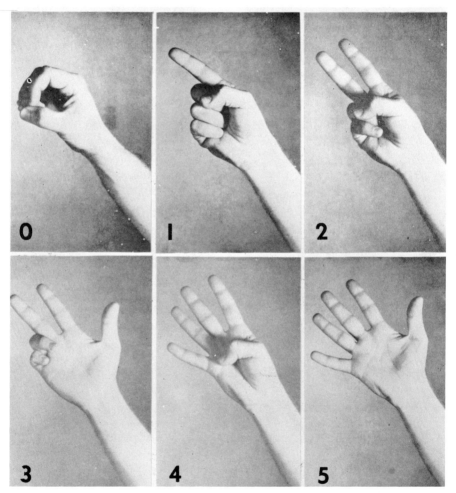

Fig. 8. Underwater hand signals (*cont.*). *0.* Sign for 0. *1.* Sign for 1. *2.* Sign for 2. *3.* Sign for 3. *4.* Sign for 4. *5.* Sign for 5. (U.S. Navy)

Among the safety rules to be observed while working in strange harbors and on objects underwater are:

1. Always post floating signs and rope off the area in which a diver is working.

2. Make sure that all underwater tools are counter-balanced to make them almost weightless in water.

3. When working with props, remember to turn them with the utmost care.

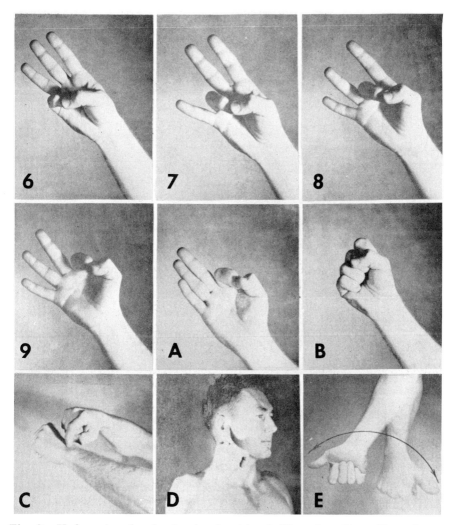

Fig. 8. Underwater hand signals (*cont.*). *6.* Sign for 6. *7.* Sign for 7. *8.* Sign for 8. *9.* Sign for 9. *A.* "All right." *B.* "Hold everything." *C.* "What time?" *D.* "I am having trouble with my ear." *E.* "What direction?" (U.S. Navy)

The author has no record of divers being killed by speed maniacs driving their "hot rod" speed boats around a harbor, but that does not prove that it cannot happen. Divers should never take any chances, especially with some crackpot and his boat. It is better that the diver surface and go ashore.

ROPE SIGNALS

Tender to Diver:

Signal   Meaning
1 pull   Are you all right? (When a diver is descending, 1 pull also
          means stop.)
2 pulls   Going down. (When the diver is ascending, 2 pulls means he
          has come up too far, and to go back down until he has
          signaled to stop.)
3 pulls   Diver. . . stand by to surface.
4 pulls   Diver. . . start ascent now.
5 pulls   Diver. . . I understand you.

Diver to Tender:

1 pull   I am O. K.
2 pulls   Give me more slack, or lower me deeper.
3 pulls   Please take up my slack.
4 pulls   Haul me to the surface.
2-1 pulls   I understand you.

Diver's Emergency Signals to Tender:

2-2-2 pulls   I am fouled up. Send another diver to assist me immediately.
3-3-3 pulls   I am fouled up, but I can get myself cleared.
4-4-4 pulls   Emergency. Take me up immediately.

Work and Search Signals:*

3-2 pulls   Give me more air (for use with the Hookah or lift bag).
4-3 pulls   Give me less air (for use with the Hookah or lift bag).
5 pulls   Send me a lifting line(s).
   *Work signals come only from the diver. Search signals come only
from the tender.

Signaling on the Lift Line:

1 pull   Stop lifting.
2 pulls   Slack the line.
3 pulls   Take up the slack.
4 pulls   Haul it up.
   (The size and weight have been predetermined and the size and
number of lines to be used to lift an object will be adjusted accordingly.)

Searching Signals:

1 pull   Stop and search where you are.
2 pulls   Move directly away from the tender if given slack.
                 Move toward the tender if a strain is taken on the line.
3 pulls   Move to your right.
4 pulls   Move to your left.
1-2-3 pulls   Send me a buoy marker.

SUGGESTIONS FOR SETTING UP A SALVAGE BUSINESS

A diver who wishes to enter the field of salvage has more to do than let it be known that he wants business. He must first check all the possibilities where his services can be used in his area. After a thorough check has been made and the diver has all the findings on paper so he may study them, he will then be able to determine if his business has a chance of success. Places to check in setting up the business are coastal areas, resort areas, fishing industries and fishing fleets, shipping industries, boatyards, inland bodies of water and popular fishing areas.

These are but a few possibilities in the salvage game. Places such as these often have need of a diver. If your locality contains such areas and businesses, your chances of establishing a salvage business are good.

A small business card should be printed to mail to prospective clients. With this card, the diver can also include a mimeographed form letter printed on the company's stationery. The business card should contain essential information. For example:

SMITH DIVING SERVICE
Anytown, Maine
Salvage, Recovery, Restoration
Tel. 10-000

Here is a sample of a standard form letter:

Now, in 1966, the Smith Diving Service brings to (name of state) its professional diving service. Our underwater work consists of salvage, recovery and restoration. Experienced divers, using self-contained diving equipment (now commonly called Scuba for "self-contained underwater breathing apparatus"), are ready to accept any task or challenge offered.

Camp owners, fishermen, sportsmen, civic, state and federal agencies, plus boatyards, contractors, dredgers, waterfront businesses and ship lines, need the services of a diver.

In the past, it was an expensive undertaking to employ a commercial diver. The cost of transporting his hundreds of pounds of bulky equipment could only be afforded by insurance companies, large businesses, wealthy individuals, or government offices. Since the invention of self-contained diving gear, which is light, easy to transport and inexpensive to operate, divers have been in great demand for all types of jobs.

Smith's Diving Service will tackle any job in the small salvage and recovery field. Each job will be completed quickly and satisfactorily. The price for underwater work is reasonable. We are confident that our new diving service will be welcome news to business owners, to sporting and recreational camp owners, sportsmen, shippers and governmental offices. We will do our utmost to give the people of (name of state) the finest, speediest, most inexpensive and guaranteed diving service possible.

For further information, write us. We will give your inquiry prompt attention.

Sincerely yours,
John Smith
President

Here is a list of places to which the business cards and letters should be sent.

1. State police headquarters in the county and state.
2. City and town police and fire departments.
3. County sheriff's and county attorney's offices.
4. State Fish and Game departments.
5. State Sea and Shore office.
6. Sporting goods store managers.
7. Hotel and resort managers.
8. Marine insurance companies, head and field offices.
9. General insurance companies, head and field offices.
10. Sporting and recreational camp owners.
11. Official sport guides.
12. Hydroelectric companies.
13. Outboard motor and boat sales companies.
14. Boatyards.
15. Waterfront warehouse owners.
16. Waterfront oil storage companies.
17. Waterfront businesses.
18. Harbor patrol stations.

Undoubtedly, a smart diver will think of or discover many other places to send his business card and letter. The salvage and recovery business is a good one. If you persist and do dependable work, you will receive a good income from your underwater jobs.

Always keep one fact in mind: keep your price right; never try to "stick" the customer. Good businesses are built on good principles and your business should be no different. When you enter the diving business, you are working in a field that is fascinating to millions of people, and you represent not just yourself but all divers and their work.

A contract for a job is signed only when the diver or divers have given the job every consideration as to the total underwater hours, total work topside to prepare for and accomplish the job, and the total number of hours spent by all connected with the job. When all the figures have been compiled, together with the materials used, the contract deductions can be made as the signers agree. Divers signing contracts should allow themselves plenty of time for the job to be performed, as the weather can ruin time-limited contracts. Divers should avoid them whenever possible.

Chapter IV

UNDERWATER CONSTRUCTION AND REPAIRS

Although underwater construction has been decreasing during recent years in some areas because of the invention of machinery capable of performing the work at less expense than hiring a diver, underwater construction jobs for the Scuba diver have definitely increased. For general underwater repairs, large construction companies have found it less expensive to hire divers to perform a job than to use costly equipment. And, even with the best of machines there are still underwater construction jobs which must be tackled by divers.

A diver who wishes to enter the underwater construction business must have some knowledge of carpentry and be able to make sound preliminary estimates and preparations. Underwater construction is not an easy occupation.

Scuba divers starting out in this particular field would be wise to stick to building such items as docks, piers, floats, moorings, boathouses, and other small structures which do not require much technical knowledge and know-how. A State like Maine, with over 5,000 bodies of water and a 3,000-mile coast line, is ideal for Scuba divers in the underwater construction and repair business. Floats, piers, moorings and boathouses are being built in great numbers, and some of the construction work is being done by divers. Many waterfront buildings require constant repairs. It costs far less to hire a Scuba constructioneer than to import deep-sea men or to employ a building firm which will, in turn, hire the divers.

Docks, piers and boathouses will offer the biggest challenge to the beginner. Because the underpinning of a dock is constantly buffeted by the water, it must be solidly constructed. The cedar log, which has been used for years, is gradually being replaced by cement, metal and other materials that have been proved better able to withstand the deteriorating action of water.

STRUCTURES

The structures selected for inclusion in this chapter are easily built, require the least equipment, and can be used for many types of jobs.

The more commonly known word, "notch," will be used instead of the term, "gain," which is used in naval architecture.

55

Small Tide-adjusted Wharf. The tide-adjusted wharf, shown in Fig. 9, is exceptionally simple to build and requires a minimum of tools and materials. It will be an added piece of valuable property to any camp-owner. Since it is made adjustable, it can be set in either fresh water or tidewater.

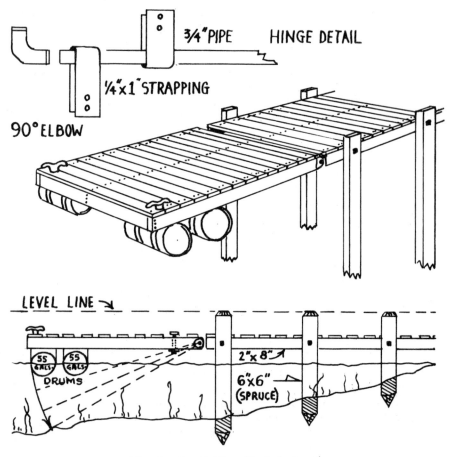

Fig. 9. Small tide-adjusted wharf.

The pilings for the wharf are 6″ x 6″ spruce, and the underpinning for the walk is 2″ x 8″ spruce. The pilings are leveled off on the top and fastened to the walk underboard by ½″ x 10″ monel bolts. At the points where the pilings will be attached to the underboard, they should be notched.

The pipe used to serve as the swinging pivot is ¾″ with a 90° elbow on each end. The metal strapping material is ¼″ x 1″ and made from brass, bronze, or galvanized iron. Two 55-gallon drums are used to float the adjustable section of the wharf. These are secured to the underside by rope, metal straps, leather straps, or wood. They may be fastened as shown in the diagram, or, if the wharf is over 8 feet wide, placed end-to-end.

A good feature about this type of wharf is that it does not have any definite measurements and may be constructed as long and as wide as desirable.

If the wharf is going to be built in salt water, all the material, including the planks for the walk, should be spruce. The drums should be covered with two or three coats of marine paint and the owner advised to repeat this at least every two years.

Caution: When strapping on the adjustable section of the wharf, do not have too little or too much of the strapping, and fasten the strappings with monel bolts. Use monel type, anchorfast nails when nailing the wharf.

This adjustable wharf is one of the simplest, yet one of the best in the low-price field.

Piers and Supports. The piers and supports in Fig. 10 may have the dimensions changed to meet the specifications of each particular underwater job.

The concrete-type support is one of the strongest yet devised. Built in fresh water for piers, docks, etc., it will withstand spring thaws and ice movements. Other material may be substituted for the railroad rails, but the substitute material must be equally as strong.

When making the form for the cement, construct the four sides and put it together under water. Have plenty of bracing so it will hold together. Concrete poured in salt water loses approximately 10 percent of its strength. When mixing concrete designed for underwater use, mix it with city water preferably. Do not use water which contains any organic matter, such as swamp water, etc.

The stone-filled pier base is made from spruce or oak and treated with a waterproofing compound, such as tar, etc. This structure is built in pyramid style. It is best to use wooden pilings which are fastened erect before the stones are filled in.

The concrete pallet makes an exceptionally good base for piling. The thickness of the pallet is determined by the diameter of the piling, the weight it supports, and the length of the piling. For example, a piling 12 inches in diameter and approximately 12 feet long should have a pallet measuring 3 x 6 x 8 feet. The forms for the pallets are constructed topside and lowered into the water prior to pouring the concrete. Underwater concrete must have at least 24 hours or, better still, 48 hours to harden before removing the forms.

For a small tie-up pier base with a walk built to reach the shore, the wooden-crib pier made from railroad ties filled with rock will prove excellent. The ties do not have to be the best of material and, occasionally, may be bought from a railroad company.

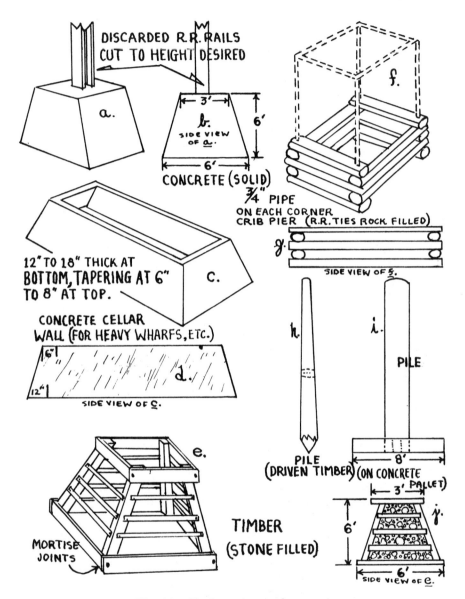

DISCARDED R.R. RAILS
CUT TO HEIGHT DESIRED

a.

b.
SIDE VIEW
OF *a.*

3'

6'

6'

CONCRETE (SOLID)

f.

¾" PIPE
ON EACH CORNER
CRIB PIER (R.R. TIES ROCK FILLED)

g.

SIDE VIEW OF *f.*

12" TO 18" THICK AT
BOTTOM, TAPERING AT 6"
TO 8" AT TOP.

c.

CONCRETE CELLAR
WALL (FOR HEAVY WHARFS, ETC.)

6"

d.

12"

SIDE VIEW OF *c.*

h

i.

PILE

e.

MORTISE
JOINTS

TIMBER
(STONE FILLED)

PILE
(DRIVEN TIMBER) (ON CONCRETE
PALLET)

8'

3'

6'

j.

6'

SIDE VIEW OF *e.*

Fig. 10.   Various piers and supports.

At the corner of the crib form, ¾" pipe is used to fasten it securely. These pipes should extend at least 4 feet above the last tie and 3½ feet driven down into the mud or earth bottom. The top 6 inches is cut by a hacksaw down the length of the pipe and pounded back. This serves to secure the top of the crib. When this has been completed, the rock fill is put in.

If exceptionally long sections of ¾″ pipe are available, they may be allowed to break the surface of the water approximately 6 to 9 inches and, by drilling in the underside of the baseboards of the pier walk, they may serve as pilings. If this type of structure is built where there is a tide, cut the pipe at the above-given measurements at high tide, never at low tide. A swamped pier is worthless.

The concrete cellar wall is built for heavy wharfs or piers. The entire wooden form must be built above and assembled below. It is important that the proper amount of taper be observed in the construction of this underwater base. It may be constructed to any desired length and width. Since each job will require a different set of measurements, none have been included on the diagram. Each constructioneer can supply the needed dimensions for his particular job.

Although the concrete base is the most difficult type to build, it will withstand the elements longer than any other.

LAUNCHING RAMPS AND PIERS

The launching ramps and piers in this section have been prepared by the engineering department of the Outboard Boating Club of America. The units have been simply designed for anyone interested in a basic small boat facility. The OBC took into consideration all sections of the United States and the water conditions when designing these facilities. The installation of a basic small boat facility is no monumental project; it can be done quickly and economically.

The sketches are designed to present ideas on the various kinds of ramps, docks, piers and the particular values of each. They are intended to cover a wide variety of conditions.

Procedure. In order to have the best facility for a particular location and a particular purpose, follow this check list:

1. Carefully check the site, determine boundaries, grade elevations and all other existing conditions.
2. Determine the type of facility best to use. Select one of the systems depicted.
3. Estimate the cost of the proposed facility selected and all other required work. Always verify the costs.

Permits and Local Regulations. Most communities require a building permit for facility construction. Before starting a facility, check with community officials to determine the proper building permits, building codes, or other necessary documents and regulations.

There are state and federal regulations covering the distances from shore structures can be placed out into the water. Be sure to check with the appropriate authorities and learn if there are any specific restrictions.

Employment of Local Firms. When the diver has checked the under-water construction, it is best to consult with local builders to assist in constructing the above water portion of the facility.

Floating Structures. A variety of materials may be employed to support floating structures:

55 gal. drums	plastic foam
wooden box floats	wooden logs
pre-cast concrete floats	

Cognizance must be taken of the degree of floatation offered by different materials in considering what construction materials and method to employ.

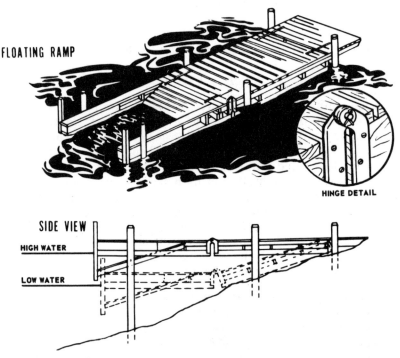

FLOATING RAMP

HINGE DETAIL

SIDE VIEW

HIGH WATER

LOW WATER

Fig. 10A.   Floating ramp.   (Outboard Boating Club of America)

Air. One (1) cubic foot of air will support approximately sixty-two (62) pounds of weight. Since air must be contained, some form of metal, wood, plastic or concrete tank must be used. Allowance must be made for the weight of the container by adding it to the weight to be supported.

Wood. Wood used as a floatation material has a wide range in the amount of weight it will support. Most woods have a moisture content, and within a species the moisture content will differ. Woods commonly used for floatation purposes will have a positive buoyancy of approximately 22 pounds per cubic foot. The wood should be properly treated with preservative materials to resist rot and marine growth.

Plastic Foam. Plastic foam is available either in precast shapes or in bulk capable of being foamed in place. Plastic foam will support approximately fifty-five (55) pounds per cubic foot of foam. Exercise care in selecting foam for each individual job, i.e., resistance to solvent attack, abrasion, marine growth, etc. If plastic foam is encased, the same allowance for its buoyancy must be made as in the case of air tanks.

Calculating Floatation. Determine the weight to be supported by the floating facility.

Add the weight of the structure itself to this figure. This will be the total weight to be supported.

Determine the buoyancy per cubic foot of the particular floatation material to be used.

Divide the total weight to be supported by the buoyancy of the material. This is the number of cubic feet of floatation material necessary to do the job.

This is the minimum amount of floatation material necessary to support a structure. It is well to apply a safety factor in any design to give some reserve buoyancy. For stability, long, thin, wide shapes are better than short, narrow, high shapes. The preferred shapes will result in a structure that will vary less in depth of submergence of the floats as increasing weight is placed on the structure.

Floating Ramp. This type of ramp is ideal for tidal water locations or other areas of moderate water level variation where the shore bottom below high water is muddy, rocky, uneven or otherwise undesirable as a launching area at low tides or low water. The floats are anchored to the shore and held in place by piling. At rocky locations, the floats are secured by anchors and cables.

Materials

Stringers	2″ x 8″
Decking	2″ x 8″
Tie Beams	4″ x 8″
Hinge Plates	½″ galv. plate
Lumber	select fir or pine
Floatation	2500 pounds

Ramp with Pontoon Floats. Using this facility, small boats are easily launched and recovered by means of a trailer. It is suggested for use at sheltered water locations, with maximum four to five feet (4′ to 5′) variation water level and where waterfront bulkheads have

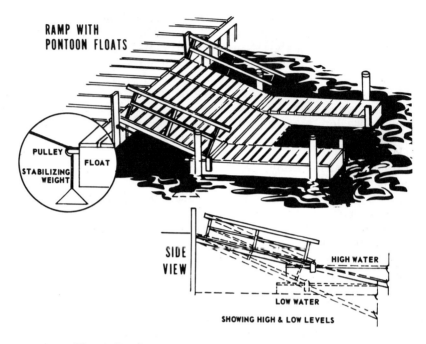

Fig. 10B.   Ramp with pontoon floats. (O.B.C.A.)

been established. The ramp is supported by two (2) floats maintaining constant water level at the underwater section of the ramp.

Materials

Stringers	2″ x 4″
Tie Beams	2″ x 4″
Decking	2″ x 6″
Upper Ramp Stringers	2″ x 6″
Tie Beams	2″ x 4″
Decking	2″ x 6″
Cleats	1″ x 2″
Walkways, stringers, tie beams	2″ x 4″
Decking	2″ x 6″
Railing	1″ x 3″
Posts	2″ x 4″
Lumber	select fir or pine
Floatation	2500 pounds

Submersible Launching Ramp. This unit is suggested for any sheltered water. It is economical and convenient to build. The submersible ramp is supported at the outer end by a movable float. The

SUBMERSIBLE
LAUNCHING RAMP

Fig. 10C. Submersible launching ramp. (O.B.C.A.)

opposite end is hinged to a shore bulkhead; by means of a winch and cable mechanism, the float is moved toward the shore bulkhead, submerging the ramp and floating the boat free. A V-guide on shore helps in lining up the trailer with the ramp. Ramp is level, overcoming traction problems in launching and recovering.

Materials

Framing	4″ x 4″ or steel channel
Float Guides	steel channel
Treadways	2″ planking or metal grating
Float Carrier	1″ planking or metal
Floatation	2500 pounds

Floating Piers. Floating piers are recommended for use where water levels vary or where changes in weather or other conditions make it necessary to remove the installation.

Materials

Decking	¾″ Marine Plywood
Frame	2″ x 8″
Frame Cross Members	1″ x 8″ (not shown)
Lumber	select fir or pine
Floatation	900 lbs.

Permanent Small Piers. The pier illustrated in Fig. 10E is simple in design and can be constructed at the site in a fairly short time. The

Fig. 10D.   Floating piers.   (O.B.C.A.)

Fig. 10E.   (Left) Permanent small pier. (Right) Finger pier. (O. B. C. A.)

construction of small piers is usually a part of a launching ramp development on lake shore or river. After the boat is launched, this type of pier offers a landing place for boaters to get aboard. Pier is of single split cap construction. Pilings are driven to solid footing, or set as described in Fig. 10.

Materials

Split Cap & Stringers	2"x 6"
Decking	1" x 6", spaced ½" apart
Pilings	6" to 8" dia. pine, oak, or fir
Lumber	select grade, fir or pine

Finger Piers. Launching ramps constructed in groups of two or more should have some type of dock structure separating the ramps. One type of dock is the small finger pier. Structures of this type allow easy access to the boat during launching and retrieving operations and also facilitate boarding and unloading while the boat is in the water. The structure is supported on single piles and driven to a solid footing. Length of piles varies depending on depth of water and penetration.

Materials

Stringers	2″ x 10″
Decking	2″ x 10″ x 2′-6″
Lumber	select grade fir or pine

The absence of measurements has been intentional as each situation would call for varying measurements. Each builder and customer will have to make the decision as to what size, length, and type of facility is needed.

Hill Printing Co., P.O. Box 151, El Paso, Texas published *The Lumber Calculator.* Price $1.00. This handy little booklet gives the amount of board feet as calculated by the thickness, width, length and number of pieces from sizes 1″ x 4″ x 20′ to 2″ x 12″ x 22′ and beam stock up to 8″ x 8″ x 22′.

When the size of the structure has been agreed upon, the builder can determine exactly how many pieces of the various sized lumber it will require. Referring to *The Lumber Calculator* the builder can then order the appropriate number of board feet of lumber from the lumber dealer. Generally, lumber is sold by the board feet measure.

Protective Equipment. The contractor should always provide or give a list of planned protective measures for the facility being built. Customers appreciate this service, as it limits or restricts injury, and saves the customer's equipment.

Bumpers. Bumpers can be attached either to piers or boat. They protect boats from rubbing against the pier and are an economical means of protecting boats from this kind of damage when craft are moored at the pier. Bumpers are available from commercial marine supply houses, or can be made with sponge rubber encased in a lightweight canvas. Bumpers are usually hot-dog shaped.

Rubber Tires/Garden Hose. Sections of old rubber tires or canvas-covered garden hose make easy-to-install rub rails for piers. Tires are usually placed at the corners and the hosing along the sides of a pier. This material is inexpensive, and rubber makes an excellent shock absorber.

Fire Hose. Fire hose is available in many areas at a very low cost. Surplus houses carry a variety, and at times public works departments or fire stations sell old or used hose reasonably. Fire hose is a very satisfactory padding material for the edge of a pier.

Plastic Foam. Half round sections of plastic foam have excellent qualities of absorbing shock and resisting abrasion. They can be attached either by bonding or by criss-crossing strap.

Mats. Plastic or rubber matting materially reduces the chances of injury to persons who may slip or fall on the pier.

The shipping containers for most typewriters are made of plastic. These units can be obtained from most dealers for the asking, and they have excellent floating capabilities.

Preservation. The maximum service of any facility cannot be realized without proper attention to preservative techniques, regardless of the excellence of design or craftsmanship in the construction. There are numerous methods of treating or protecting materials to make them last.

Wood. Unprotected wood is subject to damage from a number of causes: Rot, termites or other insects, or marine organisms. Preservatives are commercially available to treat these conditions. These materials may be applied either by pressure or by paint-on processes. Where severe conditions exist pressure treatment affords more permanent protection. Where it is desirable to paint above-water wooden structures preservatives should be used that are compatible with surface finishes. Care should be taken to treat these structures thoroughly in areas most vulnerable. These areas can be found: Around bolt holes, where wood rests on wood, where wood rests on cement or on the ground, on the end grain and in joints, cracks or crevices.

Metal. Most metals will give satisfactory service if protected with proper finishes. Base coats of metallic oxide or aluminum paints will effectively guard against corrosion or oxidation. Attention should be given to metal joints, or where dissimiliar metals are used and an electrolysis action may take place.

Areas where corrosion or oxidation is found to have occurred should be scraped free of loose deposits and thoroughly coated with a resistant finish.

On portable and adjustable structures, bolts and fasteners should be properly cleaned and oiled before use to facilitate ease of removal or adjustment at later dates.

There are other plans available for the construction of monorail hoists, launching derricks, etc. These plans may be obtained by writing to the author at International Undersea Services, Eastern Office, 43–45 Maple St., Brewer, Maine, 04412, USA.

A Simple Boat Shelter. The boat shelter shown in Fig. 11 is a simple one. It calls for two short and four long pilings, a few bolts, monel anchorfast nails, seven cross members, and planking for the walk.

When the width of the boat has been determined, construction may start. The diver or contractor decide whether to drive the pilings into the bottom as shown in the diagram or to use any of the piling supports described previously. Of course, the bottom condition will present some problems, and the diver may suggest the type of piling support that would be most satisfactory.

CANVAS COVER GROMMETED and TIED
TO SHELTER BOATS

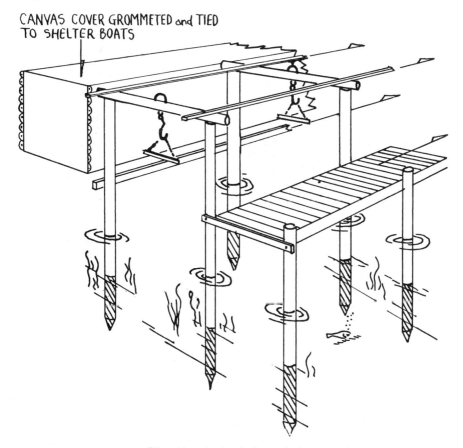

Fig. 11.   A simple boat shelter.

When the six pilings have been set, they are bolted securely to the cross members. The next step is to lay the walk and nail it securely. Then the outside dimensions of the shelter are taken, minus the walk area, and the canvas is ordered to specific size.

The canvas cover is grommeted, as shown. If this shelter is built on the coast or near salt water, monel grommet eyes will be necessary. In fact, it is a good idea to have monel eyes in any type of canvas used for a shelter covering.

This same style of boat shelter has been built and sits on a lake in Maine. It works very well, was inexpensive, and withstands severe Maine weather.

Many changes can be made in this type of shelter. Wooden sides can replace the canvas. Wooden pilings may be replaced by metal ones. In general, the complete structure may be built to cost fifty times the cost of the one pictured. Should divers want diagrams of

Fig. 12.   Navy divers doing underwater repair work. (U.S. Navy Photo)

more elaborate boathouses and shelters, they may write directly to the author, who will supply them.

Underwater repair work is not simple. Replacing a section of rotten piling is extremely difficult—not that cutting out a rotten piling and replacing it cannot be done if the stress and strain points are taken into consideration. Many mathematical problems will arise when repairing pilings and piers. Unless a diver has had courses in marine engineering, he should sub-contract this type of job to someone who is experienced.

BUSINESS TIPS FOR CONSTRUCTIONEERS

The construction field is closely related to salvage and recovery, and many of the men in the salvage field will undertake jobs dealing with construction and vice versa. Consequently, the same job setup suggested for the salvage business can be used in the construction business.

Your business card should be sent to the following people and places:

1. State police headquarters (each barrack in the entire state).
2. City and town police and fire departments.
3. State fish and game departments.
4. State sea and shore departments (in states with these offices).
5. Sporting goods store managers.
6. Hotel and resort managers.
7. Lumber yard owners.
8. Insurance companies, home and field office managers.
9. Construction company owners.
10. Sporting camp owners.
11. Official sport guides.
12. Hydroelectric companies.
13. Boat-sales companies.
14. Boatyards.
15. Waterfront business owners.
16. Shipping companies.
17. Waterfront warehouse owners.
18. Harbor patrol stations.
19. Local coast guard installations.
20. Local naval installations.

In looking for good business areas to start work in your particular state, you will find many other officials and businesses that could use your special underwater services. It will pay to advertise as much as possible.

There are few books written specifically on marine construction, and the greater part of your work will have to be thought out on the job. Of course, if you read those books or manuals on naval architecture and construction that are within your technical grasp, you may gain good ideas that can be adapted to the jobs you undertake.

Chapter V

UNDERWATER PIPELAYING

In the underwater diving field, pipe-line installation has unlimited possibilities for two or more interested Scuba divers. Divers who install these pipe lines may be classed as marine hydro-engineers. Recently, the author and his associates successfully installed 2,000 feet of underwater pipe supplying water for a newly constructed State of Maine Fish Hatchery and Rearing Pool Station. Four divers and two stand-by divers worked more than one thousand hours to place

Fig. 13.   Floating line 24″ i.d. C.I.M.J. pipe. (International Photo)

the 24″ inside diameter cast iron pipe line. The job was not a simple one and much was learned about handling big pipe under water.

The Engineering-News Record, a valuable trade magazine, gives information concerning the numerous pipe lines being installed throughout the country. It lists the jobs, the general contractors, some information about the projects, and jobs which have been approved for the near future. A check into the November, 1958 issues shows that some ten pipe-line projects are underway in the United States. In some cases, it is entirely possible that the marine portion of a job has not been sub-let or the divers have not been employed. In this event, the Scuba diver interested in underwater pipelaying and desiring to become a sub-contractor can submit bids on the job.

Cast iron mechanical joint pipe, which will be designated as C.I.M.J., is manufactured in many sizes. Water intake supply lines range in size from 12″ i.d. to 36″ i.d. There are two methods of installing the pipe in a river or lake—the floatation method and the sectioning method.

Fig. 14. Floatation method: barrels are used to float this intake water system. (Cast Iron Pipe Research Assoc.)

FLOATATION METHOD

Cast iron pipe in sizes from 16″ i.d. to 24″ i.d. can be successfully sectioned together at a point on shore and floated on the water. As each length of pipe is bolted in place, a crane or backhoe pushes it out into the water. There are enough square inches of air inside the length of pipe to support its own weight in the water. If a single 18 ft. section of 18″ i.d. pipe is capped on both ends and slid into the water, the section would have a positive buoyancy of approximately 275 lbs. If the pipe has a lesser inside diameter than 16 inches, or greater than 24 inches, sectioning is the only safe method of installation.

When a pipe line is to lay on the bottom of a lake, the fastest, easiest and cheapest method of installation is to float the pipe along a marked course. When the last section has been bolted securely, a riser (*see* Fig. 15) on the far end is filled with water, thus causing the line to sink to the bottom in one piece.

C.I.M.J. pipe of the floatable sizes mentioned will have, in most cases, an intake pipe and trap located on the far end of the line. This intake and trap is constructed from a 90° elbow (belled both ends) and a piece of pipe cut to any desired length from a standard section of pipe. The cut piece is called the riser. The trap is fitted on the open end of the riser, serving to keep the line free from underwater debris. There are many types of traps and each job calls for a different fitting. The riser section is the first step in putting together a floating line.

Fig. 15.   The riser section in place. (International Photo)

C.I.M.J. pipe is manufactured in many lengths, but the standard length is 18 feet plus. The pipe is of solid cast construction with a bell end and a smooth end. The bell end is cast with a number of grooves. The innermost groove, approximately 2½″ deep, accommodates the smooth end of the length of pipe being fitted to the line. The next groove is made for a rubber gasket and the last groove is for the sliding flange. This flange serves the dual purpose of "driving home" the rubber gasket and bolting the two lengths of pipe together. When the gasket is in place and the bolt holes in the sliding flange lined up with the holes in the bell, the bolts are set in place and tightened with a ratchet-type socket wrench.

Equipment Needed. There are certain tools required for the installation of C.I.M.J. pipe, including sets of sockets for the ratchet wrenches, a pail for water-resistant vegetable soap, wire rope slings with looped ends, anchor shackles and a chest of carpenter tools. When a job is taken by divers, the prime contractor can supply the crane or backhoe to handle the pipe, or the divers can engage their own heavy equipment. In the latter case, a standard daily, weekly or monthly rate of pay for the machine is included in the contract, plus the wages for the operator and a sum for fuel and minor repairs. These will have to be estimated.

Construction of the Riser Section. The crane moves the elbow of the riser section to the water's edge. Using 6" x 6" timbers and 55-gal. drums, a float is constructed as shown in Fig. 16. When the riser float is built, the vegetable soap is applied to the grooves in the bell with a whisk broom and the gasket is immersed in the soap solution before it is stretched over the riser piece.

The flange is slid over the smooth end of the riser piece, the gasket is pulled on and, while the crane picks up the riser piece, two men hold the flange to keep it from forcing the gasket off before it is

Fig. 16. Constructing the riser section. (International Photo)

seated in the bell of the elbow. Figure 17 shows a safe method of handling vertical pipe with a Manila rope sling. When the riser piece is bolted to the elbow, the trap may be put on. However, it is not necessary to install the trap at this point unless it is an extra heavy one.

When the riser section is completed, the crane can swing the first full-length section of C.I.M.J. pipe to be installed.

Installation of C.I.M.J. Pipe. Four to five pieces of mechanical joint pipe can be jointed to a line in an hour. The grooves in the bell receive a healthy application of vegetable soap. With a man on each side of the pipe to steady it, a hand signial is given to the crane operator to move the pipe forward slowly. The two men jockey the pipe up or down or to either side until it is seated. At the rear of the piece, a third man holds it fast as the forward men tighten the flange bolts, "driving home" the gasket and securing the joint.

The crane operator is signalled to lift the section slightly and move it forward out into the water. The forward motion is stopped when the end of the pipe is about 4 or 5 feet from the water's edge. A 6' piece of 8" x 8" hardwood is placed about 3 or 4 feet from the shore end for the pipe to rest on while the flange bolts are tightened. This process is repeated until the desired number of lengths have been attached to the line. Several thousand feet of pipe can be installed employing this method.

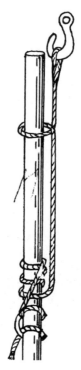

Fig. 17.   Safe method for handling vertical pipe with a Manila rope sling.

Working speedily and during daylight hours, a 4-man crew and a crane operator can install approximately 700 feet of pipe per day. When the pipelaying is started at daybreak, work should not stop. A sudden windstorm can tear 300 or 400 feet apart, scattering it all over the bottom. The 8-hour working day cannot apply in this work.

While laying pipe line, the divers should set heavy mooring blocks on the bottom directly under the pipe in the path to be followed or use any available bottom material, such as rocks or logs, onto which mooring or anchor lines can be tied securely to the pipe. This is important if the line must float in the water overnight. The riser section should have mooring or anchor lines going off in three directions to avoid swinging and breaking off causing the remainder of the line to sink.

If the pipe line is left floating overnight, a bell and lantern should be placed on the riser section and 3 or 4 pot lanterns secured on the line at intervals.

When all the sections are in place, if the pipe is not along the desired path or channel, it can be moved (to some degree). Each section has from 9″ to 11″ of play and this will give the line a tremendous bow or bend if it is needed. However, it is highly recommended that the floating pipe be kept in a straight line. To dodge exceptionally large boulders or patches of rocks, the line can be swung a little.

The line is straightened or bent simply by attaching stout lines to the pipe where the straightening or bending is to take place and attaching the other end to the diving boat. This process takes time, but is efficient. Once the pipe line is in position, all mooring and anchor lines are released.

Sinking the Line. The wooden float and barrels are removed from the riser section. The weight of the elbow and the riser piece will cause it to sink into the water until the riser piece (with the trap, if it has been attached), protrudes approximately 1 to 2 feet above the surface. A pail or suction pump is used to fill the riser section. The added weight of the water will soon pull the riser under. Each section of pipe will fill with water going to the bottom until it comes gushing out the end on shore. The shore end of the pipe should be secured so it cannot slip into the water, causing an air pocket to form along the line and break it. The load line from the crane can be used to hold the pipe fast.

After the line is in place, the divers make an inspection tour. The underwater inspection usually takes place the following day. Where the bottom is mud, the settling pipe will throw up a sediment, making a complete inspection impossible. After the inspection tour, the divers use ratchet wrenches to tighten bolts which may have loosened during the sinking. Missing bolts should be replaced. Anchor and mooring lines are removed from the bottom, and any channel or course marker buoys are taken in.

SECTIONING METHOD

The sectioning method is the safest way to place the line on the bottom in one piece. Though it requires more time, more diving hours, more equipment and costs more money, it is the author's opinion that the sectioning method is the best. If the divers involved decide to use the sectioning method, any size pipe can be handled and jointed. All work will be done under water and the cost of the job estimated accordingly.

Equipment Needed. The primary equipment needed for the sectioning method consists of two large floats with winches. The floats can be made from 55-gal. drums for light pipe and 275–500-gal. storage tanks for heavy pipe. The floats are constructed as shown in Fig. 18.

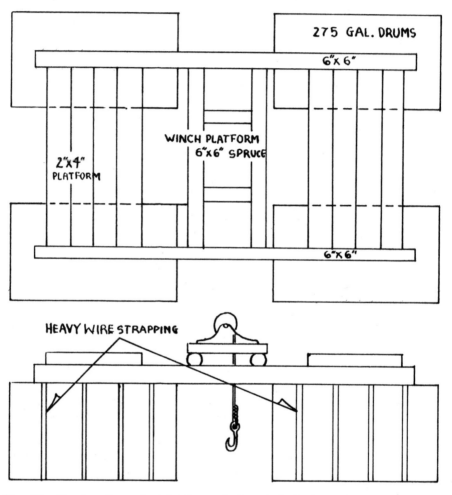

Fig. 18. Constructing a float by the sectioning method. (Cast Iron Pipe Research Assoc.)

If they are used in salt water, metal floats must be inspected regularly for corrosion, breaks, etc. Tank-type floats, made from pine or other soft woods, have proved to be more rugged and less costly to repair over extended periods. When these floats are built, they must be caulked and a coat of water-resistant material, such as tar, applied inside and outside of the tank to prevent leakage.

The length of the pipe sections will determine the distance between each float. C.I.M.J. is manufactured in various lengths. Knowing the size pipe to be installed is important in the construction of the sectioning float. The best all-purpose drum float is made from 275-gal. oil storage tanks. Using 6 of these tanks, as shown in Fig. 18, 3 sections of pipe can be jointed on shore and hoisted by crane with slings and a 3-eye spreader bar into water deep enough to allow the section float to pick it up. A power boat or the diving craft with a heavy-duty outboard tows the float to the spot where it will be in line with the pipe on the bottom. The divers have been warned of the arrival of the float by the tenderman. The float is anchored with drop-pins and the 3 sections of pipe are lowered at the divers' commands or signals.

The C.I.M.J. pipe is jointed on shore in the same manner as described for the floatation method, the only difference being that 3 sections are jointed with the actions being repeated until the desired number of sections have been jointed, taken out by the float, lowered and attached to the line.

The Scuba divers jointing the pipe line under water can use hand signals to control the raising and lowering of the sections:

<pre>
1 pull...............up
2 pulls..............down
Quick series.........stop
</pre>

Some type of communications to the surface is a *must* for this work. Using a dry-type rubber suit, the throat mike and earphone setup can be employed. If the divers use the "Look-Out" Full Face Mask (U.S. Divers Corp.), a small mike can be built into the side of the mask with the phone jack going through the rubber to the outside, thereby having the wires from the phones and the mike easily accessible to attach to the life line.

Spreader bars, wire rope slings, anchor shackles and spud wrenches are equipment used by crane operators and contractors in the rigging and mechanical moving field. Slings, shackles and spud wrenches should be purchased; spreader bars are easy to make after examining ready-made ones. Even though slings are expensive, always buy new ones. Used slings can be dangerous. Remember, all tools should be in excellent condition and every move should be made with care. When handling pipe weighing thousands of pounds, any slip could cause serious injury or death.

SUBAQUEOUS CONCRETE PIPE

The Lock Joint Pipe Company is one firm which manufactures reinforced concrete underwater pipe. This type of pipe is used considerably more in underwater work than cast iron pipe. It is exceptionally heavy, weighing as much as 116,000 lbs. per section. The pipe is made in standard 16 ft. lengths with the normal inside diameters ranging from 24 to 156 ins.

This pipe is handled strictly by the sectioning method, one section at a time (unless the sections have been doubled by the manufacturers). Jointing the pipe is simple. The joint, which is always rubber and steel, referred to as an R & S joint (Fig. 19), is composed of two special self-centering steel joint rings which fit neatly, one

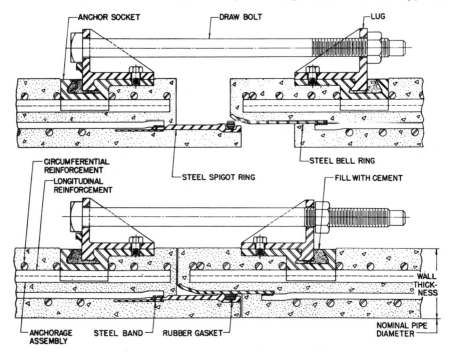

Fig. 19.   Rubber and steel joint.   (Lock Joint Pipe Co.)

within the other, to form practically a metal-to-metal joint. A round rubber gasket seated in the annular groove on the periphery of the spigot ring is tightly compressed between the joint rings when the joint is pulled together. This forms a watertight seal between adjacent pipes. The heavy bolts which pass through the lugs make it possible for the divers to assemble the joint easily and rapidly under water.

This pipe is not only sturdy, but its weight is sufficient to keep it from floating when de-watered. Both the joint and harness of the pipe will allow for expansion and contraction and are flexible enough to allow for normal ground settlement.

Installing Concrete Pipe. Scuba divers should, for the most part, hire only their services on the installation of such a pipe line. In this manner, they are always assured of a weekly paycheck and are released from the problems of big business.

Normally, a channel is dug in which this type of pipe is laid. Before the first section of pipe is lowered into the water, the divers descend and install pile bents. These pile bents are the cradles upon which the pipe rests. Referring to Fig. 20, the pile bents are placed in the following manner. Where the pipe is supported by only one pile bent per section, the bent is set just back of the open end of each pipe as it is placed. Where the pipe is supported by two pile bents

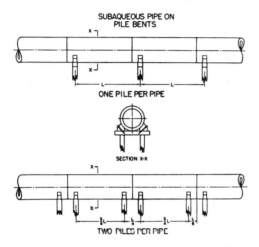

Fig. 20. Placing pile bents. (Lock Joint Pipe Co.)

per section, these bents are set in from each end of the pipe a distance equal to ⅛th. of the total length of the section. Wooden blocks should be wedged firmly beneath the pipe and spiked to the cross member of the bent to prevent the pipe from rolling. When the pile bents are placed, the pipe is lowered and sectioned together.

Care must be exercised in placing the slings around the pipe to lower it. The harness lugs *must* always be on the center line of the pipe. To check for accurate positioning, a spirit level can be placed across the bell end of the pipe in direct line with the lugs. This insures that the harness lugs will be in perfect line with the pipe on the bottom.

Coat the gasket and the surfaces of the bell and spigot ring with vegetable soap before the gasket is seated in the annular groove on the spigot ring.

After it is below the surface, the divers guide the lowering and moving of the pipe. When the lugs are lined up, the draw bolts are put in place and tightened. The two draw bolts will pull the joint together. Then, the nuts are backed off slightly to permit some flexibility in the joint. The wooden blocks are wedged under the pipe and spiked to the bent.

This section of pipe is now ready to be backfilled. In placing the backfill, it is important to deposit the bedding as equally as possible in order to give the pipe even support throughout its entire length and to distribute the cover evenly over the pipe so that the line will not be thrust off the pilings by the weight and pressure of backfill introduced on only one side of the line.

Laying underwater concrete pipe is not easy; one of the smallest diameter pipe lengths weighs 2¾ tons. Every safety measure possible must be taken. Rules governing the handling of pipe must be set down and strictly enforced and obeyed. Mistakes can be costly.

OTHER TYPES OF UNDERWATER PIPE

There are other types of pipe used as underwater lines, and divers should be thoroughly familiar with the particular type of pipe which is to be installed on a job. Manufacturers will gladly send full details concerning their products.

Ball and socket river crossing pipe has been used on many river projects. It is similar to C.I.M.J. and is jointed in much the same manner. Its one big advantage over C.I.M.J. is that it has a ball socket capable of a 15° angle of turn. This is a good feature for pipe of this type can be used when it is desired to avoid clearing underwater obstructions or blasting rocks from the direct path of the pipe line.

Be familiar with the method of installation of the pipe to be used before undertaking a job.

REPAIRS TO DAMAGED LINE

Sometimes, when using the floatation method, underwater pipe-layers are confronted with underwater damage to the line. The trouble may be caused by loose joints, underwater debris or rocks, or the elbow and riser section furrowing into a mud patch before it has time to straighten itself out.

International Undersea Services worked on a 1,600 ft. C.I.M.J. water intake pipe line of 20″ i.d. 18 ft. sections which went to the bottom in one piece. The floatation method was used successfully. Recently, the author's company laid a line of 1,350 ft. 24″ i.d. C.I.M.J. pipe by the floatation method and, upon inspecting the line, it was found to have separated in four places and broken in six places. However, an 18″ i.d. line of 780 ft. was successfully placed alongside the larger one. This second line was installed in one day, inspected and found to be perfect. What, then, caused the 24″ line to break and come apart?

There are many factors involved in this particular case. The first day saw some 700 ft. of pipe floating out on the water. Just before work was to be suspended for the day, a sudden windstorm whipped over the lake, causing the large bend which can be seen in Fig. 13. As a result of the bend, each joint was loosened, not enough to cause the line to sink, but enough to cause the weakest points to separate when the line was filled with water. Each C.I.M.J. joint can only stand approximately 200 lbs. of pressure before it comes unseated. Care must be exercised in handling this type of pipe.

During the second day, operations had to be suspended because of the wind, but after three hours it had calmed down sufficiently to resume work. On the third and final day of jointing, the complete 1,350 ft. of pipe lay floating on the water. Again the wind came, causing a bigger bend in the line. Many boats came to offer assistance in straightening the bend, but when the wind proved stronger than man's mechanical devices, it was deemed best to sink the line in its present position and hope for the best. The best was four separations and six breaks.

Two of the separations were slight, no more than 4–5 ins. apart; the other two were more than 5–6 ft. apart. Three of the breaks were caused by the landing impact and loosened joints; the cause of the others was not determined immediately. On the last two breaks, it was discovered that the pipe not only had broken, but had come apart and overlapped the next section. The first overlap was approximately 6 ft.; the second measured almost 18 ft.—nearly a full section of pipe.

Five divers spent over 50 hours surveying the damage, drawing diagrams on underwater slates and bringing the sad news back to the surface. When the information was gathered, it was found that the last two breaks and overlaps were caused by the riser section driving itself into the lake bottom some 4–5 ft. down. When the mud stopped the sinking line as it tried to straighten itself, it snapped, broke and overlapped. When the total amount of damage was determined, the next step was to effect the necessary repairs.

Repairing Small Separations. Small separations are easy to repair. Each smooth end of a length of pipe is "driven home" approximately 2½ inches. If the smooth end was in the bell portion of the next pipe only an inch, the line would still be solid and watertight. A float similar to the one used in the sectioning method was constructed. This float can be made from 16 55-gal. drums. It is not necessary to use larger tanks, since the float would not be handling more than two pieces of pipe.

Using Coffing Safety Load Binders of 6,000 lbs. capacity and wire rope slings attached to the pipe in the manner depicted in Fig. 21, the small separations were repaired. This is the single binder rig.

One binder can easily move two lengths of pipe, but by moving it to the side of the pipe and arranging another in the same manner, two divers can work the pipes back in place with the double binder hookup.

After the slings are wrapped around the pipe and the binders set in place, the divers loosen the bolts on a piece of pipe one or two lengths back, depending upon the number of inches which must be gained to close the gap. Then the bolts are tightened on the piece which the lengths are being pulled into. When the piece of pipe has been brought out from its seat 1–1½ ins., the bolts are tightened again.

If the divers must close a 4″ separation, they go two lengths back on one side of the pipe line. When a couple of inches have been gained from the two lengths, the bolts are re-tightened. The work is then reversed. The binders are slacked off and turned over so as to pull from the other direction. The same process is repeated until the line is repaired.

The winch line on the float serves to keep the pipe lengths off the bottom and in line while the divers are working on them.

In cases of separations up to 12 ins., usually the pipe can be lifted 5 or 6 ins. off the bottom by the winch and float. When this has been accomplished, only the bolts on one side of a flange are loosened, and the pipe section can be pushed over by muscle power, cant dogs or other lever devices. The same is done to the other separated piece. This changes the course of the line only slightly, but brings the pieces closer together.

Each group of diving pipelayers will find varying underwater problems and experimentation may result in a simpler method.

Repairing Large Separations. Large separations are easier to repair than small ones. If the separation is greater than a foot, a replacement piece is cut from an extra piece of pipe and joined to the line. When cutting the piece, always remember to cut the bell end as it will be needed to fit over the smooth end on the big separation. Another sliding flange and rubber gasket will be used to make the union complete. When cutting the pipe, remember to make all measurements as close as possible. The smooth end of a pipe section need only be seated in an inch or so to make a tight seal and secure joint. The pipe does not have to be driven home completely.

Repairing Overlaps. Overlaps are the hardest sections of a damaged pipe line to repair. When a 24″ i.d. pipe has overlapped, it means that at least 48 ins. of pipe is laying side-by-side. In order to effect the necessary repairs, the overlapped section is removed from the line after careful measurements have been taken to determine the amount to be cut off. The two sections of the line will not line up, so it is necessary to lift the lengths and move them from side to side until they do line up. The pieces that were cut on shore are lowered and rejointed.

Care must be taken when moving a full length of pipe sideways because, if the piece is moved too far to the side, it will come out of its groove in the bell. In order to bring the pipes in line to make the connection, sometimes it is necessary to move back several lengths to start the side swinging of the line. In some cases, it may be necessary to attach a 275- or 500-gal. tank at a joint, inflating it in order to swing the pipe on line.

Repairing Breaks. Replace the broken length with another full section of pipe. Extra lengths of pipe should be kept on hand for such emergencies.

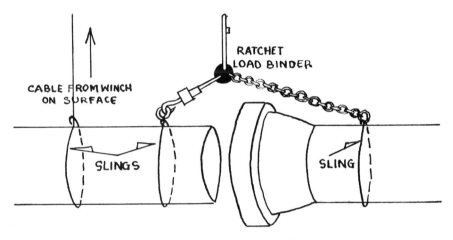

Fig. 21. Single binder rig.

BIDDING THE JOB

Unless the proper bids are made, a group of divers couldn't pick an underwater profession which can break them faster or—make them faster.

It would be difficult to present all the facts covering all types of jobs because each underwater pipe-line project is different and presents varied problems. However, the author will try to cover the most important principles of submitting bids for underwater pipe-line work.

Assuming a job is at hand and that a portion of it pertains to underwater pipelaying, the diving pipelayers should determine the following: (1) The type of pipe to be installed; (2) The total length of the line(s); (3) If the prime contractor wishes to sub-contract the entire underwater installation project, or install the line himself and employ the divers to handle the underwater work; (4) Obtain a copy of the project specifications and study them; (5) Know all data concerning the pipe, including weight, flange types, jointing methods, manufacturer, gasket types, bolt sizes, nut sizes, etc.; (6) Gather all possible information concerning the underwater portion of the project, especially engineering reports and grade charts.

The author feels that divers would derive greater benefits from hiring their professional knowledge of underwater pipe installation to the general contractor rather than assuming the added responsibilities of a prime or sub-contractor.

If it is possible to sell your professional services alone, the remaining problem is setting up the hourly, daily or weekly pay scale for the divers and the tendermen. The following pay scale has been established by the Pile Drivers and Dock Workers Union for commercial divers:

Sixty-five dollars for any day or part thereof to a depth of 50 feet. (Remember, a diver's day is six hours.)

Beyond 50 feet—

Ft.	Per ft. extra
50-100	$ 1.00
100-200	1.50
200-220	2.00
220-240	4.00
240-260	6.00
260-280	8.00
280 and over	10.00

Divers providing their own basic equipment receive the base pay of $85.00 per day, or part thereof. When the diver supplies his own tenderman and is covered with insurance for a particular job, the pay rate is $145.00. (The tenderman is paid from this amount.) When diving requires entrance into a cave or pipe line, the rate is $8.00 per ft. from 1–150 feet, and $32.00 per ft. from 150–200 feet. (Courtesy: Underwater Instructor News, 1958.)

The pay rate is agreed upon by the divers and the contractor, and it should be remembered that the scale should not go too low. Frequently, there are long intervals between jobs. Bear in mind that when the contractor took the job, he knew the pipe installation would be an expensive undertaking. He is familiar with divers' fees and it is well to assume that his bid covered the cost of full installation and an extra sum for emergencies.

Prime Contractor Bidding. Whenever possible, it is advisable *never* to be a prime contractor. However, after a few years of experience, if the business heads of the diving concern feel capable of handling a job, they may wish to act as prime contractors.

The prime contractor must submit a bid consisting of the price for which his firm will do the entire project of installing an underwater pipe line. The majority of underwater pipe lines are installed by government, state, county, city or big business firms. Engineers draw up plans and specifications for these agencies. Monies are set aside to pay the contractors who are awarded the jobs. Usually, the lowest bidder receives the award—if the agency feels his concern capable of handling it. When it is announced that a certain job of underwater pipelaying is up for bid, or a water supply line is being laid, and that a number of contractors will be called upon to undertake the project, the prime contractor for the underwater pipelaying portion of the project receives a copy of the specifications and a set of the blueprints, together with all engineering data. After these have been carefully studied, the cost of the pipe is determined. The prime contractor sends letters to several manufacturers describing the amount of pipe needed, the size, the number of lengths, elbows, Tees, flanges, gaskets, bolts, nuts, etc., and requests a bid price from them. Their prices should include delivery, either to the job site or to the nearest town, city, rail junction, or by rail as close to the job as possible. It should be made known in the price request that other manufacturers have been contacted for the same information.

After the price for the pipe has been established, the cost of transporting it from the rail head to the job site is determined. The contractor contacts all available truckers and movers, telling them what has to be hauled, the approximate weight per section, the distance to be travelled, and the responsibility they will bear for broken pipe. Naturally, the lowest bidder in this group would be awarded the contract for transportation. However, the bids from all pipe manufacturers and truckers should be kept on file.

The next step in figuring a prime contractor's bid is to consider the amount of heavy machinery which will be required to handle the pipe, dig excavation, etc. The Associated Equipment Distributors, Chicago 1, Illinois, publish a book for contractors which lists the daily, weekly and monthly rental fees for all types of construction equipment. If the prime contractor feels the job can be completed in 60 days, provided there are no set-backs, the bid figure should be based on the rental fee totaling 90–120 days. This serves to protect the contractor in the event of unforeseen delays in the work. All contracts should have a clause including circumstances covering Acts of God and Nature.

If the work is completed in the time originally estimated, the monies which would be paid out in equipment rental will then be job profit. It is wise to contact local small contractors with the equipment, explaining the type of equipment needed and the specific details of the job, and asking them to submit bids as sub-contractors.

Equipment rental fees are rarely as high as those quoted in the book. It is intended to be used merely as a guide and a basis for renting machinery and making bid estimates. The prices quoted are not fixed; for that matter, they are very flexible.

When a prime contractor hires machinery from an equipment rental firm, the machinery operators' salaries must be figured as part of the job cost. In the case of sub-contracting, the sub-contractor figures the price of his equipment, necessary crew, the costs of fuel consumed, depreciation of equipment, repairs and insurance. If there are to be no sub-contractors, the prime contractor must estimate the cost of equipment repairs, fuel consumed, etc. The figure should never be too low, but it takes experience to estimate judiciously.

The amount of labor, classified as unskilled, semi-skilled, skilled, craftsmen and professional, together with the pay scales for each, must be determined. Overtime hours must be estimated for each class. Some jobs will require the prime contractor to pay the local union scale for all employees, while other jobs will be classed as non-union. In the latter case, the unskilled and semi-skilled can be paid a fair salary below union scale, but the skilled and craftsmen will always demand the union scale. When bidding the job, it is best to figure on existing local union pay scales.

The bid must include office help, job insurance, bid bond costs, Social Security taxes, unemployment compensation, hospitalization, etc. This is classed as job overhead and the figure is determined after the rest of the job has been totaled. The overhead figure ranges from 20% to 30%. An average figure is 21% of the total job cost.

Clever bidders will refer to the bids submitted by the pipe manufacturers and truckers; taking the highest and lowest bids, the contractor will use a balance between the two when submitting his formal project bid.

Last, but uppermost in the prime contractor's mind, is his profit on the job. The usual profit percentage figure is 10% to 20%. Any amount over this figure can be termed "emergency" security.

Sub-contractor Bidding. A sub-contractor is released from many responsibilities. However, sub-contracting can be hazardous.

Assuming a general contractor has been awarded the bid for the construction of a water supply pumping station, and the contractor desires to sub-let the installation of the underwater intake supply line, the pipelaying divers inform the contractor that they would like to be sub-contractors on this part of the contract. The prime contractors will then invite all interested parties to submit bids for the job.

To arrive at a price, the sub-contractors should do the following: (1) Obtain all specifications and blueprints of the job; (2) Make underwater surveys along the channel(s) where the pipe is to be laid and take accurate soundings of the water depths. Observe the bottom and make notes as to whether it is sandy, rocky, muddy or with ledges. It is important to measure carefully the rocks and widths of sandy, muddy and ledge patches and areas; (3) Receive all data concerning the pipe—length and weight per section, manufacturer, flange type, gasket type, bolt and nut sizes, etc.; (4) Find out how the pipe will be delivered to the job site. (Prime contractors usually have the pipe already purchased.); (5) Find out if the prime contractor will deliver the pipe to the job site at his own expense or if the sub-contractor is responsible for doing this; (6) Find out if the prime contractor will supply the necessary equipment to install the pipe, such as cranes, backhoes, and/or barges, or whether this action is the sub-contractor's responsibility; (7) Find out the cost of a length of pipe(s) and the total cost of the entire line (if it has already been purchased by the prime contractor); (8) It is possible that the Project Engineer would divulge the amount the prime contractor has been allowed per foot for the pipe (this will include installation, also). Knowing the actual cost of the pipe would aid greatly in determining the bid.

Study the specifications and the underwater survey information. If the pipe is to be set in a trench or channel, knowledge of obstructions in the pipe-line path will have a bearing on the price. If the line proceeds through a rocky area, the rocks will have to be removed. Blasting may be necessary. For each cubic yard of rocks removed, there must be an added price. When the pipe line is blocked by ledge, the price increases for each cubic yard that must be removed. To arrive at a fair price, it is best to contact local excavation contractors, consulting engineers, etc., and ask what they would charge for doing the same job.

The amount of equipment necessary to do the job should be estimated. If the equipment is already owned, the sub-contractors should set an hourly, daily or weekly rental on it. Some new equipment may be charged to the job, but big items which must be purchased should have only the hourly, daily or weekly rental rates set on them. Other jobs will help pay for this newly acquired equipment.

Totalling the number of men required to do the job and their rates of pay, overtime, the 21% figure of the total job for overhead expenses and a small miscellaneous expense, will produce a bidding figure. After the profit percentage figure is added, the proposed bid is submitted.

If the bidders have been fortunate enough to receive a pipe installation figure from the Project Engineer, the proposed bid can be as close to that figure as desired.

Sub-contractors should insure their personal equipment, company equipment, rented equipment, employees, the pipe line(s) and the job. As sub-contractors, a performance bond may be required, or the prime contractor may include a special clause in the contract to protect him in the event the sub-contractor cannot fulfill his portion of the contract.

Assuming that the State Water Department has awarded a contract to the A-B-C Contractors, Inc., and they, in turn, have sub-let the underwater pipelaying portion of the project to your firm, the Marine Pipe Installation Company, a contract must be drawn up. Prior to signing any contracts, certain agreements are made between the contractor and the sub-contractor.

It has been agreed that the prime contractor will supply all necessary pipe and deliver it to the shore and job site, and further, the prime contractor will supply the machinery with which to install the pipe and to make all necessary excavation. A sample contract covering such an agreement follows:

A CONTRACT, made this_____day of_____,19___, by and between the A-B-C Contractors, Inc., a corporation duly existing under the laws of the State of Maine, having a usual place of business at Southridge, county of York, State of Maine, and the MARINE PIPE INSTALLATION COMPANY, a company having a usual place of business in Bangor, county of Penobscot, State of Maine.

WITNESSETH:

Whereas, the said A-B-C Contractors have entered into a contract with the State Water Department, State of New York, for the construction of a water supply pumping station in the City of Long View, in the county of Long Island, State of New York, and,

Whereas, the said A-B-C Contractors, Inc., is desirous of sub-letting certain of the work to be performed by them under said contract, and

Whereas, the said Marine Pipe Installation Company are desirous of accepting and performing said work,

IT IS AGREED AS FOLLOWS:

The said Marine Pipe Installation Company agrees to perform that part of the contract listed below for the sum price of $6,500.00.

The said Marine Pipe Installation Company agrees to place in an acceptable manner in Long View Lake an estimated quantity of 1,200 l. feet of 20-inch Cast Iron pipe and an estimated quantity of 750 l. feet of 16-inch Cast Iron pipe.

The said A-B-C Contractors, Inc., shall supply all of the pipe at their expense, and shall deliver or have caused to deliver the aforementioned quantities to the job site on the shore of the lake.

The said Marine Pipe Installation Company shall be responsible for any pipe breakage or damage done by their placing of the pipe and it shall be paid for by them. Under no circumstances shall the said Marine Pipe Installation Company be responsible for broken or damaged pipe caused by an Act of GOD and/or Nature, or by the handling of those persons or things other than the employees and personnel of the Marine Pipe Installation Company.

The said A-B-C Contractors, Inc., shall be responsible for all excavation, whether on land, the lake shore frontage, or out into the reaches of the lake under water.

The said A-B-C Contractors, Inc., agree to supply to the said Marine Pipe Installation Company all necessary mechanically driven and/or motor driven machinery, such as cranes, backhoes, compressors, water pumps, barges, heavy winches, etc., to complete the installation of the pipe. This equipment will be assigned to the said Marine Pipe Installation Company and be under their commands and instructions. In no event will the said Marine Pipe Installation Company be held responsible for any damage whatsoever inflicted upon the equipment in the discharge of their duties in installing the underwater pipe.

All charges for operators, assistants, laborers, repairs, replacements, fuel, etc., shall be borne by the A-B-C Contractors, Inc.

The said Marine Pipe Installation Company shall commence work as soon as the pipe arrives for placing and agrees to proceed in an expeditious manner, and to perform said work in accordance with the terms of the contract between the A-B-C Contractors, Inc., and the State Water Department, State of New York.

The said A-B-C Contractors, Inc. agrees to pay the sum of $6,500.00 in the following manner:

(a) An advance deposit for working capital of $1,000.00 within seven (7) days after the said Marine Pipe Installation Company has commenced its work, and,

(b) Upon the installation of_____number of feet of underwater pipe, to pay the amount of $_____, and to continue to pay this amount for each_____number of feet thereafter until the completion of the installation, whereupon the balance of monies due shall be paid in full within seven days after acceptance of the work by the State inspector on this project.

Signed on this_____day of_____in the year of Our LORD, One Thousand, Nine Hundred and Fifty Nine.

Witnessed by:

---------------------------   --------------------------------

Lloyd Whiting, Attorney   W. Clarence Bigelowe, President
                                                 A-B-C Contractors, Inc.

Official   John R. Smith, MSD, President
Seal   Marine Pipe Installation Company

Do *not* sign contracts that stipulate payment upon the completion of your work or the job only. When a newly established diving pipe-laying company is operating on limited funds, this should be explained to the prime contractor. It may be the case that all but a small percentage of the underwater work has been completed, but, due to lack of experience or proper equipment, it is necessary to call in some assistance. Always get paid for the work you have performed satisfactorily.

Clause (a) can be any amount, and the amount is established on the number of employees that must be paid and the amount of bills which would be due at that period, plus a sum to be kept in reserve.

Clause (b) insures that the firm will receive money for the work that has been performed. In drawing up a contract and Clause (b) is agreed upon, estimate the number of feet capable of being installed in a period of one or two weeks and use that figure. For example, the contract calls for 1,950 feet of pipe to be laid at the cost of $6,500.00. The crew is capable of installing five lengths of pipe per day. Figuring the installation at approximately $3.25 per running foot, a day's pay would be $292.50. Therefore, the number of feet of pipe could be established at 500, and the amount of pay for the work would be $1,500.00. Each additional 500 feet installed would bring the same amount. Regardless of the number of days actually required to install the stipulated 500 feet of pipe, the monies would be payable when that number of feet have been properly installed.

The following is another sample clause which can be used in place of the designated Clause (b).

The sum of $_____shall be paid the said Marine Pipe Installation Company for the performance of work under this contract for a period of_____days upon acceptance of the said performed work by the State inspector on this project. The sum of $_____is payable for each like total number of days thereafter until the completion of the installation, whereupon the balance of all monies shall be paid in full within seven days after acceptance by the State inspector.

If this clause is used in the contract, figure the amount of time in which the job can be completed and have the payments due and dates conform with the expenses. Referring to the project mentioned previously, the totals to fill in the latter clause would be: the sum of $1,500.00 payable by the contractor for each 7-day work period, and a like sum for each 7-day period thereafter.

Using either of the clauses in the contract, the small diving company is protected by having money deposited to their account to pay bills, salaries, and other necessities.

It is wise to seek the advice of a contract lawyer to assist in drawing up a contract.

POINTS TO REMEMBER

1. Have and know all types of u/w pipe data.

2. Study all project specifications.

3. Receive all u/w information possible and make personal underwater surveys.

4. Never overestimate your abilities.

5. Never undersell your services.

6. Before making any job bids, contact a Consulting Engineer for valuable information.

7. Never sign contracts or papers until an attorney has been consulted.

8. Protect the company, equipment and employees with proper insurance coverage and maximum safety devices.

9. Keep accurate records of all expenditures, working and diving time, Social Security and Income Tax deductions, and Technical and Work Progress Reports.

Chapter VI

UNDERWATER CUTTING AND WELDING

The field of underwater cutting and welding is fast becoming as important as the salvage field. More and more, metal is replacing wood in the construction of boats. In steel craft, a jagged tear or hole often can be repaired by underwater welding. In the case of bent props or shafts, the underwater cutter is employed to sever a bent section and perhaps weld on a new piece. Bridge construction companies can use underwater cutting and welding experts in many of their operations. There are many other profitable jobs for the torchman. Although underwater cutting and welding manuals have been written with only the deep-sea or shallow-water diver in mind, a Scuba diver, with experience and ingenuity, can adapt the information in these manuals to his needs.

The field of underwater cutting and welding is a new one, like most of the other underwater jobs done by divers. Very little work was done with torches of any type prior to World War II. But, since Pearl Harbor, great strides have been taken to develop better underwater cutting and welding equipment, for it was urgently needed in the salvage of our damaged warships. The U.S. Navy deserves much of the credit for the development of new and more efficient underwater cutting and welding equipment.

In principle, underwater cutting and welding equipment and procedure are approximately the same as those for surface cutting and welding. Water, of course, imposes certain limitations and these must be taken into consideration. Today's equipment will perform satisfactorily at any known depth. The success of any underwater cutting and welding operation depends upon the diving gear used, the depth of water in which the diver and gear work, the underwater currents, the water's temperature, and the visibility conditions.

UNDERWATER CUTTING METHODS

The two common methods of underwater cutting, the Arc-oxygen method and the Oxy-hydrogen method, depend on the chemical reaction of oxidation of metals and are, in general, limited to plain carbon and low-alloy steels; that is, metals which oxidize easily. In these techniques, heat is applied to the metal and on the intended line of the cut. When the metal is at "kindling" temperature, pure oxygen is released on the immediate spot and the metal burns rapidly. By

moving the heat source and oxygen supply along any given line, the
metal will fall away. The third method, the Metal-arc method, is a
melting operation. Corrosion-resisting and austenitic steels or other
unoxidizing metals are cut by this method. Sufficient heat is applied
from a concentrated source, such as an electric arc. This completely
melts through the spot where the heat is applied, and the process
is continued along any intended line of cut.

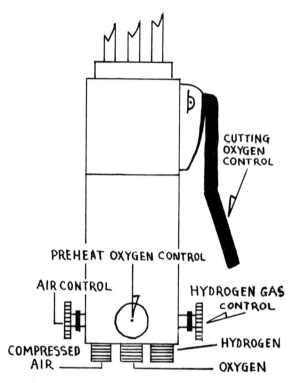

Fig. 22.   General scheme of gas underwater cutting torch controls.

There is no set rule as to which type of tool to use in any given
operation. The diver can use that tool which is available and do a
satisfactory job; or by surveying a torch job, he can determine
which tool would be most suitable.

The Arc-oxygen Torch Cutting Method. The modern arc-oxygen
cutting torch has been in use for some time but it is still being improved. The arc-oxygen torch used today was developed through
the combined efforts of the U.S. Naval Engineering Experiment Station, Annapolis, Maryland; Experimental Diving Unit and Deep
Sea Diving School, Naval Gun Factory, Washington, D. C.; and the
U.S. Naval Training School (Salvage), Pier 88, New York City.

These departments of the Navy made the following improvements in the arc-oxygen cutting torch: new electrode design, new torch design, simplification of the techniques for using the new materials, standardization of the new procedure, improved safety features, and performance equal to that obtainable with oxyacetylene method in air.

Operating Principle. The metal is preheated. When incandescence is reached, a jet of pure oxygen is released on the local preheated spot. The oxygen jet performs double duty whereby it oxidizes, or

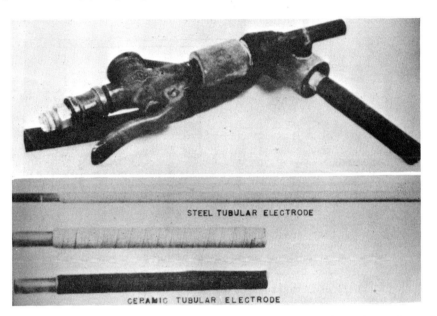

STEEL TUBULAR ELECTRODE

CERAMIC TUBULAR ELECTRODE

Fig. 23. (Top) Standard arc-oxygen torch. (Bottom) Ceramic and steel electrodes.

burns, the core of preheated areas and removes the products of combustion. The electrode is drawn along the line of cut and, because it brings the metal to incandescence so swiftly, cutting can be accomplished with great speed.

The elements of the arc-oxygen cutting torch are as follows: A chuck or grip for holding the tubular electrode and permitting entrance of oxygen into the tube; an oxygen valve; an electrical connection; a flash-back arrester for use with steel tube electrodes; an insulating coupling installed between the valve and the chunk to safeguard the operator from electrical shock and to prevent deterioration of the valve as a result of electrolysis; complete insulation (such as rubber tape) for all exposed current-carrying metallic parts of the torch. Only electrode holders should be used which have been specifically designed for underwater cutting and are of a sufficient capacity for the maximum rated current required by the electrodes with which the holder is intended to be used.

The Navy Department's standard arc-oxygen torch is shown in Fig. 23 (top).

DC Welding Generator. The best electrical power source is a DC welding generator of 300 amperes connected for straight polarity (*see* Fig. 24). The cables are welding cable stock, size 0 (105,000CM) and size 2/0 (133,000CM), and should be extra flexible. Size 2/0 is used for work that will be carried on a considerable distance from the power source, as this size will afford low resistance in the lines.

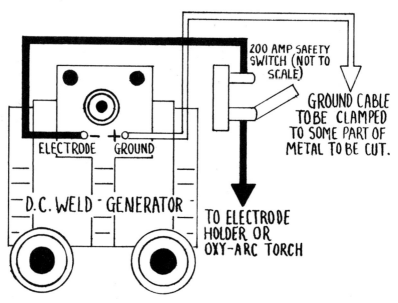

Fig. 24. DC welding generator. Generally, all underwater cutting and welding is done with straight polarity, as shown.

A safety switch should be connected to the lines of the arc-oxygen torch. A knife switch, unfusible, single pole, single throw, 200 ampere, 250 volts, is standard for the arc-oxygen torch.

Since the arc-oxygen cutting torch is still being improved upon, the primary consideration is in the design of the electrode holder. All of the current-carrying parts of the electrode holder must be completely insulated.

Determination of Polarity. If the markings on the welding generator are not legible, polarity may be determined as follows: (1) with the generator dead, connect the ground and welding leads to the terminals; (2) clamp a covered electrode to the ground lead and insert another electrode into the holder or torch; (3) place the tips of

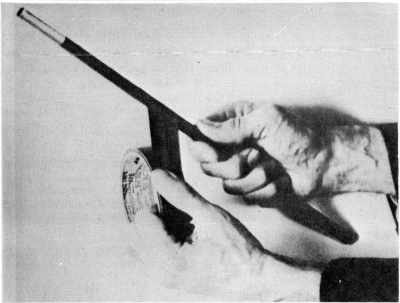

Fig. 25. (Top) Cigarette style wrapping of emergency tubular electrodes.
(Bottom) Spiral wrapping of electrodes.

the two electrodes into a container of salt water; (4) be sure that the operator is properly insulated from the current; (5) hold the tips an inch or two apart and switch on the current. Bubbles will flow from the negative pole, but practically none will flow from the positive pole; (6) the polarity is correct if the bubbles rise from the electrode in the holder. Otherwise, the leads must be reversed.

Types of Tubular Electrodes. Ceramic and steel electrodes are used. Both electrodes will give excellent performance with power. The ceramic electrode will outperform the steel electrode for plate thicknesses up to $3/4''$; but the latter is best for cutting thicker plates. Both electrodes, shown in Fig. 23 (bottom), have been used by the Navy to cut $3/4''$ manganese bronze plate.

The ceramic electrode has three advantages over the steel electrode: long life, due to slow rate of burnoff; suitability for working in a confined space, due to its $8''$ length; and lightness of weight.

For cutting thin and medium thickness steel plate, one ceramic-tube electrode is equal (in terms of length of the cut) to approximately ten steel-tube electrodes. The steel-tube electrodes have the following advantages: the very simple and readily-mastered technique; ease of operation for all thicknesses of metal being cut; performance with AC nearly equal to that with DC; rapid rate of cutting neat, trim cuts; and power requirements within the capacity of a 300-ampere welding generator or transformer.

Both types of electrodes have proved successful in underwater arc-oxygen cutting operations.

Emergency tubular electrodes can be made if there are no standard electrodes available. Rigid safety precautions should be observed in their insulation and use. They can be fabricated from tubing or pipe by utilizing $5/16''$ steel tubing or $1/8''$ extra strong iron pipe in $14''$ lengths and covering all except the grip end with masking tape or paper to the thickness of approximately $0.020''$. This may be accomplished by using 3 wraps of masking tape, ordinary wrapping paper or writing paper, or 4 wraps of newspaper.

The wrapping may be done spirally or cigarette fashion, as shown in Fig. 25.

"Wet or dry" masking tape is used on these emergency electrodes. When untreated paper is used, a waterproof glue or cement is employed to insure a neat cover. A coating with varnish, shellac, paint, or wax can be used in extreme emergencies.

The author strongly advises that these emergency measures be used only when absolutely necessary and by experienced persons.

The arc-oxygen torch requires cylinders of oxygen for underwater operations. Oxygen is expensive and can be wasted needlessly. The following tabulation presents plate-thickness and oxygen rations which were found to be most economical.

Plate Thickness	Oxygen Pressure
1/4 in.	20 psi
1/4 in.	30 psi
3/4 in.	40 psi
1 in.	50 psi
More than 1 in.	75 psi or more

The values given in the table are those that should obtain at the torch. They do not include the pressure drop with a hose more than 50 feet in length nor the pressure change due to the depth of water. To compute the additional regulator pressure necessary to compensate for operating depth, multiply the depth in feet by the factor 0.445.

Cutting Technique. The technique of using steel tubular electrodes for cutting steel plate thicker than 1/4" is as follows:

1. To start to cut, hold the electrodes perpendicular to the surface to be cut, place the tip of the electrode against the work, open the oxygen valve, and call for "current on." Withdraw the electrode slightly, if necessary, to start the arc.

2. To advance the cut: as soon as the cut is started for the full thickness of the plate, "drag" the electrode along the desired line of cut, maintaining it perpendicular to the work. The tip of the electrode should be pressed against the advancing lip of the cut. Pressure should be exerted in two directions, inward to compensate for electrode burnoff and forward to advance the cut. Do not hold an arc as when welding in air.

3. An incomplete cut due to some fault of manipulation is evidenced by back-flare. Stop the advance and go back immediately to complete the cut.

4. When the electrode has been consumed, be sure to signal "current off," before attempting to change electrodes. Maintain the torch in cutting position until the tender acknowledges "current off." This safety precaution is mandatory regardless of the type of electrode being used.

The technique for cutting 1/4" and thinner steel plate is slightly different from that used in thicker plate. The electrode in this case barely touches the plate surface as it advances along the line of cut.

The technique for cutting steel plate employing the ceramic tubular electrode is almost the same as that using the steel tubular electrode. The electrode is held in the same position, and the current is turned on at the diver's command. The ceramic electrode is held so that it is barely touching the plate. A very light touch is applied between the work and the electrode, and there is no exertion for the inward pressure. Should the electrode be pushed into the cut, it will cause a flare-back, which is indicative of an incomplete cut. When the electrode has been used up, the diver again commands that the current be turned off and, before touching the electrode or electrode holder, he waits for the tender to report "current off."

Piercing holes in steel plate is readily accomplished by the arc-oxygen method. The process is rapid and is as follows:

Touch the plate lightly at the desired point, open the oxygen valve, and call for "current on;" hold stationary for a moment, withdrawing momentarily, if necessary, to permit melting of the steel tube back inside the covering; push the electrode slowly into the hole until the plate is pierced.

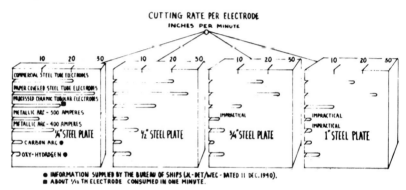

Fig. 26.   Cutting rate per electrode (ins. per min.).

By this method, 3″ plates can be pierced without difficulty.

Figure 26 shows the cutting rate per electrode in inches per minute.

Advantages. No preheat time is necessary; positive action, no flame adjustment necessary; applicable to all thicknesses of metal; can be used to cut laminated plating; skipped areas and slag can be cut easily; torch is light and easy to handle; oxygen is the only gas necessary, thus simplifying storage problem and danger inherent in explosive gases; less skill and practice are required for diver to master the technique.

Metal-arc Cutting Method. Metal-arc cutting is the process of applying the heat of the electric arc to melt the metal. No oxygen is necessary. Compressed air may be used to blow the molten metal out of the cut.

The nonferrous metals—brass, copper, nickel-copper, and manganese-bronze—and cast iron are not readily oxidized; with them, underwater cutting becomes a melting process.

The recommended power source for metal-arc cutting is a DC welding generator having a capacity of 400 amperes, connected for straight polarity. However, satisfactory cutting can be accomplished using a 300-ampere generator. Extra-flexible cable, size 2/0 (133,-000CM) is used, except for a 10-foot section attached to the electrode holder, which may be 1/0 cable, to aid the diver in maneuvering the holder.

Safety switches described for the preceding method are used. The electrode holder and the cables must be fully insulated.

In an emergency, any properly waterproofed, covered, mild-steel, welding electrode of a suitable size may be used. However, the two commercial brands which performed best under laboratory test are Alternex, a product of the Metal & Thermit Corporation, and Flexarc S. W., a product of Westinghouse Electric Company.

These electrodes are waterproofed like those used in the arc-oxygen cutting process.

Table 5. Comparison of Electrodes

Arc-oxygen cutting	Unit	No. of electrodes (approx.)	Steel plate cut in ft./box of electrodes			
			1/4" thick	1/2" thick	3/4" thick	1" thick
Commercial steel tubular electrodes	50 lb. box	167	240	170	170	160
	Tanks of oxygen (200 cu. ft.) per box of electrodes		2.7	2.0	2.0	2.0
Ceramic tubular electrodes	6-1/2 lb. box	25	475	375	275	175
	Tanks of oxygen (200 cu. ft.) per box of electrodes		6	6	6	6

Table 6. Metallic-arc Underwater Cutting

Electrode size	Unit	No. of electrodes (approx.)	Power source	Steel plate cut in ft./box of electrodes		
				1/4" thick	1/2" thick	3/4" thick
3/16"		410	300 amps.	185	102	
3/16	50 lb. box	410	400 amps.	307	135	58
1/4"		220	400 amps.	176	77	44

Note: With 300 amperes available for underwater cutting, use 3/16" diameter electrodes; 5/32" may be used, but the burnoff rate is very rapid. With 400 amperes available, use 3/16" diameter or preferably, 1/4" diameter electrodes.

When employing 3/16" electrodes with a power source of 300 amperes at about 40 volts, steel plate up to 1/4" thick can be cut by simply dragging the electrode along the desired line of cut. The thickest plate which can be cut using this drag technique is about 1/4" where the capacity is 300 amperes, and about 3/8" where the amperage can be increased to 400. To cut thicker plate, a slow, short stroke, sawing motion must be used to push the molten metal out of the far side of the cut. Skillful application of this sawing technique makes the metal-arc cutting process practical over a wide range of thicknesses, even where the large electrodes and heavy currents recommended for use with the drag technique are not available. Where large electrodes and heavy currents can be had, the drag technique has the advantages of speed and simplicity of operation. Mastery of the cutting technique will be aided by the operator's understanding clearly that the metal is merely melted, not oxidized or consumed in any way, and that if the molten metal does not run out of the cut by itself, it must be pushed out by manipulation of the electrode.

Advantages. Can be used to cut nonferrous metals and alloys; no source of fuel gas is required; standard surface welding holders and electrodes can be adapted in any emergency for underwater use.

The Oxy-hydrogen Cutting Method. The oxy-hydrogen cutting torch operates on the combined processes of compressed oxygen, compressed hydrogen and compressed air. The torching method is approximately the same as cutting in air except the diver must accustom himself to working with relatively high pressures. The major difference in the underwater torch is the presence of a third hose to transport the compressed air. The compressed air is delivered to a bell-like shield or "skirt" that surrounds the cutting tip and sheathes it with an air bubble. The purpose of the skirt is to stabilize the flame and keep water away from the metal being heated.

Cutting Technique. The metal to be cut is brought to ignition temperature by a preheat flame of hydrogen and oxygen. This preheat flame is kept on during cutting to maintain cutting heat. A narrow kerf is burned or cut by the action of the oxygen cutting jet upon the heated metal. The cut is progressed by advancing the torch along the line of cut at an even speed. The torch must be moved fast enough to keep the cut going, yet slowly enough to cut completely through.

Uses. The oxy-hydrogen torch has a very wide field of application, although it is generally used in cutting steel—hulls, decks, bulkheads, wire cable, bolts, fittings, etc. Wrought iron and cast iron are extremely difficult to cut underwater with the oxy-hydrogen torch. Unfortunately, wrought iron can be found in ship's hulls, those having all riveted seams. Machinery parts and bed-plates, of massive design and thick sections, are usually cast iron. Steel, wrought iron and cast iron may be detected by a small horseshoe magnet, though it is almost impossible to determine which of the three metals is present.

Aluminum, brass, copper, bronze, CRS, monel, and other nonferrous metals and alloys can sometimes be melted by the flame and blown away by spurts of the cutting jets. The thickness of the metal is an important factor in the oxy-hydrogen cutting method. Thin steel plates should not be cut by the oxy-hydrogen method, as the surrounding water cools the plates quickly and decreases the torch's preheat temperature.

Steel from ⅜″ up to and including 1½″ thick is considered the best for this cutting technique. The torch can also be used to cut steel wire rope, wire cable, and even manila rope, because it offers less danger of damage to nearby metals. Although the torch may be used at any depth in which a diver can work, it is suggested that it be used in moderately deep water.

Equipment Needed. The following is a list of equipment and supplies required for underwater oxy-hydrogen cutting:

1. Oxy-hydrogen underwater cutting torch.
2. Oxygen in cylinders.
3. Hydrogen in cylinders.
4. Compressed air (in cylinders or straight from a storage tank, loaded continuously by a compressor).
5. Regulators and gauges for oxygen and hydrogen.
6. Hose for oxygen, hydrogen, and compressed air.
7. Underwater electrical lighters (optional for the beginner, as the torch may be ignited on the surface).
8. Valve wrench.
9. Protective clothing.
10. Manifolds.

Fundamentally, the torches now in use are all the same.

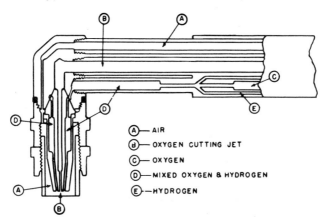

Fig. 27. Operational functions of gases in underwater cutting torch.

Figure 27, showing the operational functions of gases in the underwater cutting torch, gives a cross-sectional view of the gas passages and the head of the torch.

A number of cylinders are needed to store oxygen, hydrogen, and compressed air. Using the standard U.S. Navy Cylinder Color Code, a diving-torchman will avoid accidents caused by having the hoses attached to the wrong cylinder.

Color Code

Compressed Air	All black
Oxygen	All green
Oxygen, aviator's	Body green Top 6" green Band 3" white
Hydrogen	Body yellow Top 6" yellow Band 3" black

Once these colors have been applied to the torchman's personal cylinders, which may be purchased through salvage and surplus outlets, they should never be changed. It is important to remember that cutting cylinders containing any type of gas should never be loaned. If a diver buys cylinders from a manufacturer, the cylinder serial number is sent to the Bureau of Explosives and the Interstate Commerce Commission. These cylinders are charged to him, and a part of their care involves periodic checking by hydrostatic tests, pressure tests, valve checks, regulator checks, etc.

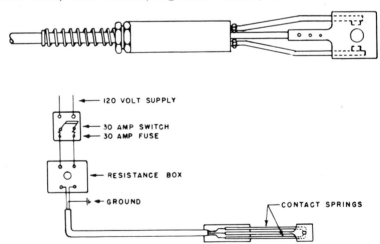

Fig. 28.   Underwater torch lighter (diagram of connections).

Regulators should be handled with the utmost care. If they get out of order, they must be shipped to a certified regulator repair company. Never attempt to make adjustments or try to repair regulators.

Hoses for acetylene, hydrogen, air, and oxygen are purchased under Federal Specification 33-H-7. The color code is as follows: red for hydrogen (or acetylene), green for oxygen, and black for air.

This color code should be observed and hoses should never be interchanged. Oil, which is present in compressed air, unless filtered, may settle in oxygen hoses and cause a violent explosion.

The 5/16" inside diameter hose is recommended for underwater cutting. Hose couplings are made of specified copper base alloy. Fuel gas hoses are equipped with left-hand thread couplings; oxygen hoses have right-hand threads.

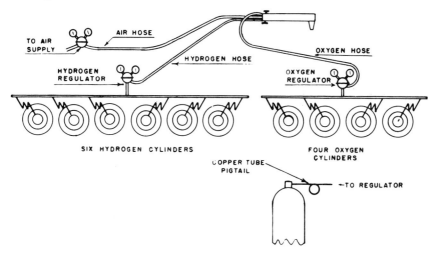

Fig. 29.   Manifold for underwater gas cutting.

Underwater lighters are commonly used in the oxy-hydrogen cutting method. It is preferable for the diver to light the torch after descending, when he is ready to start the job. An electrical type of igniter has been developed for this purpose. The lighter, shown in Fig. 28, should be used only to ignite the torch flame underwater. The igniter operates on 120 volts DC, and is not usable in air-surface operations.

Manifolds are necessary to connect two or more cylinders together. Two different types of gases are never connected together by means of a manifold. The diagram of a manifold setup (Fig. 29) will give the diver an idea of how the manifolds are used and the approximate number of cylinders of gas needed for a lengthy cutting operation. The manifolds should be treated with the same care given other diving gear. Oil and other by-products should never be allowed near any of the manifolds or manifold connections. All pigtail connectors should be of the highest hydrostatic strength possible (3,000 psi or better). A nonreturn check valve should be connected between each hydrogen cylinder and the manifold.

Setting Up the Equipment. To prepare for underwater cutting with the oxy-hydrogen torch, the following procedure should be used:

1. Place cylinders so that they will not be knocked over.
2. "Blow out" cylinder valves by a quick turn-on of the valve. This serves to clear any foreign matter from the gas outlets.
3. Set the hydrogen and oxygen regulators of their respective tanks and tighten them firmly with the valve wrench.
4. Connect the hoses to the regulators and screw the hose nuts up lightly.
5. Purge the hoses to the open air for a few seconds. This serves to remove any air in the hoses.
6. Attach the torch. Connect green oxygen hose to torch needle valve marked "Ox," and the red hydrogen hose to the valve marked "Fuel Gas." The black hose is connected to the valve marked "Air."
7. Select the proper tip size according to Table 7 to cut the known steel thickness.

Table 7. Tip Sizes

Recommended for Airco Oxy-Hydrogen Underwater Cutting Torch

Thickness of Steel	Style 35	Style 164
1/4"	4—3	6—4
1/2"	4—4	6—5
3/4"	4—5	6—6
1"	4—5	6—6
1-1/4"	4—6	6—7
1-1/2"	4—7	6—8
1-3/4"	4—8	6—9
2"	4—8	6—9

8. Adjust the regulators. Hydrogen working-pressure adjustment is made by opening the fuel gas torch needle valve, adjusting the hydrogen regulator to the required working pressure, and closing the needle valve. Adjust the oxygen working pressure in the same manner.
9. Light the torch to test the flame and make sure everything is working properly. To light, turn the torch away from everything, open the hydrogen needle valve, and ignite with a spark lighter. Adjust to proper flame by opening and adjusting the oxygen needle valve.
10. The gauges will be adjusted in the manner prescribed in Table 8.

Precautions. When lighting the oxy-hydrogen cutting torch in air, these precautions should be observed:

1. Wear gloves, goggles and suitable clothing.
2. Use a friction type lighter.
3. Point the torch away from persons and inflammables.
4. Follow this sequence in lighting the torch:
   a. Turn on hydrogen part way (open the needle valve ½ to ⅔ turn).
   b. Light flame.
   c. Increase hydrogen flow.
   d. Turn on oxygen by opening oxygen needle valve.
   e. Adjust the flame.

5. The compressed air valve should be opened to the amount determined by the length of bubble, as described below in adjusting the torch under water.

6. The correct gas mixture is determined by watching the flame color. A neutral oxy-hydrogen mixture burns with a pale yellow flame. When the torch is properly adjusted, the preheating flames burn with a colorlessness, almost invisible, indicating an excess of hydrogen beyond what is actually necessary for perfect combustion. Experimentation will give the correct adjustments.

Table 8. Recommended Pressures (Gauge Pressure at Surface) for Oxy-hydrogen Cutting Torches

Working depth (ft.)	Water pressure, pounds (approx.)	Length of hose (ft.)	Pressures		
			Air lbs.	Hydrogen lbs.	Oxygen lbs.
10	4	100	55	55	75
20	9	100	60	60	80
30	13	100	65	65	85
40	17	150	75	75	95
50	22	150	80	80	100
60	26	200	90	90	110
70	30	200	95	95	115
80	35	250	100	100	120
90	39	250	105	105	125
100	43	300	115	115	135
125	54	300	125	125	145
150	65	300	140	140	160
175	76	400	155	155	175
200	87	450	170	170	190
225	97	450	185	185	200

Testing the Flame. Once the correctly adjusted preheat flame has been obtained, the flame should be tested before it is lowered to tne diver. This is done in the following manner. The tenderman holds the hose about 6 feet back (or more) and then drops the lighted torch into the water so that it is at least 3 feet under. If the tenderman is close enough to the water, he may hold it in his hand and move it back and forth. Under these conditions, the torch should not go out. Should the torch go out, the tenderman will again light it and make more necessary adjustments and proceed with the testing process until the torch remains lit. Before lowering the torch below, the tenderman should test its cutting ability with a piece of·scrap metal. A torch that will not cut in air certainly will not cut under water. Care should be taken not to foul the tip.

The lighted torch may be lowered to a diver in very shallow depths or in easily accessible locations, or it may be carried by hand by the diver. In the latter case, the diver should be prepared to make adjustments to the flame to compensate for the increased water pressure during his descent. *Never* lower a lighted torch until the diver gives the signal for it, and this should only be when he is in position and ready to start work. An unlighted torch may be carried below by the diver or sent down to him by using a finder-line.

Underwater Lighting. The following procedure is to be used when lighting the oxy-hydrogen torch under water with the electric lighter:

1. Open the air valve until the bubble coming from the tip is 3 inches long. Note the setting and close the valve.
2. Open the hydrogen valve until the bubble from the torch tip is about 3 inches long. Note the setting and close the valve.
3. Open the preheating oxygen valve until the bubble is about 2½ inches long.
4. Reopen the air and hydrogen valves to the settings determined in (1) and (2) above.
5. Signal the tenderman to turn on the igniter.
6. Hold the torch horizontally with the tip pointing away from hoses, lines, and person.
7. Hold the igniter so that the gas from the tip of the torch blows through the hole in the igniter guard and past the igniter points.
8. Squeeze the igniter contacts together and then release. The spark formed as the igniter points spring apart will ignite the preheat flame if adjustment of the torch valves is correct.
9. If the torch fails to ignite, open the hydrogen valve a little more and try again.
10. If the torch still fails to ignite, enrich the mixture by turning on a little more oxygen.
11. Adjustments may be continued, first turning on more hydrogen and then more oxygen, until it is certain that adjustment of the mixture is not at fault.

The following may be used as indications for guidance in adjusting compressed air flow and preheating flame under water:

1. Length of bubbles from torch tip:
   a. Hydrogen bubble   3 ins.
   b. Oxygen bubble   2½ ins.
   c. Compressed air bubbles 3 ins.
2. The torch gives off rumbling and bubbling noises under water. A diver, with practice, can gain an indication of the condition of his flame by listening.
3. Maximum brightness is obtained from a properly adjusted preheat flame.
4. The torch is held in the cutting position slightly raised from the steel plate, and the preheat flame is allowed to play on the plate for a few seconds. Bright sparks will fly if the preheat flame is properly adjusted.
5. Indications of too high or too low pressure are:
   a. Compressed Air. Too high: Cools metals too rapidly. Excessive force is required to hold torch head against work. Too low: Will not displace water, causing the flame to flicker and sputter.
   b. Hydrogen. Too high: Will "blast" or "flare" and may melt the torch tip. Too low: Will not maintain flame, or may not light, may backfire into tip.
   c. Oxygen. Too high: Torch sputters and flares. Excessive force is required to hold the torch to the work. Too low: Preheat flame will not light or will pop out.

A diver may find on his first trip below with the oxy-hydrogen cutting torch that it will light on the first try; but more than likely, it will require a little practice to get the flame going and stay lit after the initial ignition period.

There are required pressures in all underwater cutting operations. The pressure required in each case will be the sum of the pressure required to operate the torch, the pressure due to depth, and the pressure required to overcome friction in the hose. For most oxy-hydrogen underwater cutting torches, a pressure of about 40 pounds on the hydrogen and 65 to 70 pounds on the oxygen will be sufficient to operate the torch. Additional pressure due to depth increases at the rate of approximately ½ pound per foot of depth. The exact figure is 0.445 pounds increase in pressure for each foot of added depth in sea water, or 14.7 pounds (1 atmosphere) for each 33 feet.

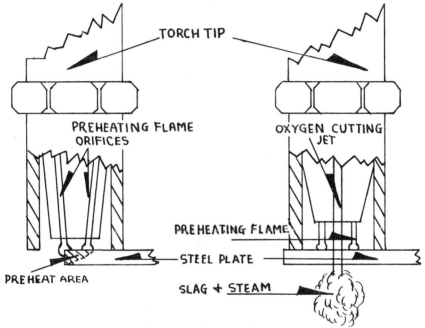

Fig. 30. Starting the cut.

A tenderman should never change the pressures on the hose lines without first telling the diver of the change.

Table 8 gives the recommended pressures. The pressures are calculated to furnish sufficient gas for satisfactory adjustment and operation of the torch, but do not include the pressure required to overcome friction loss in the hose and fittings.

Cutting Technique. The cut may be started on the edge of the plate, as shown in Fig. 30. The torch head is held, as shown, so the edge may be heated. When the small sparks fly, the metal is hot enough to start the cut. Press the cutting lever on the heated area. Better results are obtained by opening the cutting jet about half way for a few seconds at the start.

Fig. 31. (Top) Bringing the torch tip to heat. (Bottom) Finishing the underwater cut.

If the cut is started in the middle of a plate, the process is known as a "blow through." The torch tip is held on the spot until it is brought to heat (Fig. 31, top). Then the cutting jet is gradually turned on, while, at the same time, the torch's head is raised slightly so the slag will not blow into the tip (Fig. 31, bottom).

The cut is advanced with a steady speed, slow enough to cut through the metal, but not too slow to cool it; and fast enough to keep the pre-heat area in advance of the actual cut, but not too fast so as to leave places uncut. Retracing a cut is extremely difficult.

If the cut is lost, it can be re-started by going back ½–¾ inch and starting on the side of the old cut. Figure 32 shows how to re-start a cut.

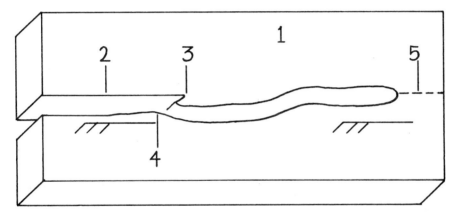

Fig. 32. Restarting the cut. 1. Steel plate; 2. Scarf; 3. End of cut; 4. Start of new cut; 5. Line of cut.

The last operation in the process of underwater cutting with the oxy-hydrogen torch is to extinguish the torch while below. There are four easy steps:

1. Turn off hydrogen valve to preheating flame.
2. Turn off oxygen valve to preheating flame.
3. Turn off compressed air, leaving the valve slightly open to keep torch clear of water.
4. If the flame shows a tendency to "hang on" and burn back up in the torch, it may be extinguished by momentarily opening and closing the oxygen preheat valve.

Upon completion of these steps, the diver may signal the tenderman that the torch has been extinguished and is ready to be hauled to the surface.

Advantages. No danger from electrical shock; can be used to cut nonmetallic objects; special diving gear is not necessary—can be used with shallow water outfit; equipment can be loaded easily in motor launch for operations away from mother ship or base.

The three methods of underwater cutting that have been explained are the ones used by the United States Navy at the present time, and it may be taken for granted that they are completely safe. The safety precautions mentioned previously and in the next section are to be followed to the letter for the safety of the diver as well as of the men tending him and the property involved in the operation.

Underwater cutters are in demand by many of the country's leading construction companies. Our country is in the middle of its greatest period of building, especially bridges, and cutters and welders can always find work. This is a great field, one which requires study, practice, some experimentation, and patience. Previously, only the deep sea diver with his bulky gear could be assigned the job of underwater cutting and welding; but now, Scuba divers can do the job equally as well.

UNDERWATER WELDING

Underwater welding is of recent development. The first successful repair job employing the use of underwater welding equipment was in 1939. This operation was carried out on a damaged ship at sea. It was so successful that the ship was able to reach port under her own steam.

Principles. The principles of underwater welding are comparatively simple. Welding is the joining of two pieces of metal by heat and/or pressure. Arc welding is a process whereby the metals to be welded are brought to the proper temperature, and then the metals fuse together, forming a solid mass when hardened.

The metallic-arc technique employs the use of an electrode. The arc occurs between the electrode and the metal. Under the arc's heat, part of the work is almost instantly brought up to the melting point. At the same time, the electrode's tip is melted and deposited in the molten area, forming a weld bead.

Although there is not as much demand for underwater welding as for underwater cutting, any torch man should know both techniques and have the tool available in case such a job should present itself.

The Navy Department uses the underwater welding holder in the repair of their ships. It has been used for other work, but, for the most part, it is limited to the repair of ship's plates, cracks, and seams.

The size of the patch to be applied, the purpose of the patch, the contours encountered, and protuberances determine the scope of operation. When plates are being welded to a ship's hull, the curvature of the hull must be taken into consideration. In most instances, replacing a plate under water is impractical, although it has been done both successfully and unsuccessfully. Leaky rivets and split seams have been welded under water, but, because of the movements of a ship, these welds must be inspected frequently. However, in bridge construction, pier repair, tower operations, etc., the welder may use his skill without fear of breakage, splitting or pull-aways. It is important to remember that faying surfaces and edges to be welded must fit as closely when working under water as when working topside; the design and attachment for underwater work must provide equal or greater structural strength than for similar work in air. The additional factor of safety must take into account any reduction in efficiency due to the nature of the work or the skill of the welder.

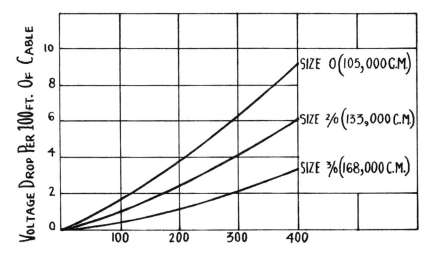

Fig. 33. Voltage drop in welding cables (current in amperes). To compensate for voltage drop, increase the output of the welding machine.

Equipment Needed. The power source used in underwater welding is a DC welding generator of at least 300-amperes capacity, connected for straight polarity. In an emergency, a 200-ampere DC generator may be substituted, but it must be run at peak or near peak capacity. No welding is done below without a safety switch, like those described previously, connected to the generator and holder.

Size 2/0 extra-flexible welding cable is used in this operation, with the exception of a 10-foot length of size 1/0 attached to the electrode holder for easier maneuverability. The voltage drops for various sizes of cable are shown in Fig. 33. This voltage drop does not include contact resistance, which can be kept to a minimum by making all connections tight and thoroughly insulated.

The electrode holder used for underwater welding must be insulated, durable and allow easy changing of the electrodes . The plastic holder shown in Fig. 34 has been adopted as Navy Standard. Shown, also, is a completely insulated Micarta electrode holder developed at the U. S. Naval Engineering Experiment Station.

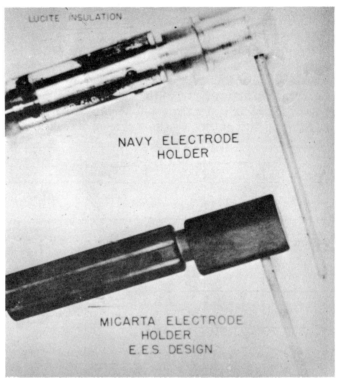

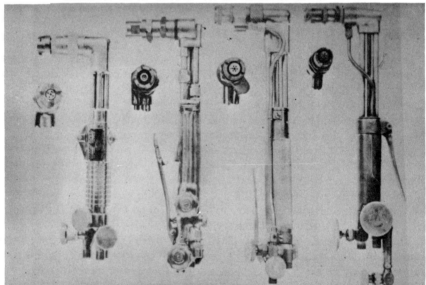

Fig. 34.   (Top) Electrode holder. (Bottom) Underwater cutting torches and tips.

Table 9. Recommended Electrodes

Electrodes	Sizes	Position	Current (amps.) (*)	Time for 12" burnoff (secs.)
		H.	170—210	54—44
	5/32"	V.	170—210	56—44
		O. H	170—190	56—50
Westinghouse		H.	220—260	59—50
Flexarc SW	3/16"	V.	220—260	59—50
		O. H.	190—210	66—61
Lincoln		H.	220—260	60—49
Fleetweld 37	3/16"	V.	220—260	60—49
		O. H.	200—220	66—60

Substitute Electrodes

Electrode	Size (**)	Position	Current (amps.) (*)	Time for 12" burnoff (secs.)
A. O. Smith	3/16"	H.	220—260	55—45
Smithweld 15		V.	220—260	55—45
	1/4"	H.	250—290	86—77
Metal and Thermit		H.	210—250	55—45
Murex	3/16"	V.	210—250	55—45
Alternex		O. H	190—210	60—55
	1/4"	H.	230—270	90—73
Hollup		H.	200—240	83—73
Sureweld "C"	3/16"	V.	200—240	83—73
Reid—Avery		H.	210—230	74—65
Raco 7	1/4"	V.	210—230	74—65
Metal and Thermit		H.	200—240	55—49
Murex	3/16"	V.	200—240	55—49
Type "A"		O. H.	170—190	61—57
General Electric		H.	180—220	61—51
G. E. W-25	3/16"	V.	180—220	61—51

* For D. C. power only; add 10% for A. C.
** These electrodes shall not be tested in 5/32" size. In most cases, 5/32" will be satisfactory.

There are no specifically designed electrodes for underwater welding, but certain commercial brands have given satisfactory results in laboratory and underwater tests. These brands are: Westinghouse "Flexarc SW," and Lincoln "Fleetweld 37." All of the electrode coverings will deteriorate when placed in water, so they must be waterproofed.

In addition to the basic equipment, the following essential auxiliary gear is required:

1. A "C" clamp (the ground lead is either bolted or brazed to it).

2. A weighted wire brush for cleaning base metal and removing slag.

3. A chipping hammer for removing slag, light rust, and paint.

4. Electrode waterproofing solution:

    a. "Sealac" No. 30-L2093, manufactured by the Duralac Chemical Corp., Newark, N. J.

    b. "Ucilon," manufactured by the United Chromium Corp., New York, N. Y.

    c. Celluloid in Acetone (approximately ½ lb. to 1 gal. will give desired consistency).

5. A supplementary face plate of the colored welding type.

6. A scraper for removing marine growth, rust, and paint.

It is necessary to select the proper size electrode for the job undertaken. All fillet welds should be made with 3/16-inch electrodes, except where the metal is too thin. Tests made at the U. S. Naval Engineering Experiment Station have shown that the 3/16-inch electrodes can be used advantageously in all positions and that single-pass fillet welds made with this size electrode, using the "self-consuming" technique, averaged nearly the same in strength as three-pass fillet welds made with 5/32-inch electrodes by the same method.

Assuming the use of the "self-consuming" technique, the procedure which yields a 3/16-inch size fillet in a single pass from 3/16-inch diameter electrodes offer the following advantages over the procedure which consists of three passes deposited from 5/32-inch diameter electrodes:

1. Only ⅓ of the welding time is required when 3/16-inch diameter electrodes are used.

2. No scraping or cleaning of weld metal is necessary in a single pass weld.

3. The groove between the plates to be welded provides a positive guide in a single pass weld, while in a multiple pass weld, succeeding beads are inclined to wander, due to lack of a positive guide.

Where the plates to be welded are thin, the use of ⅛-inch or 5/32-inch diameter electrodes is still preferable. It is recommended that fillets larger than a nominal size of 3/16 inch be made with several passes of a 3/16-inch electrode.

Fitting Up. The proper fitting up of underwater weldments of considerable size is not easy. Fitting up must be done with thoroughness and care to insure a satisfactory weld. In underwater fillet welding, it is important to insure that there is no gap at the root of the fillet before welding. Even the most expert welding is ineffective when the fit-up is poor.

Too much importance cannot be attached to proper preparation of the surfaces to be welded. A satisfactory weld cannot be made over thick paint, rust, or marine growth. In a multiple pass weld, each bead must be thoroughly cleaned before depositing the next bead. Plates to be welded on can be prepared topside before being fitted by the diver.

The preferred "self-consuming" technique for underwater welding described below involves depositing the weld metal in a series of beads or strings. It has been found in tests that these beads, when in the form of fillet, result in welds having approximately the same leg size as the diameter of the electrode used. Fillet welding is especially adapted to underwater work since it provides a natural groove to guide the electrode.

Fillet Welding Method. The recommended procedure for fillet welding in the horizontal position involves the following steps.

The safety switch is open and the generator is set to deliver the proper current for the electrode being used, in accordance with the Recommended Electrodes Chart (Table 9). This current is higher (0-30%) than the topside current for the same electrode, because the water absorbs heat rapidly.

The striking end of the electrode is placed against the work at an angle of approximately 30° to the line of weld, though this angle may vary, depending upon the type of electrode used and upon the diver. The diver then calls for "current on." The arc should start when the tenderman closes the safety switch; if it does not, tap or scrape the end against the work. This will usually start the arc burning. Once the arc has started, exert pressure against the work to allow the electrode to consume itself. Maintain the original angle between the electrode and the line of weld by moving the hand perpendicularly toward the surface being welded. *Do not hold an arc as in topside welding.* Simply keep the electrode in contact with the work. Run straight beads; do not weave. About 8 inches of weld metal is deposited for every 10 inches of electrode consumed.

When the electrode is consumed, the diver calls for "current off," whereupon the tenderman turns off the switch and leaves it thus while the diver is changing the electrode. The diver should never remove an electrode until he has heard the tenderman's reply to his last command.

Before starting to deposit a new electrode, clean the end of the previous deposit. The deposit from the new electrode should slightly overlap the old one. If a second pass is to be added, the previously deposited weld must be thoroughly cleaned.

A diver does not call for "current on" until the new electrode is in the working position. It is usually better for a diver to weld toward, rather than away from, himself. The bubbles from the weld may cause poor visibility. By welding toward himself, the diver will divert many of the bubbles.

The same technique should be used for fillet in the vertical position as that recommended for the horizontal position. Vertical fillet welds should be made from the top down; in this way, the bubbles generated do not interfere with the diver's visibility in following his line of weld. A slight variation of the electrode-to-the-work angle may prove better

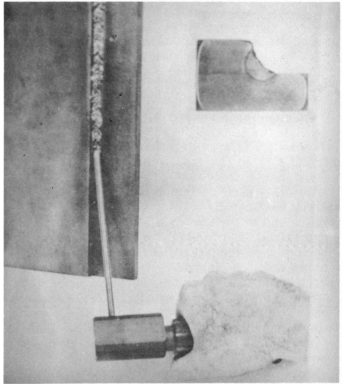

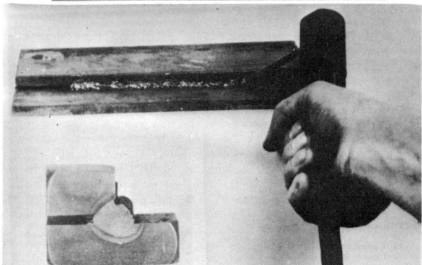

Fig. 35.   (Top) Self-consuming technique, vertical position. (Bottom) Self-consuming technique with macrograph of cross-section of weld.

to the diver. A partially completed vertical weld and the macrograph of the section through a companion joint are shown in Fig. 35.

The "self-consuming" technique can be applied to fillet welding in the overhead position when using the approved electrodes designated in the chart, provided the current is carefully adjusted. The current range for overhead welding is very narrow, and if there is any degree of current change, the bead deposited will turn out poorly. This method should be studied and practiced before a diver undertakes to attempt an overhead welding job.

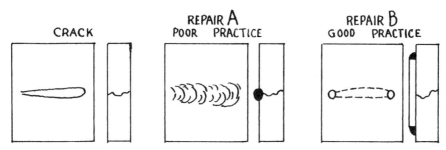

Fig. 36.   Welding cracks.

Repairing Small Cracks. The recommended procedure for repairing small cracks is shown in Fig. 36. If an attempt is made to fill up the crack with weld metal, the crack is apt to open up again through the weld. The preferred procedure is as follows:

1. Locate the ends of the crack.
2. Drill or burn small holes at the extreme ends of the cracked area to prevent further crack propagation.
3. Prepare a plate of sufficient size to cover the cracked area and fitted to the contour of the base plate.
4. Place the patch over the crack and attach it by fillet welds around all edges. Small patches can be readily attached to a ship's hull, etc., by fillet welding, as the groove of the fillet provides a ready-made guide for depositing the electrodes.

The field of underwater cutting and welding is being constantly improved and developed, and the diver entering this field will have to keep up to date on every new development. As the field expands, so must the underwater torchman.

Aside from studying about underwater cutting and welding, the underwater torcher must study about bridge construction, ship repair, pier repair, and any type of job which might require his special brand of services.

SAFETY PRECAUTIONS

In underwater cutting and welding, no matter what procedure is used, the importance of safety must be constantly emphasized. The life and safety of the diver are ever dependent upon the strict observance of safety regulations. The use of electric power in underwater cutting and welding adds one more hazard to a hazardous occupation. This is especially true of work in sea water, which is an excellent conductor of electricity. With proper safeguards and reasonable care, underwater cutting and welding can be accomplished with comparative safety if the basic protective measures which follow are strictly observed. Furthermore, personnel engaged in welding or cutting operations should exercise their imagination to insure that no hazard not specifically mentioned herein, but caused by a peculiar combination of unusual circumstances, is overlooked.

Divers who are going to operate arc-welding equipment should be thoroughly familiar with all the precautions and properly trained and instructed in the use and maintenance of the equipment.

The power supply used in underwater cutting and welding should consist of only approved electric welding machines and accessories which have been tested prior to usage below.

Electrode holders and cutting torches should be used underwater only if they are built for that purpose, and only those capable of handling the capacity of the maximum rated current required by the electrode. All current-carrying parts of the holders and torches must be fully insulated with nonconducting material capable of safely insulating against the maximum voltage encountered to ground. Standard surface or improvised holders can be used only in emergencies, and not until steps have been taken to insure complete insulation.

Welding cable and connectors should be of the insulated flexible type, and capable of handling the maximum currents required for the specific underwater task. Safety switches are extremely important. Using disconnecting switches in an electrical circuit insures full protection for the diver so that the current is on only when he is actually cutting or welding or has the electrode ready to work. Wet, bruised, or worn cables between the machine and the switch, either single or double pole, can be shorted, thus becoming dangerous. Automatic safety switches have been developed to provide for a positive automatic control of the current in the circuit. This disconnecting switch should be located in such a position that the tenderman is able to operate or oversee its proper operation at all times while the diver is below. Only upon request should the tender operate the switch and then according to the diver's directions. After each change, the tender should inform the diver and receive a confirmation.

The following precautions should be observed in the operation of arc-welding and cutting equipment:

1. The operator must make certain that the welding machine frame is grounded before the machine is turned on. Neither of the terminals should be bonded to the frame of the welder. All electrical connections should be tight.

2. Dry wooden mats or other suitable insulating material should be provided for the machine operator.

3. Always wear gloves when handling energized holders, cables or machines. The gloves should be dry and in good condition.

4. Cables should be kept dry and away from grease and oil which causes premature breakdowns of the insulation.

5. Cables should be supported overhead if they are to be strung any distance. Special care should be taken to see that welding supply cables are not in proximity to power supply cables.

Oxygen Cylinders. The following important cautions must *always* be observed concerning oxygen cylinders.

1. *Keep oxygen cylinders and fittings away from oil or grease. Oil or grease may ignite violently in the presence of oxygen under pressure.* Oily or greasy substances *must* be kept away from cylinder, cylinder valves, couplings, regulators, hose and apparatus. Do not handle oxygen cylinders or apparatus with oily hands or gloves. Oxygen cylinders *must never* be handled on the same platform with oil or placed where oil or grease can fall on them. A jet of oxygen must never be allowed to strike an oily surface, greasy clothes, or enter a fuel oil or storage tank that has contained a flammable substance.

2. Always refer to oxygen by its proper name, "oxygen," and not, for example, by the word "air."

3. A serious accident may easily result if oxygen is used as a substitute for compressed air. Never use oxygen except for its specified use in the cutting torch.

4. Do not store oxygen cylinders near highly combustible material.

5. Oxygen cylinders should be protected against excessive temperature rises.

6. Never discharge oxygen from a cylinder without first attaching an approved oxygen regulator to the cylinder valve or a manifold with regulator attached.

7 Never tamper with nor attempt to repair oxygen cylinder valves.

8. When the oxygen cylinder is in use, the valve should be opened at least one full turn, preferably all the way, to prevent leakage around the valve stem.

Regulators. Observe the following precautions in the care and use of regulators:

1. Regulators or automatic pressure reducing valves should be used only for the gas, and at the pressures, for which they are intended. Do not experiment with regulators or modify them in any way.

2. When repairs to regulators or parts of regulators, such as gauges, are necessary, such repairs should be done only by skilled mechanics properly instructed in the work. Working or low pressure gauges attached to regulators should be periodically tested to insure their accuracy. Do not test oxygen gauges with oil.

3. Union nuts and connectors on regulators should be inspected before use to detect faulty seats which may cause leakage of gas when the cylinders are attached to the cylinder valve.

General Precautions. Mixtures of combustible gases and air are very explosive and their development must be prevented. No device to permit the mixing of air or oxygen with combustible gases should be allowed unless it is to be used in a standard torch. When running tests to detect leaks in pipe systems, the torch is never used.

Metal tools for making repairs must be used with caution to avoid striking a spark. Such a spark may cause ignition if a mixture of gas and air is present.

When setting up tanks for use, the fuel-gas valve outlet should be pointed away from the oxygen tank. When the valves are opened, no one should be allowed to stand in front of the pressure gauges. And, while equipment is in use, especially in confined spaces, it should be inspected frequently for evidence of leaks in the hose, couplings, valve stem, or other points of the system. Otherwise, an explosive mixture of gas and air may accumulate and serious results may ensue.

In underwater operations, a tender should be assigned to the care and control of the gas supply. He should be so located as to have unhindered quick access to the valves in case of emergency.

In underwater operations employing electricity, it is mandatory that extreme precautions be taken to protect the diver from electric shock. The following rules are to be strictly enforced in order to provide utmost safety to the diver.

1. The diver must be so attired that his body is fully insulated from the work and torch. When working below with any type of cutting or welding equipment, he should wear a full-length rubber suit.

2. The use of rubber or rubberized canvas gloves is mandatory.

3. Shallow water diving outfits should be used only in an extreme emergency when no deep-sea diving dress is available.

4. Divers should wear a supplementary faceplate whenever performing electric arc cutting or welding. This faceplate should be made from No. 6 or No. 8 welding glass.

5. The oxy-hydrogen torch may be used under water without additional protective clothing or devices. The use of gloves and goggles is mandatory when cutting in air.

Divers should take no unnecessary chances while they are below engaged in underwater cutting and welding operations. The hazards inherent in underwater operations, such as adverse currents, unstable footing, poor visibility, confined working spaces, etc., combined with the dangers present when handling explosive gases and electrical circuits, require that the diver be constantly on the lookout for unseen circumstances resulting from a combination of these dangers.

1. The diver should make full use of the added protection afforded by the use of the disconnecting switch in electric arc cutting or welding. To make sure these devices are effective, the diver must obey the following rules:

    a. The current is off at all times, except when the diver is ready or actually working.

    b. When the electrode is secure in the holder and poised to work at the desired point, only then is the current turned on, and by the diver's direction. The tenderman informs the diver when he has turned the current on.

    c. The current is turned off when the stub electrode is ready to be replaced. Again the diver commands, and the tenderman answers upon completion of cutting off the current.

2. The electrode holder or torch is never pointed toward any part of the diver's body.

3. The diver should beware of entrapped gases.

4. The diver should make a careful examination of the work before starting to cut. There is the ever-present danger that the piece cut away may fall or roll over and pin the diver down or foul up his communication lines. The diver should always determine where and how the cut-away piece will fall and whether there are any pipes, wires, or projections which will disrupt communications or cause the piece to swing around in an unexpected way.

5. The oxy-hydrogen torch should never be pointed at any part of the diver or his gear, or left swinging or unattended. A lighted torch may be lowered to a diver in shallow depths only, and then only when the diver requests it.

6. Special safety precautions should be taken to prevent the explosion of entrapped gases which may be produced by any one or a combination of the following:

   a. Gases developed by underwater arc operations (analysis made on the gas developed have shown that it is composed of a high percentage of hydrogen).

   b. Explosive gases from the oxy-hydrogen torch (a mixture of unburned hydrogen and air, or unburned hydrogen and oxygen will produce an explosive mixture).

   c. Gasoline or fuel oil.

   d. Paint-mixing mediums, such as linseed oil and turpentine.

   e. Ammunition.

   f. Decaying vegetable or animal matter.

7. When cutting or welding is done in a corner or closed compartment, ventilation must be provided to allow entrapped gases to escape. Entrapped gases always present a hazardous problem, and it is a safety point never to be overlooked.

BUSINESS TIPS

With a few changes, the same business card and business letter recommended for the salvage business can be used with underwater cutting and welding. Your cards and letters will also be sent to the same places. In addition, send them to the following:

1. Salvage companies.
2. Shipyards.
3. Construction firms.
4. Bridge construction companies.
5. City hydroelectric companies.
6. City (or privately-owned) gas and fuel companies.
7. The telephone and telegraph company (local office).
8. City public works departments.
9. State highway commissions.
10. Federal governmental agencies.

Chapter VII

UNDERWATER DEMOLITION AND BLASTING

Although most states require that a person handling dynamite take a state test, there are a few states which do not. The author feels that there should be a federal law requiring men to pass a dynamite test before they are allowed to use it commercially.

Even though a chapter on this subject has been included, the author does not advise the inexperienced self-contained diver to start handling dynamite and try to blow under water. If an inexperienced diver has a job which requires the use of explosives, he should contact an expert, present the problem to him, let him load the charges, and then, by his directions, set up the loads for firing.

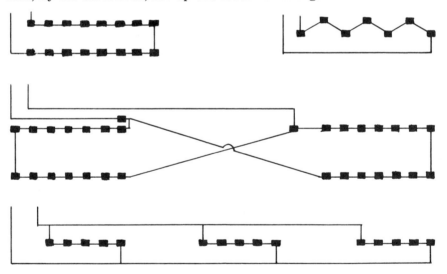

Fig. 37. Electrical firing connections for demolitions. (Top left) Straight series. (Top right) Zig-zag series. (Center) Two-circuit divider to break down resistance. (Bottom) Multi-series used with blasting machine and power current. (Jay G. O'Brien)

Lake fishermen, small-craft owners and camp owners continually suffer losses every year because of the rocks and tree stumps below the water line and those protruding slightly above the surface. As for the camp owners, often their property and beach frontage are littered with rocks and stumps. All these surface and underwater obstructions that cause so much damage could be eliminated easily and inexpensively.

Many of our nation's shipping losses were because of rocks that either project above the surface of the water or that come within a foot of the surface. These rocks could be blown away.

ROCK FORMATIONS

Most rocks have grains and, therefore, will split easily. All rocks have joints running in one direction, and some rocks have two sets of joints running at right angles.

The bedding plane or layer is lines running at right angles to both these joint lines mentioned. Knowledge about joints and the natural cleavage planes makes blasting easier. By close examination, even an amateur can see the bedding plane.

Hardness and toughness are two rock qualities which the blaster must bear in mind. These qualities have no bearing on the geological classification given them; they have been determined from actual experience at blasting. An example of rock hardness and toughness with regards to blasters would be: glass is hard, but not tough; untempered iron is tough, but not hard. Glass will shatter and break when pounded with a hammer; untempered iron is tough to pound with a hammer, but can be bent easily.

Limestone. This type of rock usually takes the form of flat boulders or is made up of ledges which project almost to the surface or above the surface, several feet in some cases. Limestone generally has two sets of joints. The bed lines are found wide apart, at least 2 feet or more. The stone is tough, breaking off rather than splitting. Its hardness varies with the age of the formation.

Slate. This type of rock is usually round, but can be found in thin, shingle structure. The leaves in the single form are less than $\frac{1}{4}$ inch thick. The stone is tough and breaks only a short distance with a small charge. By splitting along the cleavage lines, blasting is easy. The slate then becomes a soft rock and crumbles.

Sandstone. Sandstone comes in all shapes and sizes. The ledges are usually stratified—beds of a thickness of 1, 2, 3, or more feet—and frequently the joint lines run in two directions, thus breaking up the formations into irregular blocks in more or less rectangular shape. Sand particles are very hard. When the cementing material between the sandstone is silica, the stone is blue or white. It is much harder when the material is of iron origin, which makes the stone either a shade of brown or red.

For drilling purposes, blue sandstone is very hard rock; brown sandstone is classified as soft. For breaking purposes, both are listed as soft composition. It crumbles easily, but is rather tough.

Lava, Mica Rocks, Feldspar. This type of rock is found in layers from 2 to 100 feet thick. It contains infrequent joint lines. Lava is hard and brittle. It splits easily into pieces of irregular shapes and sizes.

Talc, Gypsum and Shale. These seldom exist as boulders; they are of ledge structure. There are 2 sets of joints and they lie in thin beds. These formations are fairly tough, but are inclined to crumble rather than split or crack. They are easy drilling, also.

Conglomerate. This is a mixture of various rocks, such as slate, sandstone, etc., often found in the form of pebbles cemented together. It lies in beds and may be crystalline and hard, even flinty. At times, the formation is considered medium hard. The boulders in this class are brittle. The joints in this formation run in one direction and are very far apart. Boulders of this type formation have the ball construction, and layer upon layer in the conglomerate type is approximately 1 to 6 inches thick and have joint lines every 2 to 4 inches apart. Layers of such rock crack off like the skin of an onion.

Granite. This formation is found mainly in ledge structure. It has irregular joint lines, but is easy to split. The rock is not tough, but very hard to drill.

Marble, Quartz, Trap, Porphyry. All of these rocks have fine grain. They are hard to blast for there is no distinct bedding plane. This formation does not break up in layers, as would be expected, but breaks at the joint lines. The composition is hard, but not tough, except for trap, which is tough and shatters easily. To avoid shattering of this rock, it must be blasted carefully.

General Features. Some rocks are full of irregular cavities, resembling bubbles, making the breaking easier. Cavities interfere with regular joint lines and cause the splitting to take place along new lines of weakness.

METHODS OF CLEARING ROCKS BY BLASTING

Mudcapping. Briefly, mudcapping rocks consists of placing the explosives in a neat pile on the face of the rock, covering it with about 6 inches of stiff wet clay, and then exploding it. When done properly, the force of the explosion breaks the rock.

Because of the speed of the gases, the rocks will break very easily. However, black powder and slow modern explosives cannot be used in this operation.

Of the three methods of blasting rock, mudcapping is the best one to use when the boulder is flat, brittle, and less than 5 to 6 feet across. Some sandstone is brittle, yet hard to drill; this is a good type of stone for mudcap blasting. Shale, slate, and conglomerate are rock to blast by mudcapping. Tough rock, such as trap, etc., should not be mudcapped unless they are smaller than 3 feet in diameter.

Placing the Charge. Always look for those hair-thin, but far-reaching seams. Remember that the joint lines are the best place to work a blast from. It is always best to put the charge in a hollow or depression or, at least, on a flat surface, rather than on a rounded one.

The approximate number of pounds of explosive for mudcapping per cubic yard of rock is as follows:

1. Sandstone, slate and similar soft, easily broken rock requires 1 pound.
2. Limestone and other intermediate rock requires 1¼ pounds.
3. Marble, trap, granite and other hard rock requires 2 pounds.

Table 10 gives the number of 1¼ x 8-inch sticks required for mudcapping boulders of different sizes.

Table 10

Sandstone, Slate and other soft rock			Limestone and other intermediate rock		Marble, Granite, Trap and other hard rock	
1-1/2 ft. greatest dia.	1-1/4 sticks		1-1/2	sticks	2-1/2	sticks
2 " "	" 1-1/2 "		2	"	3	"
2-1/2 " "	" 1-3/4 "		2-1/2	"	3-1/2	"
3 " "	" 2 "		2-1/2-3	"	4	"
4 " "	" 4-5 "		5-7	"		
5 " "	" 7-10 "					

Grade of Explosives. The best explosive is either 40%, 50% or 60% strength. The straight nitroglycerin dynamites or powders are quicker than ammonium nitrate. In cold, use only the low freezing grades of these explosives. Using the electric detonator, the operation must be at least 250 feet from the project and all divers must be out of the water. Because of the force of the water on the rocks, there will be very few fragments that will rise above the surface of the water, if the charge is 3 feet below the surface.

Undermine or Snakehole Blasting. To break a stone by this method, the charge is placed against the under side or bottom of the stone with the solid earth as its backing. Less explosive is required with this method than with mudcapping, because less depends on the size and shape of the stone or the ground hardness or the depth to which it is buried. Undermining works better when the stone has a flat side down and with flat boulders rather than with round ones.

When a boulder is well buried, the first thing to do is to probe about with a sharp ¼" steel rod, to learn the shape of the under side and ground conditions. The charge should always be placed as near as possible under the center of weight of the rock. The explosive should be placed against the rock. When the rock is undermined by jetting, the explosive should be packed in a compound bulk, as in mudcapping.

Amount of explosive required in pounds per cubic yards of rock is as follows:

1. Sandstone, slate and other soft rock requires ¾ pound.
2. Limestone and other intermediate rock requires 1 pound.
3. Marble, granite, trap and other hard rock requires 1½ pounds.

The number of 1¼ x 8-inch sticks required for snakehole blasting is just ¼ of a stick less than is used for mudcapping as per the cubic yard (*see* Table 10).

The extent that the boulder is buried and the nature of the ground influence the amount of explosive required.

Grade of Explosive. 30% to 50% strength dynamite of either nytroglycerin or ammonium nitrate class can be used. Because of the better confinement of the blast, stones can be broken more easily with slower explosive, such as 20% to 40% strength.

Blockhole Blasting. The size of the hole should be 1¼ inches in diameter and at least ½ way through the rock or deep into a ledge.

Grade of Explosive. 50% to 60% strength will shatter rocks; 20% will split it in pieces of good size. Ammonium nitrate is the best for this purpose. 20% to 40% is used in all types of jobs requiring this method of removal. Approximate pounds required to break boulders per cubic yard by blockholings:

1. Sandstone and other soft rock requires ¼ pound.
2. Limestone and other medium rock requires ⅜ pound.
3. Marble, granite, trap, and other hard rock requires ½ pound.

The approximate number of sticks for blockhole blasting is given in Table 11.

Table 11. Approximate Number of 8" Sticks Needed to Blast Various Diameter Rocks

Type of Rock	Size of Rock (ft. diam.)						
	1-1/2'	2'	2-1/2'	3'	4'	5'	7'
Sandstone, slate, etc.	1/4	3/8	1/2	1/2-3/4	1	1-1/2	6
Limestone, etc.	1/4-3/8	1/2	1/2-3/4	3/4	1-1/4	2	8
Marble, etc.	1/2	3/4	1	1-1/2	2	3	10

After the charge is placed in the hole, there should be 6 to 7 inches of solid clay placed on top of the charge so that there will be no air spaces.

Breaking Ledge. Drill a line of holes along the back of the edge or face of the ledge above the surface. Use half again as much explosive in a ledge blast than used for boulders. Holes 2 feet deep should be 5 feet apart in shale, slate, or other brittle composition; 4 feet apart in limestone and other medium rock; 3 feet apart in harder material.

Grade of Explosive. The grade of explosive should be 40% to 60% strength nitroglycerin.

INFORMATION ABOUT EXPLOSIVES

The explosive force of dynamite and other high explosive powders depends on another explosive chemical, which is nitroglycerin and ammonium nitrate.

The explosives marketed as "straight dynamite or straight powder" are made from nitroglycerin. Those made from an ammonium nitrate base are called "extra." Gelatin dynamite and blasting gelatin are nitroglycerin explosives in which nitro has been mixed with guncotton.

Strength and Speed. The power and violence of an explosive are two different qualities. The power, or direct strength, is due to the volume of gases. If a pound of a certain explosive gives, for instance, 1,000 cubic feet of gases when completely detonated, while a pound of

Table 12. Explosives Recommended for Different Work

Stone	(mudcap)	Straight nitro. or Ammonio	50-60%
"	(shakey) to break	" " " "	60-60%
"	(blocking) to shatter	" " " "	60-90%
"	" to break	" " " "	20%
Ditches (elec. firing)		Ammonio ni. or nitro.	20-40%
Stump Blasting		Nitro. or ammonio ni.	20%

Table 13. Explosives Suitable for Underwater Operations

Type of Explosive	Cartridge diameter	Max. depth of water	Max. duration of immersion	Weight strength
				Percent
Polar ammon. Gelignite	Less than 3 ins.	20 ft.	24 hrs.	78
Polar ammon. gelatin dy	Less than 3 ins.	20 ft	24 hrs.	90
Polar ammon. Gelignite	3 in. — 8 in.	30-100 ft.	7-30 days	78
Polar ammon. gelatin dy.	3 in. — 8 in.	30-100 ft.	7-30 days	90
"Geophex"	All	1200 ft.	24 hrs.	66
Submarine blasting gel.	All	1200 ft. or more	Weeks	95

(Courtesy, Imperial Chemical Industries, Ltd., Glasgow, Scotland)

another gives 500 cubic feet and a third gives 2,000 feet, the lifting power of each explosive will be in direct porportion to its gas volume. The violence of the gas depends on the speed of the explosives. If they are comparatively slow, they will break large cracks in the stick and leave material behind in their escape path. Nitro and ammonio powders and dynamites are of equal strength when of equal marking. The strength is indicated accurately by percentage figures. Nitro explosives are uniformly quicker and more violent in action than ammonium nitrate, and the more nitro, the quicker.

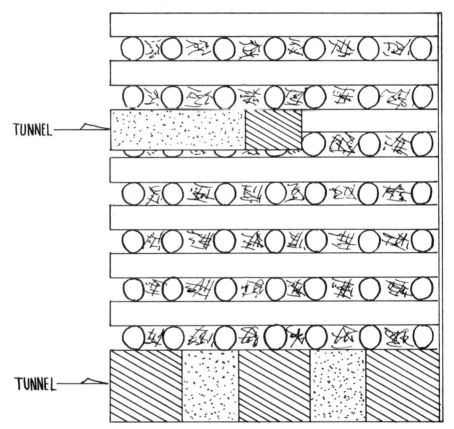

Fig. 38. Location of charges for blasting a cofferdam. (Imperial Chemical Industries, Ltd., Glasgow, Scotland)

Nitro resists water better than ammonium nitrate. Storage in a damp place will weaken explosives, especially ammonium nitrate.

Gelatin explosives resist water very well, and may be used under water with assurance that they will explode with their full power. Blasting gelatin is entirely water-resisting.

Explosives will freeze and, when in this state, they are highly dangerous. Do not try to cut, break or handle frozen dynamite. Regular nitroglycerin explosives are the quickest to freeze; they do so in temperatures below 45° and 50°F.

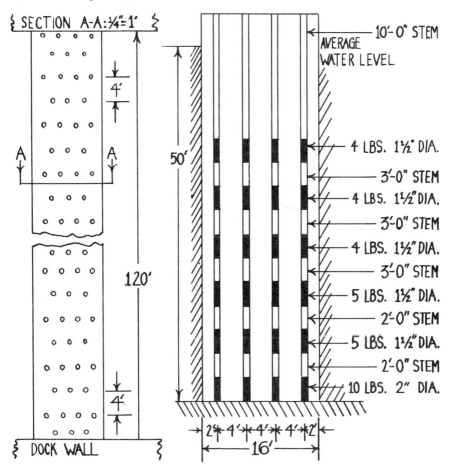

Fig. 39. Blasting a mass concrete dam. (Imperial Chemical Industries, Ltd., Glasgow, Scotland)

OTHER UNDERWATER BLASTING JOBS

For those men who choose to become professional underwater blasters, the following information will assist in the various jobs they may be called on to undertake.

Cofferdams. Cofferdams are built in the construction of many underwater structures, such as bridges, piers, etc. For the most part, cofferdams are constructed of wood and built in crib form. Rocks are placed inside the crib. In blasting a cofferdam, the main object is to scatter all the rocks and destroy the cribwork so that nothing will impede the flow of water.

Since the cofferdams are constructed in a crossing of crib timbers, the explosive charges should be placed at these crossings where they will do the most damage. The main charge is placed on the rock foundation of the cofferdam. Smaller charges should be located approximately two-thirds of the way up the dam. Employing this placement technique, the results will be a complete breaking-up and scattering of the materials. These charges are placed approximately 15 feet apart along the length of the dam, both in its front and back portions.

In blasting cofferdams of this nature, the charge amounts to 2 pounds of explosives for every cubic yard of material. The diver will give an approximate estimate of the amount of explosives needed to level the cofferdam on his survey dive. The main charge should amount to approximately three-fourths of the total amount of explosives used when the approximate cubic yardage has been determined.

Shafts are sunk along the center line of the cofferdam in placing the charges. If the charges are embedded properly, the cofferdam will be destroyed on the first fire.

Concrete Dams. During the past few years, concrete dams have been replacing the old wooden type. In most cases, the construction firm places blasting holes in the concrete during the pouring process. When a job has been completed, these dams must also be destroyed. Blasting is the easiest method.

Many diameters of explosives have been used and tested by various explosive manufacturers and, thus far, the best results have been gained with 1½-inch diameter explosives, and 2-inch diameter material—although, explosives up to and including a 4-inch diameter have been used in blasting concrete dams. If a blaster uses a large number of small diameter holes, he gets better fragmentation and does not run the risk of the vibration from larger charges damaging nearby structures.

Concrete dams, up to approximately 6 feet thick, can be broken up satisfactorily by a single row of holes located along the center line of the dam approximately 2 to 3 feet apart. These holes are drilled downward toward the base of the dam where the blast will produce its best results.

When blasting a dam constructed of the same, but thicker, material, 3 or 4 parallel rows of holes are drilled, and the holes in each row are staggered. Polar blasting gelatin is the best explosive to use for this type of job.

The explosive should be either 1½ inch in diameter or 2 inches in diameter. When estimating the amount of explosives to use on a dam of this material, the proportion of 1 pound of explosive for 1 cubic yard of material is judged the best, as it will give excellent fragmentation small enough to be handled by a steam shovel or bucket clam.

It is best to remember to fire the first charge directly on the center of the dam, for the remaining sides can be handled most easily after the main charge has been blown.

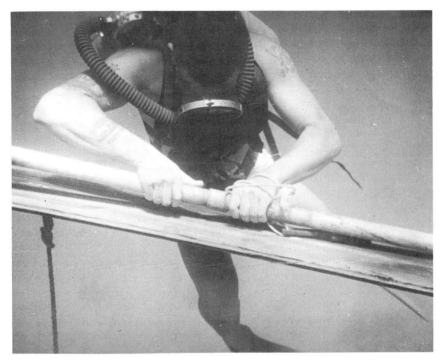

Fig. 40. U.S. Navy diver joining sections of a cylindrical section charge.
(U.S. Navy Photo)

Ships. A blaster is sometimes called upon to destroy a ship which has gone below and is a menace to navigation.

Figure 40 shows a diver handling a cylindrical section charge capable of destroying underwater obstacles. He is joining the sections of the charge along the steel structure to be demolished.

Ship blasting does not have any set patterns; each ship to be blasted is a problem in itself. However, as an example, a ship of 750 tons and 175 feet will be used.

The weight of the charge depends upon many factors which will be determined by the diver during survey dives prior to setting any charges. The length, beam, and construction of a vessel in most cases will give an idea of the amount of explosives needed to demolish it. The depth of the water must also be taken into consideration. If the vessel has been down long enough to embed in bottom sands, mud, etc., these will be important factors in determining the weight of the charge to be used.

In the case of our example ship, three heavy charges, fired simultaneously, would bring about complete leveling. The charges of explosives would be placed fore, amidships, and aft. When the charge explodes, the heavy surge of water would help in leveling the vessel by flattening plates that were loosened by the explosion itself (if the ship were of steel) or by blowing out spars, beams, and bulkheads (if it were of wood).

The following amounts of explosives would be used in the three charges to level this example ship of 750 tons and 175 feet:

Fore section charge	175 lbs.
Amidships section charge	250 lbs.
Aft section charge	400 lbs.

In a steel vessel, there probably would be boilers which would not be completely destroyed by the first blast. In this event, a charge of less than 25 pounds should be placed in the boiler door and situated as close to the center of the boiler as possible. This would finish the job.

A complete reference book, covering all types of blasting, with a special chapter on submarine diving, is *The Blaster's Handbook.* Published by the E. I. DuPont de Nemours & Co., it may be purchased from the Diving Equipment & Supply Company for $1.50.

Again, the author wishes to stress the dangers in handling any explosive. A diver, unqualified to use and tamper with explosives, not only threatens the life and safety of those around him, but also endangers his own life.

Divers, don't handle explosives unless you are authorized and trained.

BUSINESS POSSIBILITIES

Essentially the same form letter can be used by the underwater demolitions expert as was suggested for use by the salvage expert. Your card and letter should be sent to approximately the same persons and places.

Business prospects include the following:

1. Beach clearance
2. Landing approaches
3. Harbor clearance
4. Underwater obstructions (coral, mussel beds, etc.)
5. Underwater debris
6. Cofferdams
7. Concrete dams
8. Ships
9. Any menace to navigation

Chapter VIII

UNDERWATER LOGGING

During recent months, the author's company, International Undersea Services, has been engaged in the underwater logging business. It is not an easy occupation. It requires equipment, muscle power, and plenty of fly repellent!

However, by using common sense, research, good diving principles, and a little mechanical ingenuity, the Scuba diver who takes up the logging business can make a good profit during a summer school vacation, or during a working-diving season. Here in Maine, the underwater logging season begins the last days of April and can be continued up to the last week in October. In this period, a crew of divers should be able to gather 250,000 to 500,000 board feet of lumber, depending upon the type of lumber being salvaged and the total bottom amount.

Two years before our logging operation began, International Undersea Services conducted and made survey dives to determine the amount of long logs at the bottom of Maine's many lakes and rivers. Figures were compiled as to the number of long logs driven over a certain lake and river and the estimated number of logs that sink during a drive; the condition of the sunken logs was determined by the Forestry Research Laboratory, Plants Science Division, University of Maine, and salvage rights were checked into through the Forestry Department, State of Maine. After this research was completed, actual survey dives were made by staff members of International's Salvage Division.

One lake, at the northern tip of the state, proved to have more than one million feet of sunken white pine in a certain area—pine sawed in 16-foot lengths going better than 20 inches at the top. The Penobscot River, running through Bangor, the former lumber capital of the world, had four large boom houses and sites where long logs were boomed, marked, held, sorted and rafted. The boom house handling the majority of the long logs driven on the Penobscot was the Pea Cove Boom House and Boom Site. International's Director of Undersea Operations, Master Diver E. E. Guernsey, Jr., and the author made the survey dives at this site. We found that within a 3-mile stretch of the river, there were more than one million feet of sunken logs visible. This spot, only 18 miles from Bangor, offered a perfect base of operations. Property was leased, land was cleared, a log yard was set up, the beach area was swamped out, and a landing site constructed. Then, came the work—work that is still going on at this writing.

The Pea Cove Boom Site is actually a branch waterway of the Penobscot River. The current, running southerly, is at 3¾ knots with a maximum water depth of 22 feet. The water is fairly clear, having visibility up to 15 feet. The Pea Cove Boom Site stopped operation in 1927. During the last 18 years of operation, the Boom handled 18,505,549 long logs, totaling more than 1,218,448,130 board feet of lumber. It is also of interest to note that the boom site was in operation before 1900 and handled over 100 billion feet of lumber during its working days.

Lumbermen estimate that between 5% and 10% of all white and Norway pine driven will sink before reaching its destination. A smaller percentage of spruce and hemlock sinks during a drive. It can be concluded that a majority of pine will be found on the bottom in the area in which pine was cut and driven.

Today, logs cut in the Northeastern woods are usually in 16-feet lengths. In the past, logs were cut and driven in tree lengths (36 to 60 feet long). These long logs, constituting a virgin growth, are the ones that will be found on the bottom. Cutting these to size for the market often means that 2 to 4 cuts can be taken from one long log. Today's market calls for 16, 14, 12, 10, and 8 feet lengths in pine stock. White pine is usually used for boarding boards and inside finish stock, and ranges in price from $100.00 per thousand board feet to $400.00 per thousand board feet, after they are sawed, dried, planed, and graded. Norway pine is commonly cut into dimension lumber 2″ x 4″, 2″ x 6″, 2″ x 8″, etc. Although dimension lumber is usually more costly than boarding boards, the lumber mills offer less in price when buying it in the log form. As yet, the author has been unable to find the reason why.

Many people will tell you that sunken logs are worthless. This is not true. Sunken pine is better lumber than freshly cut because the water has removed the sap and pitch from the log.

Pine is rarely milled in the summer months because of a blue fungus that lives in the sap pockets and causes a blue stain. This stain, which comes only after the trees have been cut, will cause a price decrease in the value of the lumber. Lumber which is recovered from the water can be milled during the summer months without fear of blue stain, as the water has cleared the sap pockets. However, it should be added that blue stain can get into the logs as they are being driven on lakes and rivers, or when they are held in the booms for marking, sorting, and rafting. Up to the present, it has been found that less than 25% of all the logs recovered at the Pea Cove operation has contained traces of blue stain, and a greater portion have been two or more cut logs.

A SURVEY OF UNDERWATER LOGGING PROSPECTS IN THE
UNITED STATES

The underwater logging operations that have had such a promising beginning in Maine led the author to make some research regarding opportunities for similar operations in other sections of the United States. There is no question in his mind that wherever there have been extensive lumber operations involving the floatation and river driving of lumber, there the Scuba diver with energy and determination will find it profitable to undertake water logging operations.

In early logging days, the river driving of logs was common in the northern Lake States, and many sunken logs have been recovered from rivers and lakes where deep silting has not subsequently buried them. Log floating was also common in the bayous and lakes of Louisiana, Arkansas, Mississippi, and Florida where cypress was extensively logged. In the West, river driving of logs was also common. In the mountains where streams are swift and stream beds are rocky, logs did not often sink. Where the streams emerged from the steep country and deepened, some logs undoubtedly sank and are still submerged. Certain lakes and ponds were and are used for storage and may contain "sinkers." Rivers and lakes in northern Idaho, western Washington, western Montana, western Oregon, and California might be worth investigating.

Lumber Towns. The nation has had four historic lumber towns during the growth of America. The first, which is the author's present home, is Bangor, Maine. During the heyday of their lumbering operations, over two trillion board feet flowed down the blue waters of the Penobscot River.

Having worked in the Penobscot since opening business in Maine, the author knows full well that the entire bottom of the river is cluttered with sunken logs. Today, this same river sees countless thousands of cords of pulp woods in its waters, flowing on their way to feed the great paper manufacturing mills in Millinocket and Bangor. Since setting up our operation last April, other Scuba divers, who have visited the project area, have also started working in their areas. Two hundred more divers could work for ten continuous years without scratching the surface in salvaging the sunken lumber in Maine's rivers and lakes.

When the tall pine started to peter out in the great Maine woods, the lumbermen trekked to Saginaw and Muskegon, Michigan. The Saginaw Valley was the site of the logging operations in that state. Research shows that logs were floated on the Tittabawassee, Cass, Flint, and Shiawassie Rivers. This was located ten miles above Saginaw City. Sunken logs will be found in this area in the million board feet.

At the mouth of the Muskegon River, over 900,000,000 feet of logs were boomed there in a single year. If only 100th of 1% sank, which is a very low sinkage figure, there would be enough long logs to warrant an underwater logging operation.

By the turn of the century, the lumbering operations in Michigan were starting to slow down; so the men picked up their tools, heading westward to Gray's Harbor, Washington. Gray's Harbor was the Bangor of the west coast. Scuba divers will find long logs sunk on the bottoms of the Hoquiam and Chehalis Rivers.

Every state has some lumbering operations, and where there were active lumber towns at one time, there should be good prospecting for Scuba divers.

The Lumber Industry. Since the colonies declared their independence in 1776, this country's lumber industry has produced the staggering amount of nearly 3,000,000 million board feet of lumber—enough to build 300 million five-room frame houses or a boardwalk 6 feet wide all the way to the sun.

Today's lumbering is one of the major manufacturing industries in the United States. It is an intricate business structure involving growing, harvesting, transporting, and marketing wood.

The early migrations of the industry from one timbered area to another, cutting out and moving on, form a saga of American history. But it is a saga of the past. A changed national economy, based on supplying the ever-expanding needs of a fast-growing population, has brought a new concept of permanency to the lumber industry.

Today, the lumber industry is a highly competitive and complex structure of thousands of sawmills, lumber wholesalers, commission salesmen, retailers, and transportation system. According to the best estimates, there are about 50,000 sawmills; every state in the Union has some. Because the mills are widely dispersed and usually far from markets, their output is, for the most part, distributed through wholesalers. There are approximately 4,000 lumber wholesalers who together handle about 75% of the lumber produced. The retail lumber dealers—about 30,000 of them—are the largest single factor in the distribution of lumber to the American people. Most retail lumber yards—60% of them—are located in towns of less than 5,000 population.

Such a large and far-flung industry has developed many business associations to further the industry and to inform the public. Manufacturers, wholesalers, and retailers have associations to represent their special interests; and self-contained divers planning to engage in underwater logging should become acquainted with local representatives of these organizations.

Forest Regions. The country's forest lands are divided into five regions. (*see* Fig. 41). Going from the East Coast to the West Coast they are:

1. Northern Forests
   a. Northern Pine and Hemlock Region
   b. Northern Hardwood Region
2. Southern Forests
   a. Southern Pine Region
   b. Southern Hardwood Region
3. Central Hardwood Forests
   a. Appalachian Hardwood Region (Northern portion)
   b. Southern Hardwood Region (Southern portion)
4. Western Forests (Western Pine Region)
5. West Coast Forests (Douglas Fir and California Redwood Regions)

The great Northern Forest covers the following states, or parts of them: Maine, New Hampshire, New York, Pennsylvania, northern Massachusetts, western Virginia, eastern West Virginia, eastern Tennessee, western North Carolina, northern Michigan, Wisconsin, and Minnesota.

The principal timber of this forest region includes red, black, and white spruces, balsam fir, white, red, jack, and pitch pines, eastern hemlock, maples, oaks, beech, birches, and aspen. Pine is the country's leading building material, and this is a great territory in which to find it.

The Southern Forest includes parts of and all of these states: eastern Virginia, South Carolina, southern Georgia, Florida, southern Alabama, Mississippi, Arkansas, Louisiana, and a small strip in eastern Texas.

This forest area has longleaf, shortleaf, loblolly and slash pine, southern oaks, red gum, hickories, southern cypress, eastern and southern red cedars, and small amounts of other types. The pine produced in this area is tall and straight and is used for telephone and hydroelectric poles, for the most part. It is also cut up for dimension lumber—2" x 4", and larger stock.

The Southern area could well prove to be the ideal place to set up winter underwater logging operations. Arkansas and Oklahoma, in 1953, produced

953,000,000 board feet of lumber. Mississippi, another southern state, produced 1,397,145,000 board feet in the same year, while Louisiana was just a small 100,000,000 board feet short of Mississippi's output.

Florida, which was not mentioned above, has been on a steady lumber output decrease since 1939; in 1947, it produced slightly over a half billion board feet. However, since cypress, one of the better trees logged in Florida, is heavy wood and sinks easily, a lumbering operation in Florida might prove most profitable, if the operators had the proper equipment to handle the big and heavy cypress logs.

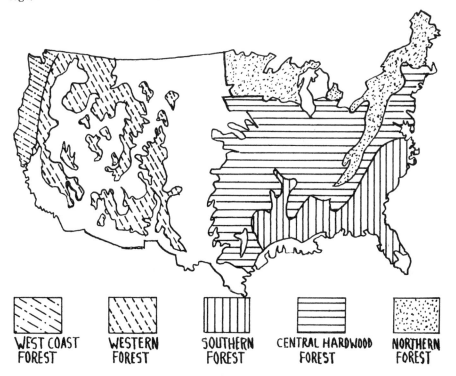

WEST COAST FOREST   WESTERN FOREST   SOUTHERN FOREST   CENTRAL HARDWOOD FOREST   NORTHERN FOREST

Fig. 41.   Forest regions of the United States.   (American Forest Products Ind.)

The Central Hardwood Forest covers a greater portion of Tennessee, Kentucky, eastern West Virginia, Ohio, Indiana, southern Michigan, Wisconsin, Illinois, Minnesota, greater eastern and southern Texas, eastern Oklahoma, northwestern Arkansas, Missouri, and eastern Iowa. This particular region grows oaks, hickories, ashes, elms, maples, beech, black walnut, pitch, shortleaf and Virginia pines, cottonwood, red and black gums, eastern red cedar, yellow poplar, and others.

It is the author's opinion that the Central Forest Region would be an excellent area for underwater logging. Black walnut is an expensive woods product, and it is likely that some has found its way below the waters. Even small amounts of this particular wood are worth diving for to salvage and market.

The Western Forests spread into Washington, Oregon, Nevada, Utah, Montana, Wyoming, South Dakota, Colorado, New Mexico, Arizona, and southwest Texas. Ponderosa pine, Idaho white pine, western larch, Engelmann spruce, Douglas fir, lodgepole pine, sugar pine, western red cedar, western hemlock, white fir, and others grow abundantly in this forest region. Divers will find that the pines and spruces bring tidy sums when marketed.

The last of the great American forests, the West Coast Forests, includes northwestern California, western Oregon and Washington. Douglas fir, western hemlock, western red cedar, redwood, sitka spruce, sugar pine, lodgepole pine, incense cedar, white fir, Port Orford cedar, and other species, will be found in this gigantic forest region. Divers working this region will need the best of floating gear if they expect to bring some of those Douglas firs and California redwoods to the surface again.

There is a sixth forest, the Tropical Forest, found only on the southern tip of Florida and in a small area in southeastern Texas, which does not produce lumber in large enough quantities to be commercially important. The author lists it because of divers in that section of the country who can well do the needed research and exploration to recover a million or so board feet—enough to pay a crew, buy a good compressor, more diving gear, a clubhouse, a boat . . . or a trip to Maine, where there is plenty of underwater logging for all!

UNDERWATER LOGGING FOR SCUBA DIVERS

Equipment. Scuba divers who desire to go into the underwater logging business will need other equipment than the diving gear they already possess. The following is a list of the basic logging equipment needed to become successful in this particular field of underwater work.

> 1 Salvage craft, hauling, w/ motor
> 6 Cant dogs
> 50 Bottleneck buoys w/ line attached
> 2 Pulley blocks
> 500 ft. 1-in. Manila hemp rope
> 2 6-ft. crosscut saws (or 1 chain saw)
> 25 Inner tubes
> 1,000 ft. 3/16-in. sisal rope (for attaching tubes to logs)
> 1 Vehicle (for twitching logs) (or 1 power winch)
> 10 ft. Chain (heavy duty, logging type)

Attaching Buoys. The diving crew starts the morning off with the tenderman assisting. The tender helps the diver into his gear and loads the buoys into the boat. The diver goes over the side with a buoy line in hand. Reaching the bottom, he selects a log, measures it by eye for diameter and length, and ties the buoy line to the top end, if possible. The tender throws him another buoy when he reaches the surface, and this action is continued until either the diver's air supply has been used or 25 to 35 buoys have been attached to logs.

When the first few logs have been buoyed up, the hauling crew starts to work. The salvage craft used in the International operation is the same as the one described in Chapter IX. It is an easy craft to construct and serves the purpose well. The hauling boat should be powered by at least a 10-hp. outboard motor.

The hauling crew pulls in beside a floating buoy, picks it up, lifting the log off the bottom to the stern of the boat and tying it fast to pins placed into the ramp deck up forward. Four to 6 logs can be hauled by employing this method.

The tie board is probably the easiet hauling method when the logs are of the softwood species or small top diameters. The tie board is a rather large plank which is attached to the rear of the craft by chain. On the top side of the board, pins are placed in it onto which the buoy lines are tied securely after the log ends have been lifted off the bottom. In either case of hauling, both ends of the logs (top ends or tied ends) will ride close to the stern of the hauling craft.

There will be logs that will not come up because of silt coverage or due to their size. The only method to bring them to the top is by floating. Two methods of floating have been used, and both worked

Fig. 42.   Floating one end of a water-logged log.

well on those occasions. First, pine pegs were used to bring some of the logs up. These pegs were cut out as wedges, taken below by the diver, and driven into the ends of the logs. As many as five pegs per end have been used to bring a big Norway pine to the surface.

Common truck tire innertubes are used to bring the unusually large logs to the surface. The tubes are completely deflated when taken below by the diver. They are then tied to or slipped over the ends of the log. When they have been secured, the filler line is sent from the surface, and the tubes are blown up. After the two end tubes have been inflated, if they still do not float the log, as many tubes as necessary can be employed to get it to the surface.

The salvage craft can haul 15 to 20 of these floating logs when rafted together, with little strain on the engine.

Fig. 43.   Hauling with the salvage craft; craft hauls in reverse.

Fig. 44.   Rowboat hauling method; logs secured to tie board.

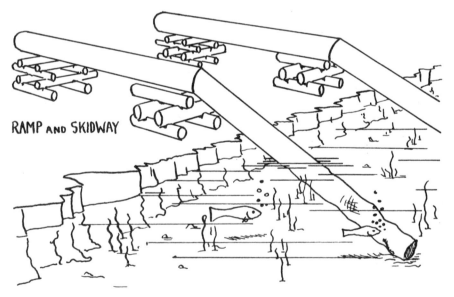

Fig. 45.   Logging ramp and skidway.

The filler device is made from a Snorkair filler yoke, a 50-foot length of garage air hose, and a tire-filler chuck. The Snorkair filling yoke is rethreaded to fit the standard hose threads. When fitted, the tubes can be filled from any tank with the K-type valve from above or below the surface. However, it is best to have the tubes filled from the boat by the tender, as the standard garage hose is made for low pressures. The tendermen can best handle the tank and filling process above, thus allowing the diver free use of his hands.

Fig. 46. (Top left) The log yard. (Top right) Trigway to get logs onto log yard easily. (Bottom left) Jitterbug twitching logs to the log yard. (Bottom right) Sizing up the big ones. (International Photo)

The Landing Site. When the hauling crew have the logs tied on or the floating logs attached to the craft, they take them to the landing site, which is located on the shore, just below the sawing yard and log yard.

The landing site is made of logs, one end placed in the water and the other lying on the bank. This landing site, or **rampway,** is kept wet to allow the logs to slide easily over it as they are twitched up to the saw yard. There are various ways to construct a landing site, as shown in Figs. 45 and 46.

The skid rampway takes time to construct properly; however, when it has been completed, logs brought up onto it require very little handling. Plenty of blocking and notching will be required to construct the double-skid rampway landing site.

The Log Yard. This same style of skid rampway can be combined to make the log yard. There are two excellent methods of constructing this combination. The first is to extend the double-skid rampway logs to any desired length. However, it is best to build the rampway and log yard combination so that the rear of the log yard will flank a rather large tree or tree butt. This tree will serve as a bumper to prevent the on-rolling logs from falling off the yard. This rampway and log yard combination is made with a movable section approximately 8 to 10 feet in length. This allows the logs to be loaded onto a truck. The log yard should have a *very* slight downward incline. The winch used to load these logs to the log yard and bring them up from the water should be located at the rear of the log yard. The front of this yard, where the logs will be loaded onto the trucks, should be at least 5 feet off the ground.

The second method employs the same double-skid rampway; but instead of extending it to the base of a tree, spread it to a Y section, thus having two log yards and being able to load from either yard. These log yards can be made to any length desired.

When employing the simple log rampway mentioned as the simple landing site, a saw yard must be set up on the shore and located on flat land. The saw yard consists of two long logs laid parallel to the shoreline. When the logs have been twitched from the water up the rampway, they are brought across the logs of the saw yard, measured, and rolled over to be hauled onto the log yard.

The Twitching Crew. The twitching crew—two men, using a power winch, a length of logging chain, and the cable—snatches the logs from the water, up the rampway, and onto the saw yard. The twitching crew is responsible for getting these logs to the saw yard in as few movements and as speedily as possible.

When the power winch is not available, a "jitterbug" will serve the purpose well. A "jitterbug" is the nickname for a cut-down Model-A Ford pickup truck, ranging in vintage from 1930 to 1941. This vehicle is regeared for low-low speeds, with oversize tires on the rear, mounted with chains for greater traction, and weighted for maximum dig. If Model-A vehicles are not available, any old truck or pickup will do the job.

The Shore Crew. As the logs are hauled from the water to the saw yard, the shore crew, headed by the shore master, handles the logs. The shore crew consists of no less than three men: the shore master, a sawyer, and an idiot-stick man. This latter gentleman is by no means what the name implies. His job is a tricky one—that of handling a cant dog. It takes experience to wield this tool, and the author, who has been on the business end of a cant dog, has no desire to make it a lifetime vocation.

Once a log has been brought to the saw yard, the shore master and idiot-stick man, armed with cant dogs, roll the log in place to be marked. The sawyer checks the proper length and makes his cut

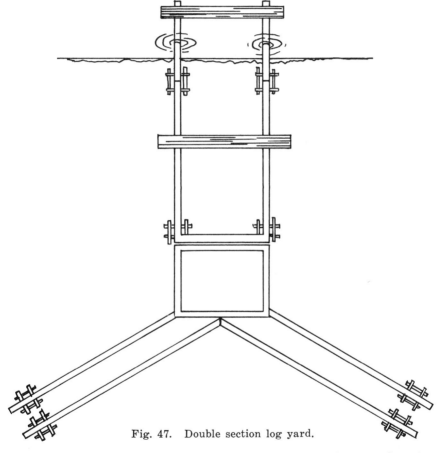

Fig. 47.   Double section log yard.

with the chain saw. When the logs are of such length that two or more cuts can be made from one log, the operation is carried on up the entire length. Then the cut logs are rolled off the saw yard to the log yard station.

The Log-yard Crew. The log-yard crew, operating either a power winch or a jitterbug and employing the use of a pulley block or snatch block, pulls the logs into the log yard in much the same way as they were snatched and twitched from the water.

If the jitterbug is used to bring the logs to the yard, it must have room in which to maneuver. If a winch is used, it should be located permanently at the base of the log yard. By employing a little ingenuity, the saw yard and the log yard can be located in direct line with the landing site, thus saving a great deal of wasted motion and cutting down on the number of men needed.

When the base logs of the log yard have been placed, a shorter log is placed across the front top. This piece is called a header. It is notched to make for a snug fit. The base logs at the front are also notched to prevent the header from slipping. Two small skids can be used to get the logs to the yard as shown in Fig. 46. However, short skids can be cut and placed on either side of the yard and the logs can be rolled up onto the yard by using the cant dogs. This method takes plenty of muscle, but it gets the logs there. When the bottom of the yard has been filled, small thin skids are laid on top of these logs, thus allowing easy passage and rolling of the second layer. The "jitterbug," or winch, eliminates the need for second-layer skids.

After the logs have been stacked on the log yard, they are ready to be trucked or shipped to the sawmill. There are times when it will pay a crew of divers to purchase an old truck and transport their own logs to the mill, but, usually, the buyer will arrange for the transportation, thus relieving the divers of that problem and headache.

BUSINESS ARRANGEMENTS

Scuba divers who have a desire to enter the underwater logging business should contact the wholesale lumber associations and/or the retail lumber dealers' associations in their area. It will be worthwhile to exchange ideas with both organizations. Some wholesale organizations will direct diving loggers to sawmill owners who will purchase all the logs they recover. And, retailers will agree to purchase the logs as they are hauled from below and pay for them as they are landed on the river or lake shore, have them hauled to a mill, and defray all costs themselves.

The author has found that, when possible, it is advisable for a diver to hire his services to a lumber concern, making a contract with the firm to buy all the logs which are on the log yard for immediate disposal. By making such an arrangement in the beginning, the diver-lumberman is assured of getting all his logs sold and having money coming in all the time. On the other hand, before a logging operation starts, he should look into all the selling possibilities in his area, even checking several hundred miles around the spot to be worked. There may be buyers in a nearby state that will pay more and have a greater need for the logs than those mills in and near the operation site. If no written contract is possible, the diver should try to find out the approximate number of board feet needed and the type of logs wanted; then, after this careful checking, he can start the operation if he feels that the prospects warrant it.

The logging business is not any easy job. But it has been done, as an experiment, by the author and his associates with a minimum of equipment and it has been done, more easily, of course, with power tools. Moreover, a profit was realized.

It is a good summer job and, at the end of the season, you will be as brown as a nut from working in the sun, as hard as a chunk of steel from juggling heavy, water-soaked logs, and as healthy as a person could possibly be. Muscles will pop out where you never expected them to develop; your hands will be tough and hard.

This particular field of diving is the only one that seems to offer diving work for divers in every state. Underwater logging is not an easy job, but the author has found that no underwater task is easy.

Chapter IX

THE UNDERWATER CRAFTSMAN

The American market has much equipment with which to supply the skin diver, Scuba diver and commercial scubaman. The author knows from experience that when a group of divers pool their knowledge, experience and equipment, to establish a diving business, there are many items which are very expensive to purchase. Therefore to overcome this big expense, the men of International Undersea Services designed and tested a great portion of the tools used in those early days. Since that time, this gear has been constantly modified and improved. This equipment was designed to cut unnecessary overhead for an individual or group of divers and is naturally inexpensive.

The engineering capabilities of the personnel at the Research & Development Dept. are available to all divers thoughout the world. Plans and designs are available at a minimum fee. Special underwater problems may be presented to the staff, and they will design and build a specific item for the special need. American and European divers may write directly to International Undersea Services, Eastern Office, 43–45 Maple St., Brewer, Maine, 04412, USA. Pacific and Far East divers can contact International Undersea Services, Pacific Office, 120 Glanmire Road, Newlands, Wellington, New Zealand, c/o The Hon. Peter I. Millar, Representative.

The list of items can be constructed as pictured, or modified and improved to best fit the needs of the individual person or the job. The sole purpose here is to present a basic idea, thereby allowing the individual to employ his imagination and creativity.

DIVER'S WORK CRAFT

Divers engaged in underwater work need some type of boat. If the group does not possess the necessary funds to purchase one of the amphibian government vehicles mentioned in the text, it will be necessary to purchase a commercially built craft or to construct a boat.

Pleasure craft and general small utility boats have been found unsuited for diving-business purposes. Since a diving work boat will receive a generous measure of rough treatment, it is advisable to build the type of boat best suited to meet the needs of the particular underwater operations in which the group will be engaged.

Mobility of equipment is a prime factor to be considered. Many underwater jobs can be lost to other divers because gear cannot be transported to the job site fast enough. Always have boats which can be transported by truck or towed on a trailer behind a car or truck.

SEARCH AND OBSERVATION SKIFF

This boat is a small, lightweight, and portable craft. It may be powered with a small outboard motor or oars. When loaded, it draws less than four inches of water. Construction is simple and cost is low. The large plexiglass observation port is situated to allow the boat's operator to observe the divers or to assist in searching for submerged objects. This craft can be transported atop any vehicle with a cartop carrier.

Sides and Bottom. The side pieces, 1¼" x 12" x 120", are measured 6" down from the top and 36" in from the front end. Make a gradual curve and saw both pieces. Save the curved cut-off pieces to be used later. Nail three pieces of scrap wood 42" long to the top edges of the sides, at the front, middle and rear. Turn the unit over.

Most plywood is available in 4' x 8' sheets, but it is available in 10', 12', 14' and 16' sheets. If possible, buy a 10 ft. sheet. If only the standard 48" by 96" sheet is available, two pieces, butted, will be necessary to complete the craft's bottom. The standard plywood sheet measurements will be used here.

Cut a 6" x 8' strip from the side of a ⅜" sheet of exterior or marine plywood. Use caulking compound or marine glue on the bottom edges of the boat's sides prior to nailing on the bottom piece.

Nail the 42" x 96" plywood piece from the bow with 4d screw nails, spaced 1" apart. Using the second sheet of plywood, butt it to the piece already nailed to the craft, mark and saw. Nail securely after gluing the end to make a solid and waterproof seam. Put a ¾" x 1½" stringer directly over the seam. This should be screwed securely from the bottom side with brass screws staggered.

Mark the area ahead of the cross stringer for cutting out the observation port. The area is 12" x 24" and should be located in the center of the boat. Save the piece cut from the observation port.

Clean off excess caulking compound or glue.

Stringers. Cut pine stock ¾" x 1½" in lengths to fit inside the boat. Place a stringer flush to the bottom edge in the bow as close to the bow curvature as possible. Nail through the sides into the ends of the stringer to hold it fast. Disregard the bend in the plywood at the bow; it will straighten when screwed to the stringer. Caulk or glue the stringer before applying the #8-⅞" flat-head brass screws, from the underside staggered slightly. Screws are turned in flush with the wood.

Place a stringer about 36″ from the bow, another to overlap the observation port ¾ inch, another to do the same on the opposite end of the observation port, and one in the stern. (Note: The observation port can be cut prior to putting the remaining two feet of the plywood bottom on the craft. If the 12″ x 24″ hole is cut then, the remainder

Fig. 48.   Search and observation skiff.

of the bottom can be put on and the stringer over the seam will serve as part of the observation port framework.)

All stringers are glued and screwed securely from the underside.

Back. Cut two plywood strips 12″ x 42″ and glue them together. When sufficiently dried, fit the piece to the stern. Caulk the stern edges and nail with 7d screw nails into the sides, and 4d screw nails into the bottom stringer. Set the 4d screw nails 2″ apart and place ⅞″ flat-head screws between the nails. Clean off excess caulking compound or glue.

The stern has extra bracing to hold an outboard motor. This is made from ¾″ pine stock or scrap plywood.

Bow. The bow piece is ¾″ x 6½″ x 42″ pine. It should fit slightly below the curvature of the bow. The leading edge should be planed to conform with the bow curve. Use caulking compound freely before nailing. A ¾″ lip remains at the top to butt the bow seat against. Use 7d screw nails on the sides and 4d screw nails along the bottom of the bow piece. Head the 4d nails to draw tightly against the bow stringer. Use nails liberally.

Bow Seat. The bow seat is ¾″ x 7″ x 42″ pine. It is glued or caulked on the leading edge and butted to the bow piece. Seven-penny

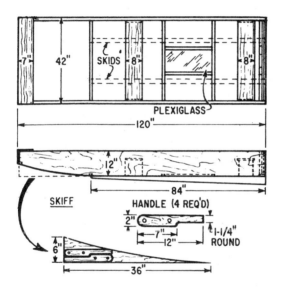

Fig. 48A. Search and observation skiff blueprints.

screw nails secure it. Nail from the top into the sides and from the front through the bow piece.

Skids. Skids are cut from 2″ x 4″ pine or hemlock, the latter considered best. They are tapered the entire length from 1″ to the full 4″ height. Two skids (keels) are cut 1″ to 4″ x 2″ thick and 84″ long, rounded at the 1″ end. Skids are mounted flush to the rear of the boat and set in about 10 inches from the outer edges. They are secured in four places where they cross the stringers. Carriage bolts are used for securing.

Countersink large holes ½″ deep to accommodate octagon nuts; drill the bolt holes through the skid, bottom and stringers. Apply caulking compound in and around the bolt holes before attaching the skids. Cut off excess thread on bolts with hacksaw.

Seats. Two solid pine pieces $3/4''$ x $7\frac{1}{2}''$ x $7\frac{1}{2}''$ serve as the seat braces for the rear seat. The pieces are set out from the stern approximately 3 to 5 inches.

Two solid pine pieces $3/4''$ x $8''$ x $8''$ are set slightly forward of the observation port (approximately $55''$ to $65''$ from the stern). Screw these pieces to the boat sides with $1\frac{1}{2}''$ flat-head screws from the inside.

Cut two pieces of pine $3/4''$ x $8''$ x $39\frac{1}{2}''$ for the seats. These are not secured. They should fit tightly, yet able to be removed with a sharp upward rap.

Observation Port. Two more braces are needed to complete the frame of the plexiglass port. These braces fit between the cross stringers and overlap the hole $3/4$ inch, thereby serving as the port framework.

The observation port is $3/8''$ plexiglass cut to fit the hole. It is secured with #5–$3/4''$ flat-head brass or chrome-plated screws. Screws are set in $1/2''$ from the edge of the glass, approximately 3 inches apart. Use a #2 Screw Hole Drill (Craftsman Mfg.) which drills the hole, makes the right shank size and countersinks in one operation. Or, if a regular drill is used countersink all holes.

Before inserting the plexiglass, apply caulking compound liberally to the port framework. Place in the plexiglass and secure carefully. Wipe off excess caulking compound inside and out.

Handles. Four handles are made to carry the boat. They are made from the pieces cut from the sides. Two handles can be made from each piece. Handles are bolted on to the bow and stern with carriage bolts and wing nuts. When not in use, handles can be bolted inside the boat for storage.

Oarlocks. The selection of oarlocks is varied. The author used the inexpensive pot metal type. This type has a lock holder which must fit into the boat's sides. A $3/4''$ x $4''$ x $4''$ pine piece was added to the top edge after the oarsman sat in the middle seat, stretched his arms halfway out, then full out, then back, making a rowing motion. This determined the best spot for the wood block in which to set the oarlock post.

Nail the wood block to the sides, but leave a $1''$ clear space in the middle to allow for the auger bit to make the oar post hole without striking nails.

Oars. Oars should be carried in all boats. A $5\frac{1}{2}$ to 6 ft. pair of ash, spruce, fiberglas, aluminum, or basswood oars is excellent. Oars should be treated: wood with two coats of clear varnish; metal with marine paint. Always leave the handles bare.

Safety. Blocks of foam plastic are secured to the underside of the middle and rear seats by two $2''$ canvas strips. In the event of accident, these seats will serve as safety floats.

Painting. The entire craft is given one coat of marine undercoat primer, and two coats of any color marine paint. Nonskid compound should be added to the mixture covering the insides. Each diving business should have its own individual colors and all equipment should carry these colors.

Port Cover. Using the plywood piece cut from the bottom when making the observation port, glue a piece of thick felt to it. This will save the plexiglass from unnecessary scratching or damage during transportation or storage. Use two screw hooks at each end of the port on the underside to hold the port cover in place.

Many other improvements and additions can be made by each individual builder.

List of Materials

Pcs.	Dimensions	Use	Stock
2	1-1/2 × 12 × 120	sides	pine
2	3/8 × 48 × 96	bottom	plywood, exterior or marine
2	3/4 × 7-1/2 × 7-1/2	seat braces	pine
2	2 × 4 × 84	skids	hemlock or pine
2	1 × 8 × 39-1/2	seats	pine
1	3/4 × 7 × 42	bow seats	pine
2	3/4 × 8 × 8	middle seat brace	pine
1	3/4 × 12⁺ × 42	back	plywood
5	3/4 × 1-1/2 × 39-1/2	stringers	pine
2	3/4 × 1-1/2 × 22-1/2	port stringers	pine
1	3/8 × 12 × 24	port	plexiglass
1	3/8 × 12 × 24	port cover	plywood

2 lbs. 4d screw nails; 1 lb. 7d screw nails; 1 can marine glue; 1 tube caulking compound; 100 #8 - 7/8 in. f. h. screws; 160 #8 - 1-1/2 in. f. h. screws; 50 #5 - 3/4 in. f. h. screws; 6 - 1/4 × 3 in. carriage bolts w/wing nuts; 2 - 1/4 × 3-1/2 in. carriage bolts with wing nuts; 2 - 1/4 × 2-1/2 in. carriage bolts; 2 - 1/4 × 3-1/2 in. carriage bolts; 2 - 1/4 × 4-1/2 in. carriage bolts; 2 - 1/4 × 5 in. carriage bolts; 2 pcs. 6 × 6 × 30 in. styrofoam plastic; 4 pcs. 1/16 × 2 × 20 canvas strips; 1 pc. 1/8 × 12 × 24 in. felt.

The following material describing a salvage boat for underwater work is an extract from pages 22 through 26 of *Underwater Logging* by John Cayford and Ronald Scott, published by Cornell Maritime Press in 1964.

SALVAGE BOAT

The home-constructed salvage boat is a heavy-duty, sturdily built craft for work and diving operations. (*See* Fig. 49.) It can be constructed in 12 and 16-foot lengths. It is a flat-bottomed, square-backed, scow-type craft especially designed with a wide, flat bottom to supply maximum lift and to draw as little water as possible.

In actual use, the 12-ft. craft carried a crew of three, 100 log marker buoys, a low-pressure compressor with reserve tank, 200 ft. of diving hose, and hauled six logs of 15-inch top diameter, 16 feet long, powered by a 10 horsepower Johnson outboard motor. With all the on-board weight, and the drag of six water-soaked logs, the craft drew less than 4 inches of water and performed well.

Construction. The boat has been simply designed of available materials. Planks, plywood, 2 x 4-inch stock, pine boards, calking com-

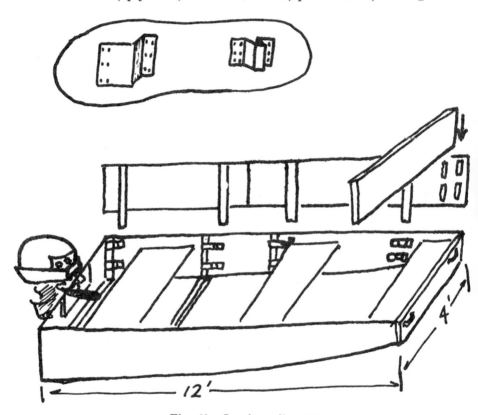

Fig. 49.   Log boat diagrams.

pound, glue, screw nails, and screws comprise the majority of building materials. Construction time is two to three days.

Sides. Pine planks, 2 x 12 inches and 12 or 16 feet long, are the sides. Use half-dried, or air-dried, stock; kiln-dried lumber has too much of the natural moisture content removed. If higher sides are desired, two planks are used. Other stock is substituted if 2 x 12-inch is not available. The stock should be no less than 2 x 8 inches.

Cut the bow curvature which is the same for both models. When using a two-plank side, glue together and secure with 2 x 2-inch braces from the outside with 3½-inch screw nails. Place the braces

24 inches on center. No brace is used in front. Turn the completed sides upright and nail exactly 48 inches apart with scrap pieces. Turn the unit over, run calking compound the length of the bottom edges, and nail a ¾-inch sheet of AD exterior or marine plywood from the bow, bending it to fit the bow curvature.

Use 7d screw nails 1½ inches apart on the bow curvature, then 1 inch apart to the end of the sheet. The 16-ft. craft will use two full plywood sheets to cover the bottom. Clean off excess calking compound when nailing is completed.

Saw off the 4-foot piece on the 12-ft. boat. This piece is used to make the back.

Braces. Braces and stringers are made by sawing 2 x 4-inch stock in half. The braces are cut to the side height determined by the builders. Use 3½-inch screw nails from the outside to secure the braces 24 inches on center. Cut plenty of 2 x 2-inch stock in 4-foot lengths.

Stringers. Cut seven stringers for the 12-ft. boat, and nine for the 16-ft. model. Place a stringer across the bow and calk it liberally. Nail through the sides to hold, then nail 1½ inches apart from the underside. Use 2½-inch flathead screws between each nail. Continue to place the stringers 24 inches apart on center positioned with the braces. Glue or calk the stringers liberally before nailing and screwing alternately as in the bow stringer.

Place a stringer over the seam where the two plywood pieces come together on the bottom. Secure this stringer with 2½-inch flathead screws from the underside in a staggered pattern 1½ inches apart. Pour plenty of glue in the seam before screwing, and after, if the seam is not full.

Back. The back on the 12-ft. boat is made from the 4-foot plywood piece, if the boat's sides are one foot high. Cut the piece in half, glue together, and put in a few 1¼-inch flathead screws to insure its holding under motor stresses and hauling strains. Calk around the sides and bottom, and nail into the sides with 5- or 6-inch common nails, 1½ inches apart. Across the bottom, 7d screw nails and 3-inch screws are used. The nails are driven into the plywood; screws are placed through the back into the stringer; placement is 2 inch alternating staggered.

The back for the 16-ft. craft is made from two pieces of ¾-inch plywood glued together. Follow the directions used for the 12-ft. model.

Bow. The bow is cut from ¾-inch pine. It overlaps slightly at the bottom and ¾ inch at the top. It is glued along the sides and calked along the bottom. Nail with 7d screw nails from the front.

Seats. Seats are cut from ¾-inch pine, 10 inches wide. Solid pieces of 2 x 10 x 10-inch stock or individual pieces of 2 x 2 x 10-inch stock are used as seat braces and nailed to the boat's sides.

The stern seat is set out from the back to allow for comfort when operating the outboard motor. The stern and midship seats are not secured.

The underside of the seats have two blocks of 8 x 8 x 12-inch foam plastic pieces attached to them by 2-inch canvas or metal aluminum strips. These serve as emergency floats in the event of accident. Space the plastic blocks to the ends of the seats leaving the middle space open to lay across or hold on to.

The bow seat is stationary. It is glued on the leading edge and butted to the ¾-inch overlap of the bow piece. Nail with 7d screw nails through the front and 8d common nails from the top.

Skid. A single skid, 2 x 4 x 96-inch tapered from 1 inch to a full 4 inches for the 12-ft. craft, and 2 x 4 x 144-inch tapered for the 16-ft. craft, is placed in the middle of the underside of the boat. The big end is placed flush with the stern and bolted with carriage bolts.

The bolts are located at the rear, middle, and near the tip of the skid. Put calking compound into and around the boltholes. Countersink a hole to accommodate the nut, then drill the shank hole. Center the holes to go through a stringer, which will give added strength to the bottom and the skid.

ACCESSORIES

Oarlocks. Selected by the builders. The inexpensive pot metal type requires a ⅞-inch hole drilled 2½ inches deep in the sides to the rear of the middle seat. Positioning is attained by a man sitting in the middle seat and stretching his arms to the normal rowing stroke.

Oars. Wood, fibreglass, or metal serve well. A 6-ft. oar is sufficient, although a short-limbed person will require a longer one.

Wooden oars are varnished at least two coats. Do not varnish or paint the handles.

Side Boards. Side boards are cut from ½-inch plywood 36 inches wide to the length of the craft. Two sheets are required to each side. They are butted together, yet work as individual units. The two forward units can be inserted in position and covered with a canvas tarp, or all four side boards can be used and covered.

Braces of 2 x 2-inch pine stock are nailed to the side boards, and positioned alongside the boat's braces. Braces will run from the top edge of the side board to the bottom of the craft. Braces are held by double-angled band iron pieces.

A 2-inch wide band iron 8 inches long is bent as shown in **Fig. 49** The angles are drilled to accommodate 2-inch roundhead screws. Each side-board brace is held by two angle straps.

There is no stringer or brace in front of the bow seat. The side-board brace is held by two U-clamps—one placed 2 inches from the top of the boat's side, the other approximately 3 inches from the boat's bottom. The front end of the forward side boards have a ¾ x 10-inch cut on the bottom edge for the bow seat. The rear side boards have cutouts for the oarlocks, if necessary.

The forward side boards will not be flush with the bow. The piece must be even with the seam in the bottom of the boat. Front side boards meet at the center of the seam brace. The fore and aft side-board braces will be placed on either side of the boat's main brace.

When the side boards are set in place, nail a ¾-inch quarter-round hardwood strip fairly snug to the bottom edge of the side board on

List of Materials

Pcs.	*Dimensions*	*Use*	*Material*
2	2″ x 12″ x 12′ or 16′	Sides	Pine
2	¾″ x 4′ x 8′	Bottom	Plywood, Ex./Marine
7/9	2″ x 4″ x 42″	Stringers	Pine
14/16	2″ x 2″ x 12″	Main Braces	Pine/Hemlock
1	¾″ x 7″ x 48″	Bow	Pine
1	¾″ x 10″ x 48″	Bow Seat	Pine
2	¾″ x 10″ x 45″	Seats, Mid/Aft	Pine
2	¾″ x 10″ x 10″	Seat Braces	Pine
1	1″ x 4″ x 96″ x 144″	Skid	Hemlock/Pine
2	½″ x 36″ x 96″	Side Boards, Fore	Plywood, Ex./Marine
2	½″ x 36″ x 48″ or 96″	Side Boards, Aft	Plywood, Ex./Marine
1	½″ x 35¼″ x 44″	Bow Board	Plywood, Ex./Marine
8	2″ x 4″ x 6″	Bow Board Blocks	Pine
16/20	2″ x 2″ x 48″	Side-Board Braces	Pine
4	⅛″ x 2″ x 10″	Brace Holders, Fore	Iron, U-straps
30/38	⅛″ x 2″ x 8″	Brace Holders, std.	Iron, dble. angle
1 pr.	Standard	Oarlocks	Metal
1 pr.	Std. 6 ft.	Oars	Metal, Fibreglass, Wood

8 line cleats; carriage bolts ½″ x 7″; ½″ x 6″; and ½″ x 4½″. 2 lbs. 7d screw nails; 2 lbs. 8d common nails; 1 lb. 3½″ screw nails; 1 box 2″ f.h. screws; 1 box 2½″ f.h. screws; 1 doz. 1¼″ f.h. screws; 2 doz. 3″ f.h. screws; 3 doz. 2″ rd.h. screws; 3 doz. 1¼″ rd.h. screws; 1 14-oz. 5′ x 13′ or 17′ canvas; 24′ or 32′ ¾″ hardwood quarter-round.

top of the boat's sides. This channel serves to strengthen the side boards.

A bow board is placed between the sides. This piece is made from ½-inch exterior or marine plywood, and held by 2 x 4 x 6-inch blocks nailed to the side boards. There are four blocks to a side; two near the top, and two approximately 3 inches from the bottom edge of the side board. Space the blocks to allow for a minimum amount of play in the bow board.

Handles. Large brass handles can be attached to the bow and stern for easier handling and transporting. Two handles are located on the back in each corner near the top, and two are bolted onto the bow piece in the same positions.

Painting. The entire boat has one coat of marine undercoat primer. Then apply two coats of any color marine paint. Non-skid compound is mixed with the paint used on the craft's interior. The compound prevents slippage of men and equipment.

The bottom of the craft should be painted white, silver, or aluminum. These colors are easily seen as the diver ascends.

Cover. Make a canvas cover to fit the entire craft. The cover should come down over the sides and ends approximately one foot. Grommets are evenly spaced around the edge of the canvas for tying purposes.

LIFTING BAG

Lifting bags are used to raise objects from the bottom. The bag described is made from heavy ten- to fourteen-ounce canvas, 36 inches wide.

Two 3-foot pieces are cut for the ends. These are trimmed to make 36-inch-diameter circles. Two or three lengths of canvas are cut and sewed together with a double overlap stitch. These pieces form a tubular body for the lift bag and are cut in lengths to fit around the end pieces with an inch extra on each side to sew it lengthwise. The

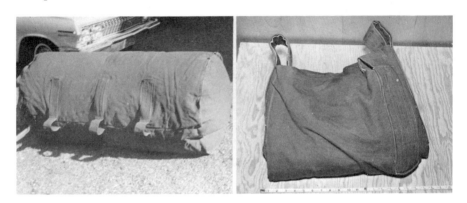

Fig. 50.   (Left) Lifting bag full. (Right) Lifting bag folded.

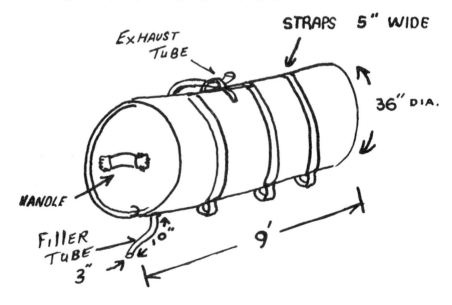

Fig. 51.   Lifting bag dimensions.

end pieces have an inch fold to sew them to the tubular body. A 10-inch-long, 3-inch-diameter canvas tube is sewed into the bottom of the bag for filling purposes, and another is sewed into the top for an exhaust tube. The exhaust tube has a small loop strap sewed near it so the exhaust tube can be tucked under it and brought back and tied.

Three 5-inch straps are doubled and sewed completely around the bag with a 3-inch loop left at the bottom.

The unit folds into a neat 20-inch package, easily handled and very portable. An 8½-ft., 35-inch-diameter bag will lift approximately two to three tons.

Prior to using the bag, it is unfolded and submerged in water. Allow a half hour for the canvas fibers to swell, making the unit airtight. Re-fold and take it to the object to be lifted. Unfold and slip the 2-inch steel pipe through the strap loops. Attach chains, wire rope cable or ropes to the pipe and to the object to be lifted.

If when the bag is filled, the object has not moved, more bags of the same size or a larger bag may be necessary to do the work.

If the object is in mud or heavy silt, the suction could be holding it from rising. Try to break the suction by working the object back and forth or run a long stick or bar under the object.

After use in salt water, wash the bag thoroughly in fresh water and allow it to dry before storage.

UNDERWATER METAL LOCATOR

John C. Bender, member of the staff of the Mecca Cable & Service Company, Houston, Texas, converted a SCR 625H Army mine detector to fit into a brass tubular housing for underwater work. The results were astounding. The reason for the success of this instrument is the relatively low frequency. Because the SCR 625 detector works on a frequency of 1000 cycles compared to other units that work at several hundred kilocycles, the depth of penetration is much greater and the results are much more satisfactory.

There are several models of the SCR 625 detector. The best unit for conversion is the SCR 625, Models D through H, and the latter model the easiest. The detectors can be purchased from numerous army and navy surplus outlets. See Figs. 52 and 53.

Conversion. The detector is not difficult to convert, however divers not familiar with a wiring diagram should check the local radio repairman for assistance in construction and parts.

Amplifier Unit Housing. The amplifier unit is encased in a brass or plastic container made to the following dimensions: Diameter 6 in.; length 14 in.; wall thickness $\frac{1}{16}$ in. brass: $\frac{3}{8}$ in. plexiglass. Face plate 8 in. diameter; $\frac{1}{4}$ in. thick brass; $\frac{1}{2}$ in. thick plexiglass. A flange 8 in. in diameter is cut to fit snugly around the top of the housing.

This housing will contain the electrical and power source of the instrument.

The amplifier strip is removed from its original case. There is a lip on the forward end with two mounting holes in it. The strip is then mounted to the rear side of the face plate. Mount the amplifier strip chassis with #8–32 brass screws ¼ in. long. Use #2 Permatex or equivalent on the screws before securing the chassis to the front plate so that no water will leak through the mounting holes when using the brass plate.

A Phaostron, 2½ in. round, Prestige 50–0–50 DCUA #247–02207 meter is mounted as shown in Fig. 53. Mount an IN 34 diode

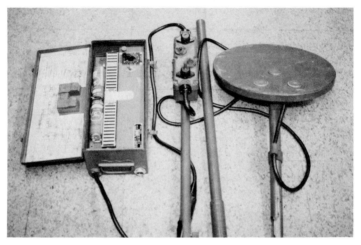

Fig. 52.   Original SCR-625, Model H, U.S. Army mine detector as purchased from government surplus outlet. (Bender)

in series with the meter. If the meter shows a reverse reading, reverse the diode.

A Keystone #176 twin battery clip or equivalent is mounted on right-hand side of the amplifier. *Be sure that the batteries are hooked up as shown in the technical manual which accompanies the SCR 625.*

The "B" battery holder is mounted on the left side of the amplifier strip. A separate holder is placed alongside the amplifier mounting strip to contain the XX-69 or equivalent battery.

This mounting is made from a 1½" aluminum angle stock. Cut a piece 14⅛ inches long. Split back the end 1⅜ inches. Bend up a lip on the end. Mount the "B" battery terminals from the original box to each end of the inner side of the bracket. Try the battery for size before spotting the holes to mount the terminals. Drill 3 holes in the lip with a #19 drill. Countersink all holes from the inside of the lip. Mount the battery holder to the front plate and to the amplifier mounting strip with #6–32 brass screws to give rigidity to the whole unit. Connect the red wire to the positive (+) terminal and the black wire to the negative (−) terminal.

Replace the large one-microfarad condenser with a 200-volt, one-microfarad tubular condenser. Mount this condenser to the frame of the amplifier chassis with a metal strip.

Replace the R–12 with a 1000 ohm potentiometer with a round brass shaft. Mount the potentiometer away from the back face of the instrument. Use a regular copper tube fitting (⅞″ x 28) with a .257 drilled hole in the center and a #6227-5 "O" ring seal in the stuffing box to prevent water leakage around the shaft.

Fig. 53. Fully converted SCR-625H metal detector with capabilities of finding ferrous and nonferrous metals. (Leiper)

The metal box in the photograph (Fig. 53) is used with the land model. The same circuitry is applied to the underwater model. The parts are so small, they are mounted on a small bakelite strip and attached to the rear side of the meter on the terminal screw posts.

There is no need to waterproof or seal off the cable leads to and from the control box. Unscrew the cap that covers the course balance control and fill with castor oil. This will keep water from leaking into the unit balance control.

The handle of the unit is mounted to the face plate. Designer Bender made the prototype from ¾ inch Masonite and mounted it to a brass plate in the shape of a "T". The three (3) corners of the "T" are drilled to take brass screws. The screws fasten to the face plate. Handles can be made from wood (well varnished) and/or metal.

The search coil is mounted simply. A screw stud (⅜″ x 16 threads x 1¾″) is threaded into the bottom of the amplifier housing unit and secured on the inside with a hex nut. The SCR–625H has a short extension shaft. This screws onto the ⅜ inch screw stud. Connect the search coil shaft to this extension. The search coil is fully waterproofed when purchased and needs no further attention.

Testing Under Water. The unit is tested under water by turning on the switch and gradually turning up the sensitivity control until the meter swings full scale. Now adjust both balance controls until the meter returns to zero. Increase the sensitivity control until it deflects full scale again. Rebalance. Keep doing this until the meter will not quite return to zero, at which point the detector is in complete balance.

The use of the 50–0–50 meter is an improvement over Mr. Bender's first conversion. The unit will discriminate between ferrous (iron, steel, etc.) metal and non-ferrous (brass, copper, gold, silver, etc.) metals.

The metal locator will afford uses for sports divers as well as commercial Scuba divers.

WEIGHT-PAK

The Weight-Pak is an improvement of the backplate manufactured by Seacraft Industries, Wilmington, Massachusetts. Donald and Stanley DeRoche of International's Research & Development Department designed, built and tested this unit. It was desired to consolidate equipment and incorporate the most advanced safety features.

Weight tubes were added to each side of the backplate and the B–275 Quick Release Box assembly replaced the original quick release buckle.

Quick Release Mechanism. The B-275 Q-R box assembly compares with the British-made *Normalair* Scuba diving release system.

The box contains four (4) posts to which four (4) strap lugs are attached. The locking knob, located on the front of the unit, is turned and pressed, thereby releasing all but one of the strap lugs. This lug remains permanently closed so the Q-R box will not become totally detached from the unit. A safety clip keeps the release knob from being accidentally pressed releasing the lugs.

The unit is turned to lock position and each strap lug is pushed into place and automatically locks securely. Maintenance is slight. The illustrated parts breakdown shows the simple operating mechanism (Fig. 54C). Vaseline petroleum jelly, or any good lubricant, keeps the moving parts lubricated.

B-275 Q-R assemblies can be purchased at: Capt. Joe's Surplus Stores, 1028 Arch St., Philadelphia 7, and David Gottlieb Co., 2820 Surf Ave., Brooklyn, N.Y. Price: $2.00. If the strap lugs are not with these units, they can be purchased from: Pioneer Parachute Co., Connecticut.

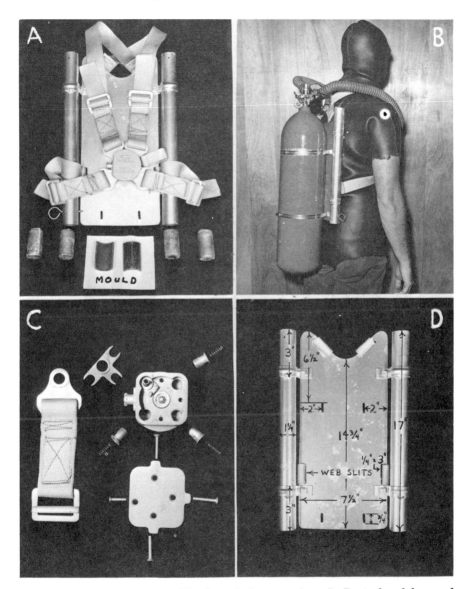

Fig. 54. A. Weight-Pak. B. Weight-Pak in operation. C. Parts breakdown of Weight-Pak. D. Dimensions of backplate with weight tubes.

Weight Tubes. Two 1¼ inch diameter, 17 inch long steel conduit pipes serve as the weight tubes. A one (1″) inch long, round, wooden plug with a one (1″) inch diameter, four (4″) inch long, light gauge steel spring is stapled to the plug. This unit is then fitted into the top of each tube. Drill through the tube and wooden plug and rivet or bolt securely.

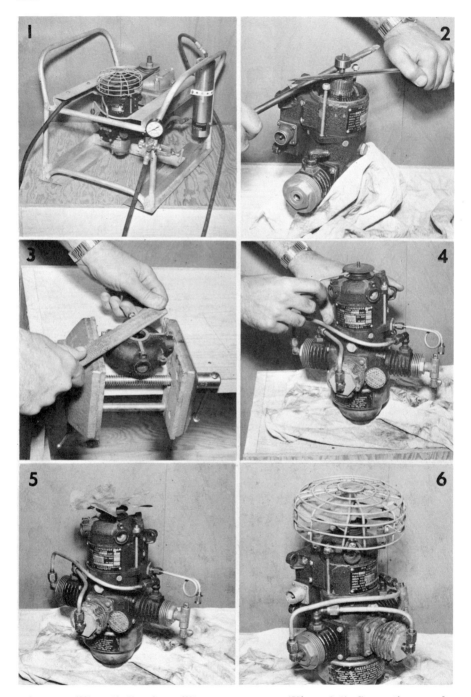

Fig. 55. (View 1) Surplus military compressor. (Views 2-6) Converting surplus compressor for diver's use.

Viking TW-1, 1¼ inch clamps, or equivalent, are spot welded to the tubes approximately three (3″) inches from each end. Line up the tubes as shown in Fig. 54D, drill ¼ inch holes in the backplate and bolt the tubes to the plate using lock washers.

Drill ⅛ inch holes in the bottom end of the tubes, one (1″) inch up on the outside. Bend a length of ⅛ inch stainless steel rod to fit into the holes. Make a full one (1″) inch loop and a straight shank 2 inches long for the weight release pins. Make one for each tube.

Weights. Weights are molded in a plain steel pipe, 1¼″ x 2½″ long. Cut the pipe mold lengthwise for easy removal of the lead weights after they are poured

Some of International Undersea Services' divers have cleaned out the cores of used size "D" flashlight batteries of the metal case type and poured lead into them. They weigh one (1) pound each and work more efficiently than the plain lead molded weights.

The weights are loaded into the tubes in the amounts needed. A one (1″) inch dowel can be used as a dummy weight to fill the space when lead weights do not make correct spring tension. When the weights have a tension on them, insert the weight release pins.

HIGH-PRESSURE AIR COMPRESSOR

Scuba commercial divers and individual divers need an inexpensive apparatus to refill diving tanks. The surplus military compressor shown in Fig. 55 refills a standard Scuba tank to 2400 pounds per square inch in approximately one hour at a cost of (15¢) fifteen cents. The highly portable compressor can be made to operate from any 110-volt electric system (or with reducing transformers for 220-volt European electrical systems), or with a 2½ h.p. gasoline engine, or both. Experiments have been conducted with two and three compressors driven by a single heavy-duty electric motor with excellent results.

This portable diver's compressor is of the low-volume, high-pressure design. When converted as directed, it will produce over 3000 pounds per square inch of free air. The air will be oil- and moisture-free, nearly 100 percent pure breathing air. Owning a portable compressor will pay for itself in a few months' time.

Several small 2-, 3-, and 4-stage compressors were converted, tested and used under actual conditions. The 2-stage compressor could only produce slightly over 2000 psi, and recharging time was very slow. The 4-stage machines are excellent, but cost from $200 to $400 on the surplus market. The 3-stage compressor will provide 3000 psi, at 1 cubic foot per minute and is available in many parts of the United States at surplus stores for less than $50.00 for the basic unit.

The best, least expensive unit is the Series 32 Cornelius 3-stage, oil base compressor originally designed to preload aircraft hydraulic systems.

Conversion. The fan guard and fan are removed; the fan has a left-hand thread. Next, remove the 2 self-locking nuts that hold the brush and bearing housing. Ease off the housing by employing two screwdrivers at opposite points and working it off carefully. When the housing is off, the bearing is removed. Place the screwdrivers under the bearing, as shown in view 2, and pry. The bearing will be damaged; however its only purpose is for comparison, so save it. The housing also has four brushes held by pins. Knock out the pins, remove the brush caps, take out the brushes, then replace the caps and pins.

The housing is placed in a vise and filed down as shown in view 3. Measurements should be followed fairly closely. The depth of cut in the housing top is approximately $\frac{1}{8}''$ to $\frac{3}{16}''$ deep, and $1\frac{1}{2}$ inches radius from the center. A metal rasp or file can be used to make this cut. When the cut is completed, replace the housing on the unit.

The original bearing is replaced by a New Departure #77R-6, $\frac{9}{32}''$ x $\frac{3}{8}''$ id x $\frac{7}{8}''$ od bearing or equivalent bearing. It is the same bearing as removed from the compressor, but thinner. Be sure it is a permanently sealed and packed, precision ground bearing. Check it carefully before purchase.

The author made his original pulley (see view 4); it was a bastard size and unavailable on the open market. The compressor pulley is $2''$ od with a $\frac{3}{8}''$ id center hole. It has been noted that some compressors in the Series 32 are heavier duty units and have slightly larger diameter drive shafts. Therefore it is best to check the drive shaft to obtain the correct diameter. The pulley is $\frac{1}{2}$ inch thick and grooved to accommodate a thin V-belt. This pulley is drilled and tapped in the groove on opposite sides for set (allen) screws. Aluminum is the easiest material to work for the pulley.

The motor shaft has two (2) flat areas near the top under the fan. Use a metal file to extend these areas down the shaft approximately $\frac{5}{8}''$ lower. The pulley set screws will rest against these areas. The fan is placed in position in view 5.

The fan guard has a section removed from it to allow the V-belt to pass around the pulley. Wire cutters or a hacksaw will clear the necessary area. File the ends of the guard wires smooth. Converted compressor is shown in view 6.

Other converted models of the same compressor have removed the armature, commutator, and motor housing. It was learned from a compressor expert that after these items have been placed on the drive shaft, the entire unit is balanced quite accurately. It was the expert's opinion that removal of these parts could throw the mechanism out of balance, causing wear to the pistons, cylinders and cylinder walls. The conversion method described herein has proven very satisfactory. The unit has worked for 48 continuous hours, and for 8 hours a day, 7 days a week for 6 mos. concurrently.

Air Filter. Clean and pack the Model 48 Cornelius high-pressure filter. The filter unscrews at the middle. Be careful not to damage the rubber O-ring when separating the sections, which will be designated as "A" for the top half of the filter, and "B" for the lower portion. Clean the sections thoroughly in carbon tetrachloride.

A fine rustproof screen is placed in the top of section "A," followed by two $\frac{1}{8}$ inch felt pads. Activated charcoal granules are poured in this section to within $\frac{1}{2}$ inch of the bottom. Two more round felt pads are inserted to keep the contents from spilling. Another fine screen, cut slightly larger than the diameter opening, is pushed into section "A."

Section "B" has a copper (only copper) chore girl (a kitchen pot cleaner) stuffed into the bottom. This serves to trap and hold some of the moisture and oil which could pass into the filter. A sanitary napkin (or portion thereof) follows the copper chore girl to further aid in trapping oil and/or moisture.

Lubricate the O-ring with a vegetable oil before joining the two sections of the filter.

The filter has an air outlet, drain plug, safety release air valve, and air outlet; all are plainly marked. A high-pressure elbow is placed into the outlet; a straight high-pressure male fitting is inserted in the inlet. Two 3-inch adjustable hose clamps, which hold the air filter to the compressor stand, complete the air purifying unit.

Motor. The best all-purpose motor using a minimum of electricity and delivering a maximum of performance is a $\frac{1}{2}$ horsepower, long shaft, ball bearing, heavy duty, 110-120 volt AC electric motor. The motor should turn up 3450 rpm.

The long shaft is used to allow for correct alignment of the compressor pulley and the motor pulley. In the event two or three compressors are employed on one stand, the extended shaft will accommodate a 2- and 3- unit pulley.

Stand. A number of different stands have been constructed from wood, and metal. Wooden and steel stands are heavy, so recent stands have been made from aluminum stocks.

A simple stand made in the shape of a box is ideal for the compressor unit shown in Fig. 55 The compressor is mounted on one end, the electric motor on the other, and the air filter is located on the side of the stand near the third stage outlet on the compressor. The third stage is the smallest cylinder.

The four corner posts are 2" x 2" x 16" box aluminum stock. Aluminum angle stock 1" x 1" x 22" is used on the sides. Four pieces of 1" x 1" x 10" angle stock complete the stand framework. The angle stock is all bolted to the box corner posts.

The angle stock is drilled $^{17}\!/_{32}$" staggered through the sides and attached with $\frac{1}{2}$" straight shank $2\frac{1}{2}$" bolts. The angle stock on the ends is drilled and staggered and attached to the corner posts with

½″ full thread ¾″ shank bolts. Locking nuts are used with all bolts.
The compressor and motor mounts are ⅛″ x 1″ x 12″ flat stock. Lay
out the pieces parallel 2″ apart, place the compressor in the middle of
the pieces, mark the holes and drill 9⁄32″ holes. Measure in 1 inch from
each end of both bars and drill 17⁄32″ holes. Attach the compressor to
the mounting bars with ¼″ full thread ¾″ shank bolts. Next, locate
the unit to the stand so the top of the fan guard is slightly below the
end frame angle piece. Mark the holes and drill 17⁄32″ holes and attach
the unit to the frame with ½″ straight shank 3½″ bolts. Use two lock
washers and two nuts to secure the unit. The bolts are purposely long

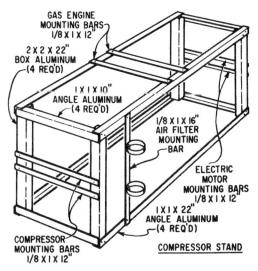

Fig. 56.   Compressor stand.

to allow for washers to be placed between the corner posts and the
mounting bars. These large washers are used as spacers to give
proper fit and tension to the V-belt if necessary.

The motor mount bars are drilled and bolted to the electric motor.
Since motor bases vary, each builder must select the proper length
bolt for attaching his particular motor. Holes are drilled in the ends of
the mount bars exactly the same as for the compressor mount bars,
and secured with the same size bolts.

A single piece of flat stock ⅛″ x 1″ x 16″ serves as the air filter
mount bar. It is bolted to the stand approximately 4 inches from the
end to which the compressor is attached. When the air filter is
attached to the bar with the hose clamps, mount it high enough to
allow for easy removal of the drain plug.

A short length of 4000 lbs. test high-pressure air hose is connected
to the compressor outlet and the air filter inlet. If the piece can be

purchased with the correct size, high-pressure female fittings will make the job simple. If the piece is not available, any firm working with hydraulics or high-pressure hosing will be able to cut the correct length piece of h.p. hose and properly fit the h.p. fittings. A 6 ft. length of 4000 lbs. test is attached to the air filter outlet and the tank filler yoke to complete the filler assembly. A filler yoke can be purchased from a number of manufacturers, or made from a Scuba pressure guage. The latter is the least expensive, and provides a gauge whereby the compressor operator can check the air pressure in the tank at all times.

This same box construction can also be used to mount a gasoline engine to run the compressor, thus creating a completely portable unit. The singular vertical shaft 2½ h.p. gasoline engine is mounted in the middle of the top of the stand with mount bars exactly as the electric motor and compressor.

Carrying handles may be fitted on each end when using the gas power, or in the middle of the unit when employing electric power. When electricity is available, by all means use it.

A 4" pulley is used on both the electric motor and the gasoline engine. When the pulley is set on the shaft and aligned with the pulley on the compressor, place on the V-belt. If there is some slack in the belt, use washers behind the mounting bars to take it up. When using the combination gas-electric unit, the pulley on the gas engine must be pushed up or removed when using the motor. The V-belt is removed from the electric motor when using the gas engine as the belts are different lengths.

Checking Out. Prior to filling a diving tank, the unit must be test run. Fill the compressor oil cup to within ½" from the top and replace it on the compressor. Ordinary mineral oil can be used. Check the V-belt tension; there should be a little play in it. Check all the fittings on the compressor and be sure they are tight. Remove the drain plug in the air filter and give the compressor its first run. If there is a pinging sound detected, the fan blades are hitting the V-belt. Stop the power, reach in through the fan guard and gently twist the fan blades. Turn the belt by hand to see if the blades clear it. Turn the unit on again. If all sounds well, stop the machine and replace the drain plug in the filter. Start the unit again; hold a white cloth over the filler yoke and check to see if there are any deposits on it after a minute or two. If nothing appears on the cloth, the machine is pumping good diving air. Next, place a Scuba tank in the filler yoke, but do not open the tank valve. Start the machine and let the pressure build up to 2000 psi. Watch it as the unit does not require much time to build up this pressure. Stop the machine and listen for leaks. If seepage is heard, put saliva around the fittings to determine which one is leaking. Tighten the leaking part. Do not let the pressure at 2000 psi hold in the lines for more than three to four minutes. This pressure backs against the cylinder pistons and could cause damage to the compressor in time.

It has been determined that all is well, so the unit is started again, the pressure is allowed to build up to 500 psi, then the tank valve is opened very slowly for the first filling. Most tanks are never sucked dry of air, therefore the compressor has a 500 psi buildup to offset any air pressure in the tank. It would be best to check each tank to determine how much air it contains prior to filling. If a tank contains over 500 psi of air, then let the compressor line pressure build up to the poundage read in the tank before opening the tank valve.

When the tank is filled, turn off the tank valve first, shut off the power, and slowly open the air filter drain plug. *Do not open the drain plug too fast.* Open it at arm's length or have a cloth rag between you and the drain plug as the trapped oil and moisture will spurt out the hole driven by a 2000+ psi air force. *Do not* remove the tank from the filler yoke until all the pressure has been drained from the lines.

The compressor may be hot; however this is natural as the little machine is turning up almost 10,000 rpm. The compressor fan, which blows air down to assist in cooling the piston housings, is unable to keep them from heating up. Large trailer-mounted and stationary compressor piston housings heat up.

Always fill diving tanks in the open where there is pure air. *Do not* fill in a garage or building where the air is stale or perhaps mixed with carbon monoxide or paint fumes. These gases in a diving tank can easily kill a diver.

When using the gasoline engine, add a flexible pipe to the engine exhaust system and lead it away from the unit. Be sure the wind is blowing away from the compressor so the exhaust fumes cannot be sucked into the compressor air intake and pumped into the Scuba tank.

In short, execute extreme care when filling diving tanks as your life could depend upon the safety measures you employ.

FLOATING MARKER BUOYS

The files of International contain many different types of marker buoys used for various purposes. A diving business should have a selection of at least three of those described in this section. They are simple to build and inexpensive.

Floating Marker Buoy. This simple buoy, shown in Fig. 57, is made from a small can (2″ inside diameter by 4″ in height), the bottom of a larger can to make the flange, a wooden spool and a rubber ball. Two washers, three dowels, a little lead, and a snap hook will complete the job.

The can should be thoroughly cleaned and dried. Using a larger can with a 4″ to 4½″ bottom, cut along the side of the can so the rim remains. File and pound the edge of the rim smooth. With a ball-peen hammer, tap the bottom to the curvature shape of a saucer. A hole is drilled up an inch from the bottom of the can for the spool and the two washers are soldered beside the holes on the inside of the can. A dowel is fitted through the spool, and a small button knob is made from any type of material to fit into the shaft so the marker can be re-used. Another hole is drilled 3/16 inch from the top rim, extending through the can. This hole should be no larger than ⅛ inch diameter, and a single dowel can be used to hold the ball inside the

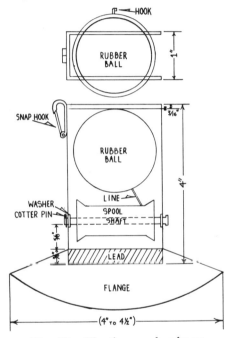

Fig. 57.   Floating marker buoy.

can, or the two-dowel arrangement, as shown in the diagram. In either case, a button knob is fitted to the dowel for easier extracting. A line should be tied to the knob and attached to the can to prevent loss of the marker security pin.

The flange can be bolted, riveted or soldered. If bolted, don't forget to use washers and secure the flange before pouring in the ⅜ inch of lead. When soldering, the lead may be poured before the flange is attached.

A thin-shanked, high-walled spool is best for this type of marker. At least 50 to 100 feet of line should be used. When the spool is placed in the can, the turning shaft (dowel) is given a generous coating of glue and slipped in place and the cotter pin secured.

The marker is either a hollow or sponge type rubber ball. If sponge, thread a large darning needle with the line and push it from the bottom of the ball, pull it out on top and tie the loose top end around the bottom line again. The same method applies to the hollow ball, but use a little tire patching glue to cement the holes around the line. The ball should be dipped in fluorescent or brightly colored paint.

The final step is soldering the snap hook on the top side of the can. The snap hook enables you to attach the marker to your weight belt or salvor's access belt.

Bottleneck Marker Buoy. Another type of safety-marker buoy is the bottleneck marker buoy, Fig. 58. This is even easier to make than the two-log floating type.

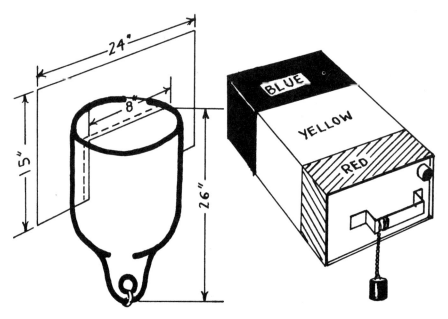

Fig. 58.   (Left) Bottleneck marker buoy.   (Right) Can marker buoy.

The log is stripped of all the bark and taken down with a draw shave to a smooth surface. With a small hatchet or a wood lathe, the bottom section is shaped, as shown in the diagram. The rough spots should be sandpapered. When this step has been completed, a

List of Materials

1	Log (Pine)	(8" to 10") x 26"
1	Board (Pine)	1/4" x 15" x 24"

9/32" or 5/16" groove should be sawed into the log at least 4 inches deep. This is to hold the sign. An anchor hole is drilled at the neck of the marker buoy to attach the anchor line. This floating marker buoy will provide the diver with a maximum of topside safety.

The square 1-gal. gasoline can has been put to many uses since it was first introduced on the American market. The divers of International's staff use it to mark areas and objects found on the bottom. This can, painted a bright yellow and red (the red is a fluorescent paint which allows night spotting if necessary), is anchored by a light chain to the object on the bottom. These markers are usually carried in the craft which follows the diver, and they are placed in the water at the diver's directions.

The cans are obtainable in many different places. If the diver has no luck finding 1-gal. gasoline cans, any type of marker about the same size will serve the purpose very well. Using these marker buoys to mark bottom objects will save divers and topside men a great deal of work.

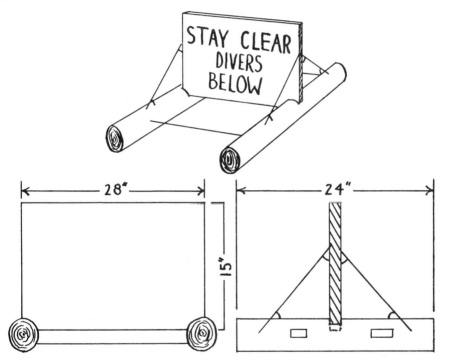

Fig. 59. Two-log floating safety sign.

Safety-marker Buoy. Safety-marker buoys are of utmost importance when divers are working below the water. They are placed in the area where the diver is working to warn motorists, yachtsmen, etc., that a diver is working down below and to stay clear of that area. Any time you go below to work, no matter where, it is best to set out these safety-marker buoys, just to be on the safe side. You can never tell when some fool will come ripping up the waterways in his flashy little skipper and hack you to pieces with his fancy speed prop. It could happen—and happen to you—so play safe and live longer.

The floating safety sign shown in Fig. 59 is simply designed and requires a minimum of carpentry ability. But it serves the purpose well.

List of Materials

2	Logs	Approx. 6" x 24"
2	Crossmembers	1" x 3" x 28"
1	Board	1" x 15" x 28"
4	Braces	1" x 3" x (?)

The logs are grooved to hold the sign, crossmembers and braces. The grooves for the sign should be cut into the center of the log to give it some support. Holes are also made for the crossmembers, which can be placed any desired distance apart. When the holes have been cleared and the crossmembers placed in, drill a hole down from the top of the log so that it goes through the crossmember. The hole should be slightly larger than a 20-penny nail. Flat grooves should be made for the braces.

This safety-marker buoy has been designed to be completely portable. The holes are drilled through the logs and into the crossmembers to allow 20-penny nails to go through them to serve as pegs. The braces will be held in place by common door hooks, such as are used on the back screen door. Four hooks will be screwed into the sign and four into the logs, thus holding the sign steady and the braces fast. Since this marker buoy is easily portable, it will take up very little room in the diver's supply compartment in the utility chest.

Signal Flag Marker Buoy. Figure 60 shows a signal flag marker buoy. The U.S. Navy has used signal flags aboard ship for many years. Most of the country's boatmen and yachtsmen know these flags on sight. The Navy uses a solid red flag, baker flag, which has among its meanings, "Diver Down."

The International Diver's Flag, which has been declared official, should be used for underwater work. It is a 15-in. square flag of red with a diagonal white stripe.

List of Materials

2 pcs.	Pine Planking	2" x 8" x 20"
1 "	Dowel	1/2" x 30"

The two pieces of pine planking are given 2 coats of shellac, 2 coats of varnish, then nailed together. A ½-inch hole is drilled 3 inches deep in the center. The dowel is glued in this hole. Or, if preferred, the hole may be drilled completely through the floating base, allowing the dowel to stick through. In this case, a small hole is drilled through the bottom of the dowel and another about 4½ inches up from the bottom. A nail can serve as a pin to stop the dowel from

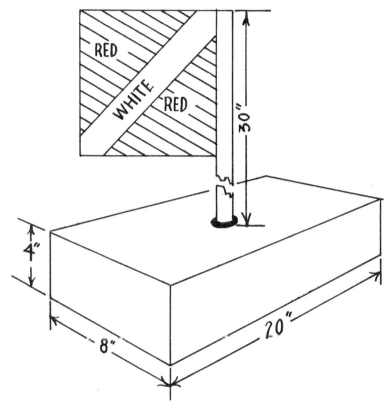

Fig. 60.   Signal flag marker buoy.

going completely through the floating base. Another nail (or brad) is used at the bottom of the dowel. A piece of red cloth is cut and sewed to fit down over the dowel. When purchasing the material for the flag, try to get material which will not run or fade when it gets wet.

AIR DRUM FLOATS

Air drum floats are made from strong metal (preferably steel) 55-gallon drums, obtainable at barrel manufacturers, garages, junk yards, etc. Examine them carefully for breaks, dents, rusty seams, etc., and be sure the bunghole is in working order.

A standard screw-handle water faucet is brazed onto the drum opposite the bunghole, and the needle valve is brazed just under the bunghole on the single A.D. Float.

On the double A.D. Float system, two barrels are welded together by metal bars, as shown in Chapter III, Fig. 7. Both ends of the barrel are joined together by this bar method. A needle valve is brazed to a manifold, which is welded in position, either between the two barrels approximately in the middle, or on the end with the bunghole and faucet, as shown.

This unit is operated by opening the bunghole and the faucet to admit water for sinking. Once it has been secured to the object to be raised, the bunghole is closed, and the hose from the topside compressor is attached to the needle valve. The compressed air will force the water out the open faucet. When air bubbles can be seen coming from the faucet, it should be closed slowly. As the object starts to rise from the bottom, the air hose is removed from the needle valve. A signal is sent to the tenderman to stop the compressor.

The salvor should stay with the rising object, but at a safe distance. However, should the unit begin to rise too fast, the diver should open the faucet, thus releasing some air to slow the ascent. Some A.D. Float systems have had hoses connected to the barrels leading to the surface for the release of the air pressure. In this manner, the tenderman can control the rate of ascent, while the diver supplies hand signals from a safe distance.

If used carefully, these drums will give long service.

UNDERWATER BLADES

One of the safety tools that a diver should always carry with him is a knife. There are many different types of knives, floating and otherwise, on the American market. Some of these knives are good, while others "wouldn't cut hot butter." Any knife carried below by a diver should be a solid weapon, able to cut most of the entanglements which divers encounter. A good blade to carry below should be at least 7 inches long with a saw edge on the back. Divers will be surprised at the number of times the saw on a knife will be used (see Fig. 61).

The members of International Undersea Services have developed a highly satisfactory knife to use in underwater operations. It is constructed from a steel hacksaw blade like those used to cut steel railroad tracks. Although it is brittle, once a good edge has been worked on it with the emery wheel, it will stay that way for long periods. A point to remember is that, while underwater, the teeth of any saw should be pointing toward the diver rather than away from him; the cut is always made on the draw.

Once the blade has been shaped as shown in Fig. 61, two holes are drilled in the shank to fasten on the handle. Should the diver choose wood or cork for the handle, these materials are easily worked.

The cork is wrapped around the blade shank and glued all the way. When the maker thinks he has wrapped enough cork about the shank, he cuts off the surplus and glues the loose end firmly. The wrapping should be kept tight. When the glue is thoroughly dry, the handle is shaped on the emery wheel to suit the diver's tastes.

If wood is used, two pieces are cut and grooved to fit the blade shank. Then, the handle may be shaped to any desired style by a knife and sander. The two handle pieces are secured to the shank by rivets.

Plastic handles are made in a number of ways. One of the easiest is to cut 1″ x 1½″ pieces, drill out a slot in the center of each and slip them down the shank until it is covered. Colors can be added by either painting the blade shank, or, to give a blend of colors, paint the inside of the slot of the pieces. Many colors can be used, and all will show up through the plastic.

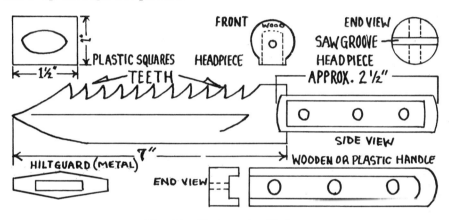

Fig. 61. Underwater blades.

When enough plastic pieces have been drilled and slipped on the shank, the headpiece is screwed on and then the handle is ground on the wheel to any desired shape.

Headpieces and hiltguards are not necessary on the wooden or cork handles, but both the headpiece and hiltguard are required on the plastic pieces. If sheet plastic is used, these pieces are unnecessary. To make a blade using the plastic pieces for the handle will require a little time and work; the other knives are comparatively simple to make.

The hiltguard is cut from a piece of marine brass. A slot is drilled in the center, so that it will fit on the blade shank. Dimensions are left to each maker.

Headpieces are made from wood and shaped as desired. They are grooved to fit over the top of the blade shank, and are attached by riveting.

Cases for the knives may be made from plastic, wood, canvas, cloth, leather, or imitation leather.

WEIGHT BELT

The weight belt is another important piece of diving equipment and, although the ones offered on the market are not expensive, weight belts can be made by the diver at a fraction of the cost of the ready-made ones.

Weight belts may consist of many things. The author once used a heavy monkey wrench, but this was a case of extreme emergency. All weight belts should have quick-release buckles. If a diver makes his own belt, he must know how to put on a quick-release buckle.

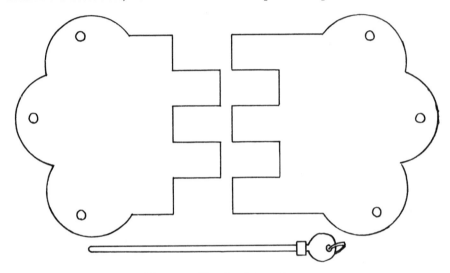

Fig. 62. Metal safety release.

The surplus Army web cartridge belt serves to make an excellent weight belt. Up to 20 pounds may be carried in the ten pouches. Since the original metal clasp is rather awkward to unhook or release under water, a different safety release is substituted (*see* Figs. 62 and 63).

Wood may be used for the safety release, but may have to be re-placed because of its swelling and warping out of shape.

A piece of pine, approximately ¾" x 3" x 5", is cut with a jig saw in the manner indicated in the diagram. A slit is cut in both ends to allow the web belt to be attached. A hole with diameter slightly larger than the pin is drilled down through the buckle, as shown. The pin can be made from a piece of coat-hanger wire. A small chain is used to attach the pin to the weight belt through one of the numerous eyelets.

The diver can taper the buckle from ¾" at the end to ½" toward the middle, if he desires. In no case should the buckle be less than ½" at the joining point.

A surprisingly satisfactory substitute for the wooden buckle is the kind of hinge used on removable seasonal doors.

The hinge is filed at the joining points so that there is some play between the connections. The locking pin is filed to be slightly smaller, and a hole is drilled in the head for a ring. The hinge is then riveted to the web belt.

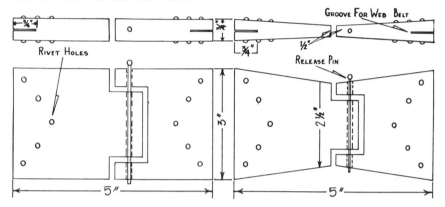

Fig. 63. (Left, top and bottom) Wooden safety releases. (Right, top and bottom) Tapered wooden safety releases.

UNDERWATER LIGHT CASING

The simplest underwater light source is the common flashlight with a waterproof casing (*see* Fig. 64). Bel-Aqua Water Sports Company, and the Pennsylvania Rubber Company manufacture waterproof cases. The Lennan Company makes the insides of a special underwater flashlight as well as the case, but a diver can make these cases at little cost and labor.

List of Materials

1 Section of bicycle innertube	1 Screw clamp
1 Round piece of 1/4" plexiglass	1 Tube of waterproofing glue

This particular case can be constructed in two different ways, employing the same materials:

Case 1. Cut the plexiglass to fit exceptionally tight in one end of the innertube. When the glass is snug, remove it, and wash the inside of the innertube with gasoline around the top section where the plexiglass sets. A coating of waterproof glue is applied to the inside of the innertube and the plexiglass lens is set in place. To secure a solid weld, the clamp should be screwed on tightly and left in place for at least 24 hours.

The other end of the innertube is folded over after the light has been inserted. Be sure you leave approximately 4 inches of rubber lapping over from the end of the flashlight. This excess material is folded over and tied or clamped securely. Test the case for water-tightness before putting a flashlight in it.

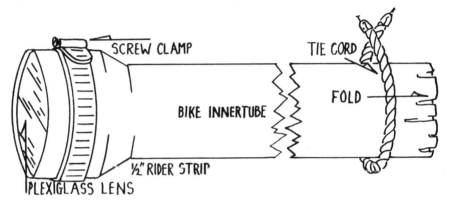

Fig. 64. Underwater light casing (Case #1).

Case 2, The same material is used in the construction of the second case, the only difference being that the plexiglass lens is not glued to the top of the innertube. Instead, the bottom of the case is glued as shown in Fig. 65. The lens and screw clamp must be removed each time the flashlight is inserted or taken out.

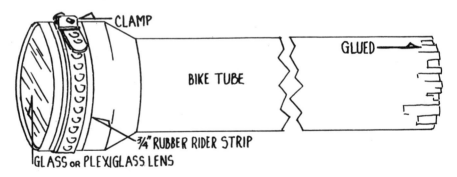

Fig. 65. Underwater light casing (Case #2).

A small ½″ strip of rubber should be glued around the outside top section of the case. This is for the clamp to ride on. The lens should not be placed below the rider strip.

Either case will work sufficiently for projects which do not require a great amount of light. Both cases can be made to fit any length flashlight from 2 to 6 cells.

Note: **Forty feet is maximum safe depth for flashlights.**

UNDERWATER LIGHTS

Underwater lights are not easy to make in the home workshop. Following is a description of two which have been constructed and tested with good results. The cost of building these lights is small, but they do require some time and effort.

These two lights are constructed of the same materials, though the portable light requires a little more equipment.

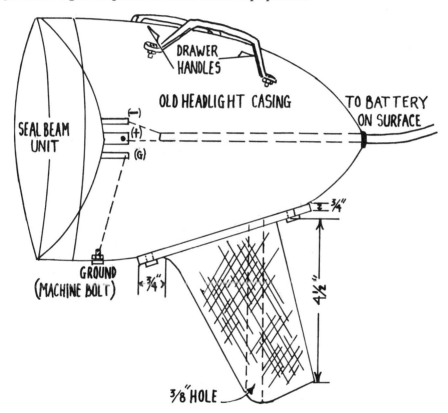

Fig. 66.   Underwater light with surface current.

Surface-powered Light. The underwater light, whose power is supplied from the surface, (*see* Fig. 67), operates on a standard automobile battery, either 6 or 12 volts; the portable light, shown in Fig. 68, operates on flashlight batteries, either 4 or 8, depending upon the voltage requirements of the light used.

The sealed-beam headlamp is purchased at any garage or automotive supply dealer—either 6v. or 12v. At the rear of the lamp are three prongs: positive, negative, and ground. The sealed-beam lamp is placed in an automobile headlamp housing usually obtainable at a local junkyard. This type of headlight casing is found on cars made prior to 1939.

List of Materials

1	Sealed-beam headlamp	2	Handles (metal)
1	Headlamp housing	1	Steel Rod
1	Automobile battery (6v. or 12v.)	1	Base (metal or weighted)
1	Wooden grip	1	100 ft. insulated rubber wire

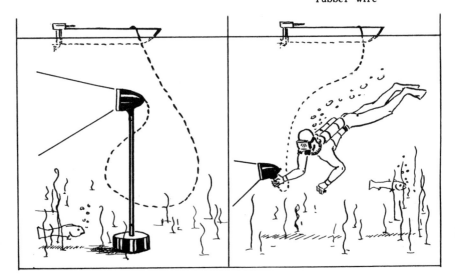

Fig. 67.   Surface-powered light.

A ¼″ hole is drilled at the rear of the housing to allow the wires to pass through. The ground wire can be attached to any part of the metal housing. The best method of grounding is to drill a hole in the housing for a metal or machine bolt. The wire from the ground prong should be soldered securely; the other end is wrapped around the bolt.

Before any wires are attached, certain steps must be taken to make over the housing. The two metal drawer handles· are bolted to the top of the lamp housing in the manner indicated in the diagram. The wooden handle grip under the housing is made from ¾″ stock (oak). The top is curved to conform to the curvature of the lamp housing, and then bolted with machine bolts at the point where the unit will balance well. A ⅜″ hole is drilled through the handle only. This is for the base stand rod when the light is maintained in a stationary position. Remember to drill the hole at such an angle that the light will lie perfectly horizontal.

All wires attached to the metal prongs of the sealed-beam lamp are soldered and then potted, the process of encasing bare wires in wax. This is a waterproofing measure. A small mailing tube will serve as the mold in which to pour the liquid wax. The ground wire is now attached to the bolt and the lamp is placed in the housing and secured.

Topside, the positive (+) wire is connected to the battery's positive pole and the negative (—) wire to the negative pole.

Portable Underwater Light. A portable underwater light is not easy to build. The materials used in this unit are similar to those used in the surface-powered light.

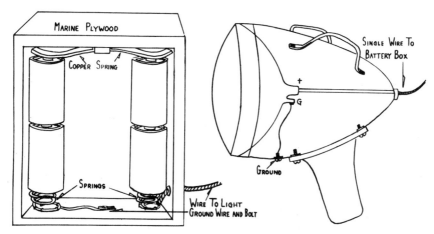

Fig. 68.   Portable underwater light.

The headlight housing is worked in much the same manner as the one described previously. A wooden pistol-type grip is bolted to the underside of the housing, and a wooden rather than a metal handle is used on the top. The bolt is placed in the underside to serve as a ground, and the wire hole is drilled at the rear of the housing.

List of Materials

1 Sealed-beam headlamp (6v. or 12v.)	1 Spring
1 Headlamp housing	1 Copper metal strip
1 Wooden grip	1 Stove bolt
1 Wooden drawer-type grip	1 Length of insulated wire
1 Watertight battery box	

The watertight container is made to contain the batteries which are of the standard flashlight type. The box is constructed of marine plywood as indicated in the diagram. It should be just large enough for the four or eight batteries (depending on which voltage light selected), the spring, copper metal strip, and wire lead.

The batteries are placed in the box head-to tail. A ½″ copper strip is attached to the top of the box by small screws and is bent so that the battery poles will touch it to complete the circuit. Between the two rows of batteries, a stove bolt is placed, to act as a ground. The ground is accomplished by running a wire from the bolt to the spring under one of the batteries, as shown.

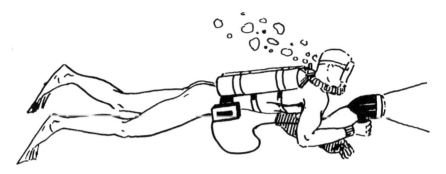

Fig. 69.   Diver using portable underwater light.

A single insulated wire is used with this hookup; it is attached to the positive prong of the sealed-beam lamp. Running from the positive prong of the sealed-beam lamp, it goes to the battery box, passes through a watertight hole, and is attached to the underside of the other spring and battery. Test the circuit to see if the light comes on. If it does not, reverse the ground wire over to the other spring and run the single lead wire under the spring and battery on the other side.

As shown in the drawing, canvas is used to make the battery-box loops, so that it may be attached to the diver. If the sealed-beam lamp prongs have been potted, and the connections are entirely insulated and solid, this circuit will produce light in good strength. However, the batteries will have to be replaced often.

The author suggests that the surface-powered light be used in most all operations. Although the portable underwater light will work sufficiently, it is expensive and tricky. As Mr. Alan Atkins, of the Department of Physics, University of Maine, who designed the circuits for this light, points out, at best the portable underwater light will last for only a few hours.

DIVER-TENDER COMMUNICATION SET

Figure 70 shows an inexpensive communication set developed by Paul Thompson, Jr., Chief of the Electronics Research Division and Mr. Ronald Atkins, of the University of Maine.

The set consists of an induction coil, a telephone transmitter, two sets of headphones, a surplus Air Force throat mike, a 4-pole, 8-throw switch, two 4-plug sockets and two 4-pronged plugs. Everything can be made on a flat board with the two 1.5-volt dry cell batteries attached to the side, back, or elsewhere.

The induction coil is the hardest part of the set to build—especially if one attempts it by hand. It is advisable to have an electric motor rewinding shop make it for you, or to purchase it from a radio supply house.

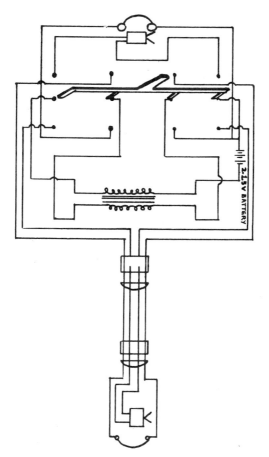

Fig. 70. Diver-tender communication set.

The induction coil laminated strips are thin, but there should be enough so that when they are squeezed together, the coil measures 3/4" high. When the bundle is completed insulation paper is wrapped around them and varnish is applied thoroughly.

Next, take the 28-gauge wire (which is known as the primary wire), and wrap it about the induction coil strips 300 turns. This should be about the length of the core. The ends of the wire should be left exposed so that the wire of the rest of the set may be soldered to them. Cut a layer of insulation paper and wrap it around the 28-gauge wire, then give this a coat of varnish.

List of Materials

Induction coil laminated strips	1 Throat microphone (USAF surplus)
3/4" x 1/2" x 6"	2 Sets headphones
Insulation paper	1 Set 4" foam rubber earphone caps
28 gauge wire	1 Telephone transmitter (speaking end)
32 gauge wire	1 4-pole, 8-throw switch
(These four items make an in-	2 4-pronged plugs
duction coil with a 1-5 ratio.)	2 4-plug sockets
2 1.5v. dry-cell batteries	

The secondary wrapping (32-gauge wire) is wound around the core 1,500 turns. When the wrapping reaches the end of the core, a layer of insulation paper is varnished about the wrapping. Then, the wrapping is reversed, going back to the starting point until the full 1,500 turns have been completed. Remember, after the wire has been wound the full length of the core, a layer of insulation paper is varnished on. The loose-end wires of the 32-gauge wire go to the receiver, while the 28-gauge wire is connected to the transmitter.

The use of the 4-pole 8-throw switch eliminates the construction of another set to match this one. The switch allows the diver to listen while the tender speaks, and vice versa. Of course, if the tender wishes, he can cut off all conversation by throwing the switch to the no-contact position.

As for the earphones and throat mike, the Palley Supply Company will be glad to assist you, and their prices are reasonable. The Allied Radio Company can furnish all the necessary parts that are unavailable in your vicinity.

This set can be built for less than $10.00, and it is a great asset in many underwater jobs.

CAMERA CASE

Figure 71 shows one of the simplest camera cases the self-contained diver or underwater explorer can build.

Cut a 24" section of innertube and, in the middle on one side, cut a 3" x 5" rectangular hole; on the other side, cut a 2" x 4" rectangular hole. The lucite glass, such as is used in the rear windows of convertible cars, can be purchased at any shop that does that type of repair. Buy a small tube of 3-M weather-strip adhesive (black) and a waterproof cement manufactured by the Minnesota Mining and Manufacturing Company.

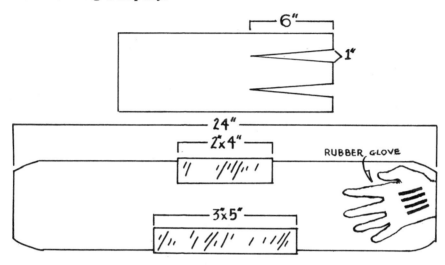

Fig. 71. Camera case.

With gasoline, wash the surface of the innertube where the front lucite port lens will fit, then wash the edge of the lens port. Apply a generous coat of the adhesive and set the lens port in place. If spots of the adhesive get on the inside or outside of the lens, a little gasoline on a cloth will remove the spots after the adhesive has dried. The rear port lens is cemented in place in the same manner as the front lens.

List of Materials

Quantity	Materials	Use
1	7 x 16 innertube, 24" long	Camera case
2	1/16" x 4" x 6" lucite (glass) 1/16" x 3" x 5"	Port lenses
1	Rubber glove (right or left)	Operating controls
8	3/4" innertube strips	Port lens coverings

Cut ¾" wide strips of innertube to cement over the outer edge of the port lenses to insure a watertight seal.

The rubber glove is cemented to either end, depending upon whether the diver is left- or right-handed. V-shaped sections of rubber are cut from the chosen end about 1" wide and 6" deep. This is to make the case hole smaller so as to fit the gauntlet of the rubber glove. When the hole is small enough, the slits are cemented together and then the gauntlet is cemented in, as shown in the drawing. The other end is left open to insert the camera.

When a camera is inserted in this case, fold over the end and secure it either with a heavy rubber band or a C-clamp (the C-clamp works best, for it acts as a handle). Before the diver enters the water, the hand is placed in the rubber glove and the camera is adjusted so that the camera lens lines up with the front port lens, and, if necessary, the back lens is lined so that the diver will be able to read the number of the next picture.

Remember to test your case before putting your best camera in it.

WOODEN UNDERWATER CAMERA HOUSING

The camera case shown in Fig. 72 is constructed from ¾" thick marine plywood. It is shaped exactly like any rectangular box, with a hole sawed in either side (depending upon which hand you use) large enough to admit your hand. This hole is for a rubber glove, which is sealed in watertight.

Around the top of the box is a ¾" lip. At the distance of every 2 inches, holes are drilled for wing-nut bolts. These holes are centered in the lip. A rubber gasket is made for the lip and holed accordingly. The top of the box is also constructed of the same material and made to fit to the far edge of the lip. Holes are drilled through the top in accordance with those in the lip and gasket.

It makes a difference whether your camera is of 35 mm. type or box-type. If it is the latter, the lens ports will be cut out of the front and rear of the housing, with the glove control hole in the side. If the camera is of the 35 mm. type, the lens port (only one) is cut on the side, and the glove control hole in either end.

If the camera has a range finder and the diver wishes to use it, a rear lens port will be necessary.

This type of housing can be constructed to fit any type of camera. It can be as large or as small as desired, but it must be remembered that there should be room left on the side in which the glove is to be sealed—room enough to allow free movement of the hand and fingers.

The lens ports are attached from the outside and sealed with a rubber gasket (innertube) and waterproof glue, plus matching bolts. The lens port is plexiglass, at least ¼" thick. All joints should have a good application of a waterproofing compound to insure against leakage.

Always remember to test your housing first without your camera. If the water does not seep in on the first two or three dives, you can then use a camera.

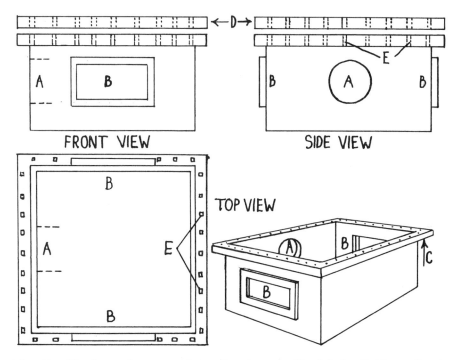

Fig. 72. Wooden underwater camera housing. A. Hand hole; B. Ports (lens); C. Cover flange; D. Cover; E. Wing nut holes. Material: Marine plywood, plexiglass, gaskets (rubber), cement (glue), wing nuts, screws, rubber glove.

Chapter X

UNDERWATER CAMERA MAGIC

There are many divers who "cut their teeth" on a camera's lens and have made money with their home-built darkrooms and equipment. When a photographer desires to combine his knowledge of camera magic and diving to reproduce the beauties of Mother Nature's great blue kingdom, there are only a few additional principles and pieces of equipment which must be employed. Aside from the watertight camera housings and a camera, the undersea photographer should have a knowledge of light conditions below.

A cameraman, depending upon his own powers of vision, imagination and creativeness, will be able to take exceptionally good pictures with a Kodak "Brownie." Many prize-winning photographs have been taken by amateurs using $5.00 cameras; on the other hand, someone without imagination and knowledge may own an $800.00 Leica camera set and be unable to produce a photograph worth a nickel. But when a good lensman has a good camera, the final results can be sheer beauty.

The author and his associates, in exploring the possibilities of marketing underwater photographic work, came up with some very promising leads.

High schools, colleges and universities can use 35 mm. color transparencies in sets or single shots for classroom instruction. Restaurants, libraries and museums use large black-and-white and color pictures for display or advertising. Murals can be sold to department stores and other businesses having a connection with the sea. Films are used by research organizations, theatres, television studios, schools, and theatrical-booking agencies. The underwater photographer might also establish a film rental library. Other possibilities will be discussed later.

THE FUNDAMENTALS OF UNDERWATER PHOTOGRAPHY

Lighting. The amount of natural light penetrating beneath the surface rapidly diminishes with each foot of depth. Not only the water itself, but small microscopic organisms like plankton, which live near the surface of the water, can diminish the light. There are times when the plankton is so thick that it would be almost impossible to take any pictures, because their density blocks out the sun's rays.

188

The effects of cloudy and bright days vary greatly in the blue kingdom. The angles of projection of light rays and the clearness and stillness of the water can distort things. Relatively smooth waters ruffled by winds and rains permit less light to penetrate beneath the surface waters than on a calm day.

Fig. 73. A plexiglass camera housing and the Hydro-pak; a camera and an adventurer are the full requirements to reproduce the beauties of Mother Sea on photographic plates. (Capt. Jordan Klein, Miami, Fla.)

Ninety percent of the white light entering the water is absorbed between 26 feet and 30 feet. At 100 feet, there is approximately 1% of white light remaining. Colors cease to be present at various depths. Red, the least penetrating ray, loses 90% of its strength at 16½ feet.

Scientists have exposed photographic plates at various depths in the ocean. Red rays were weak at 330 feet. Blue and violet rays registered on the plates at 1,640 feet. After an 80-minute exposure at 3,280 feet, only violet and ultraviolet rays appeared on the plates. Some of the plates were exposed for a long time to absorb all possible traces of color at the various depths. At ⅓ of a mile, darkness is complete. Over the depth of a mile, there is no light whatsoever.

The maximum depth for shooting black-and-white stills is 225 feet. Employing the natural light source at this depth, the pictures arc shot at 1/5 of a second with an f.2 lens opening. The underwater photographer will take a majority of his shots between the surface and 50 feet. Camera speeds, in this instance, will range from 1/25 second to 1/50 second, depending upon the type and emulsion speed of the film.

Exposures. Each film has an emulsion speed, which is normally indicated on all standard brands of films. A fast emulsion speed requires a smaller lens opening or a faster shutter speed.

If the underwater photographer uses a camera which has no iris diaphragm or shutter speeds, it is best that he use either Super XX film or the new Kodak Tri-X. Since his lens is preset, everything that comes into the camera's range is in focus, except for very close objects.

With cameras having lens openings and shutter speeds, shooting between the surface and 50 feet down, at speeds of 1/25 to 1/50 of a second, the lens opening should be f.16 at the surface and f.3.5 at 50 feet. These openings, of course, are only for standard weather conditions, such as a bright sunny day and a good sandy bottom where the sun's rays will be reflected back toward the surface. With a hazy sunlight, a ½ stop larger opening is required, and dark bottoms may require 1 or 2 stops larger lens opening.

The author has used many types of films and has found that Kodak Plus-X produces the best results in taking pictures below the waters; though, of course, Ansco Supreme also does an excellent job.

The new Eastman film, Tri-X, with an emulsion speed of 200, is proving to be outstanding for underwater photography. But the high-speed films are apt to be somewhat grainy.

Color. Though photography requires more expensive film and equipment, it also follows that more money will be gained from the sale of colored pictures. Only a few days ago, the author viewed a 20-exposure roll of 35 mm. color film dealing with the history of the sea. All of the pictures were staged reproductions; there were no real underwater scenes. But the price was enough to make a good dent in a ten-dollar bill!

However, underwater color photography presents a number of problems. The red in the spectrum is quickly absorbed by the water and "true" color balance is impossible to achieve. Actually, however, photographers taking underwater pictures are not concerned over this "true" color balance, since what they want primarily is an underwater picture that looks like a similar scene examined "first-hand" with their eyes.

The color of the water changes from hour to hour because of the color of the floating particles or rock, and the kinds and amount of plankton or minute floating plants and animals in the water. Consequently, rendering the underwater scene in its natural condition is quite convenient. Usually, it requires only one set of filters ranging from light to pale rose. Without a filter, color pictures taken at a depth of 15 feet are very bluish. Employing a filter, good pictures are taken without a bluish cast on them at depths up to 50 feet.

These previous comments, of course, have applied specifically to making color photographs under water. The problem involved in black-and-white picture taking are not nearly so complex, being primarily concerned with exposures (and occasional filtration) for various depths. Table 14 shows underwater exposures for both black-and-white and color picture taking and, while illumination conditions may vary rather widely with specific subjects and in particular localities, this exposure information will provide an excellent basis for making first tests.

Table 14. Table of Underwater Exposures Bright Sunlight—Light Bottom*

	2-5 ft.	10 ft.	20 ft.	50 ft.	Hazy Sunlight
Black & white Film Plus-X & K2 Filter					
Movies at 24 f.p.s. Stills at 1/50 sec.	f/16	f/11-f/8	f/8-f/5.6	f/3.5-f/2.8	1/2 stop larger opening
Kodachrome Film Daylight Type With Wratten No. 86**					1/2 stop larger. No wave action
Movies at 24 f.p.s.					
Stills at 1/50 sec.	f/11-f/8	f/5.6-f/4.5	f/4.5-f/3.5	f/2.8 at a 1/30 sec.	seen on bottom gives unreal effect

* Dark bottom may require one or two stops more opening.
** At depths greater than 40 to 50 feet, use 86B Filter.
(Courtesy, Eastman-Kodak)

A very simple method of determining the strength of the red rays is to paint a 2″ round rock red, have your diving partner drop it from the surface, and you follow it down. Normally, at 15 feet, it will become almost green, though local conditions may vary this figure somewhat. When the color change begins, the diving photographer should mentally check the depth on his depth gauge. Thus, by using this simple method, a diver can adjust his camera lens openings and filters to produce good color shots.

The 35 mm. color film is about the least expensive to use. Rolls are available in 20 and 36 exposures. Daylight type film is the best for underwater work. The Wratten 86 and 86B filters are used for correcting color loss. The Wratten Filter Series can be used with all types of color film.

Cameras. Schools, universities, laboratories, research organizations, and lecturers are more likely to purchase 35 mm. color transparencies than color films of a larger size. The 35 mm. projectors are inexpensive, small and portable; whereas the opaque projector, which produces actual pictures, either black-and-white or color, on a screen, is rather large and expensive. The 35 mm. transparencies are small (2¼″ x 2¼″) and a rather small case can hold as many as 250 prints.

Because 35 mm. cameras are being used by so many millions, the price for most of the cameras is reasonable. One of America's finest, in the author's opinion, is the Argus C-3, which comes complete with range finder, set of filters, and a good fast lens, which is of great help in taking underwater photographs. Underwater engineering firms have turned out many good usable camera cases to fit all types of 35 mm. cameras. The new Argus C-4 has been used by the author, and its automatic resetting of the shutter button rates it as a leader in the field of cameras to be used in underwater photography operations. Naturally, the simpler the operations of a camera, the more popular it is bound to become with underwater photographers. Since camera housings are so expensive, with the exception of a very few models, automatic cameras eliminate the need for "extra" outside controls, thus cutting the purchase price by many dollars.

On the other hand, 116 and 616 color films produce better murals and large pictures for display and advertising work. A larger negative can be enlarged with less grain, and thereby insure a clearer, more detailed photograph. So, if you have a camera that uses the larger film sizes, don't discard it for a 35 mm., because you may find that you can put it to good use.

Color photography requires only patience and experimentation to determine the proper lens opening and filters. The type of color films used, whether American or foreign, is left to the lensman's judgment. Most foreign color films are pastels, giving no "true" colors, but a beautiful blend of soft, well-balanced shades. There will be many times when the Agfa pastel-color film will present a better picture of life below the seas than the color films manufactured in the United States. Pastel colors are indeed beautiful, and would appear to the general public to be authentic underwater color. On the other hand, photographs for popular magazines or for display purposes should be taken with American-made film.

Movies. The same principles that govern still black-and-white and color photography are employed with movies. The same lens openings and filters are used, but your frame-per-second speed should read 24. Pictures taken on land can be shot at 32 f.p.s. and the human eye will see no difference. The reason film companies had to change the frame speed was the addition of voice. Films shot at 16 f.p.s. with a sound track added had a voice drag, like playing a 78 r.p.m. record at 45 r.p.m. speed, and with the 32 f.p.s. speed, the voice was slightly too fast. The 24-frame speed meets with eye approval as well as ear approval. If you own a motion picture camera which has a range of frame speeds, a camera repair man can adjust the frame speed governor to an exact 24 f.p.s.

U.S. Camera Magazine carries many advertisements of used motion picture cameras, and at reasonable terms. Many photo hints can also be picked up from this fine magazine. The March 1956 issue, for

Fig. 74. Diver-lensman using oxygen rebreather lung and the Franke and Heidecke Rolleimarin camera housing with flash attachment. (Burleigh Brooks Photo)

Fig. 74 A. Navy underwater diver-cameraman maneuvers an Aquarri 35 mm movie camera at a depth of 180 feet in Nassau waters. (U.S. Navy)

example, has plans for the construction of a plexiglass housing to fit the Bolex H-16 motion picture camera.

When purchasing a motion picture camera, almost any 16 mm. type will do the job. Commercial work should be shot with 16 mm. only. Along with the camera's standard lens, there should be an adapter for a revolving lens turret. In order to produce ultra-fine work, especially for science films, a 15 mm. to 20 mm. wide-angle lens, and a 50 mm. to a maximum of 75 mm. telephoto lens is essential.

Care must be exercised when purchasing used cameras and lenses. The lens should be carefully looked over for scratches or bubbles. Footage speeds should be tested against those of new cameras. Focus distances are checked by using a piece of ground glass against a known distance. Take a small light bulb and test the camera for light leaks in the case.

Subjects. The subject matter of your underwater film can range from collections of coral and plant life to the shooting of the blue kingdom's more dangerous creatures, such as sharks, moray eels, barracuda, and octopus . Whatever the subject matter may be, a film script and shooting schedule should be drafted and expedition plans laid out before each filming attempt.

Shooting Techniques. Your film will have professional qualities if you employ a number of the shooting techniques listed below:

Fade In. This is a simple method of introducing the subject matter of your film. If your camera has an iris diaphragm, shooting starts with the diaphragm closed and gradually opens until the proper setting is reached.

Medium Shot. This is the standard distance shot for a scene which has a good deal of action in it. The camera is generally about 15 to 25 feet away from the subject; thus the foreground and background, which are always important in an underwater picture, get into the camera's framer. In taking underwater pictures, it must be remembered that the water magnifies all objects. Your eyes notice the difference and can make the corrections in size and distance, but your camera does not have this power. You will have to judge for yourself.

At 13 feet under water (measured distance), your camera's focus range should read approximately 10 feet.

Medium Close-Up. This is, of course, a closer shot, usually taken at 10 to 15 feet away, On land, as a rule, this would take in a person from head to toe. But, again, remember the magnification of the water and keep a close check on your distances.

Close-Up. The words are self-explanatory. The camera is usually brought within 10 feet of the subject.

Pan. This term (coming from the word, panorama) means to swing the camera horizontally or vertically, arc style, in order to film a larger area or to follow action, such as fish swimming in and out of coral or divers going through their performances. A panning action should always be done slowly and steadily. To get the best results in a panning action, hold the camera steady on the subject for at least 3 seconds, and then swing it very slowly over the complete scene of action or the area where the action is going to take place. Do not, under any circumstances, reverse your direction. At the end of the panning action, you again hold the camera still for another 3-second period before stopping the film.

Titling. When your film is done, it needs a title. Simple titlers may be purchased at any good camera shop or at some of the better mail-order houses. These machines offer great versatility in titling.

There are many other techniques which you will learn as you progress in the underwater movie business; those listed above are intended as an introduction to the subject.

There will be many times when the creatures of the sea will "drop in" on the scene. Sometimes they will be "just what the doctor ordered", whereby the scene receives that much-desired look of authenticity. Good shots of underwater life can also be cut from a scheduled shooting and used in a short film which is designed for just that purpose. Almost all good underwater scenes can be used in some manner; for example, as the background for a film's title, for extra footage between scenes, and for finales. Don't throw away even the smallest piece of good film footage.

Planning a Script. Filming life in the blue kingdom is not a tremendous undertaking; it only requires planning and the assistance of Mother Nature and Mother Sea. The author and his associates contacted H. E., the Governor-General of Jamaica, for permission to photograph the famous pirate stronghold, Port Royale, which lies at the bottom of Kingston Harbour, Jamaica. When Sir Hugh Foot's "Lettre de Cachet," granting the royal permission, was received, the filming expedition plans were formulated.

With a fairly clear idea of the subject of the expedition and filming work, maps of the following types were ordered from American and British map companies: hydrographic, topographic, full-scale maps of Jamaica and enlarged maps of the Kingston Harbour area. Information about the tides, currents, weather, bottom conditions, undercurrents and animal life was also obtained. With this data, the type of diving equipment and emergency gear for this operation could be partially determined.

As soon as these data were a fixed part of each diver's knowledge, the draft script was written up. An overall script was the guide for each day's operation. From this script, which was to be followed as closely as possible, a diving and photographing schedule was designated for each day of operations.

A schedule was also drawn up for the photographic laboratory specialists. Of course, these men were also members of the diving-photography team, but, because of their talents in the lab, a special breakdown had to be set up. At the end of each day, all of the day's filming was taken to the laboratory and developed. In this manner, shots which were out of focus or too dense could be cut from the film strip and rescheduled for another day, or for the beginning of the following day.

A diver who wishes to become a photographer, or vice versa, should read all the literature he can about taking photographs under water. Articles have been written about camera housings and underwater photography since 1928. At first, most of these articles appeared in scientific and trade journals only, but during the past three years, many popular publications, especially the men's magazines, have carried accounts of undersea photographers and their exploits. *The National Geographic* magazine has published some excellent articles and pictures concerning underwater photography. *The Skin Diver*, the best magazine in the world devoted to the skin diver and his world below the sea, is probably the best for self-contained divers to subscribe to, for it carries all types of articles, including underwater photography and its advances.

The bibliography lists selected articles and books which should be read by the diving-photographers. Chapter IX contains plans for camera cases which novices will be able to construct to fit their own particular cameras.

Darkroom Equipment. The following list is included for the photographer who plans to set up his own darkroom to develop and print his film and pictures.

3 Trays	Print washer (wooden or metal)
Chemicals:	Negative washer
Developer (film and paper)	Negative drier
Stop bath	Ferrotype plates (for glossies)
Acid fixer and hardener	Drying blotter (for matte prints)
Timers and thermometers	Contact printer
Mixing vessels	Enlarger (4" x 5" or 5" x 7")
Chemical containers	Easel
Roll film developing tank	Paper stock (8" x 10")

Regarding paper stock, most of the prints a diving-photographer would be making up would be for sale and more than likely for reproduction purposes. So keep in mind that prints used for reproduction are printed on 8 x 10 inch and on glossy paper.

Murals that are to be hand-tinted with transparent oils, should be printed on double-weight matte paper. A photographer who has learned to mix and apply oils can create textures in undersea pictures which actual color films cannot reproduce. Murals and pictures oil-painted by hand command high prices.

Those diver-photographers who have their own darkrooms and have had considerable experience in processing their own film, might like to advance to color processing. Color processing is a bit more difficult than standard black-and-white. There are more steps in color processing and it takes over an hour to process a roll of color film. Also more chemicals are needed, plus a lot of patience and experimentation.

Movie film requires special handling through a machine built to process the rolls. These machines are somewhat expensive, but they do an excellent job. By inquiring around, sometimes it is possible to find a surplus government model or a used one that may be purchased reasonably.

If a diver who used a 35 mm. camera and color film looked over his negatives, he may find enough good shots to make up a small roll of 20 different pictures, closely related, or running in a pictorial history sequence. These single negatives may be reprocessed to make up a roll of 20 to 36 or more exposures. Such series are extremely valuable to teachers of biology, zoology, and physical science.

The Eastman Kodak Company has many inexpensive small booklets covering all phases of photography. It would pay a diving-photographer well to read over a few of these booklets pertaining to the type of photography work he plans to do.

Where to Sell Underwater Photographs. The science departments of high schools and colleges that offer courses in biology, botany, and/or zoology are good prospects for 35 mm. color transparencies, singles and in sets; for 35 mm. color films of sequences; for 5 x 7 and 8 x 10 black-and-white and color singles and sets; and for 16 mm. motion picture in black-and-white and in color, 5 minutes in length, or longer.

Department heads and individual teachers, if you can secure their names, will be interested in receiving your list or catalogue. It should also be sent to marine research organizations and to biological supply houses.

Magazines, department stores, restaurants, advertising agencies, libraries, and museums are always in the market for good black-and-white and color photographs for illustration, advertising, and display.

Types of Photographs Most Easily Sold

5 x 7 b & w and color singles
5 x 7 b & w and color sets
8 x 10 b & w singles and color singles
16 mm. motion pictures, b & w and color (any length)

8 x 10 b & w sets and color sets (story picture series)
35 mm. color singles and color sets
16 mm. motion pictures, b & w and color (5min.)

8 x 10 b & w sets and color sets

Types of Subject Matter

Sea creatures
Fish
Hard shelled animals: lobsters, shellfish, etc.
Sea plants (all types)

Divers in action (singles or picture series for story work)
Soft bellied animals: octopus, jellyfish, etc.
Collections of coral

Seascapes of fish and coral gardens

Chapter XI

THE WONDERS OF PHOTOMICROGRAPHY

Photomicrography is another of the profitable underwater businesses a Scuba diver can enter. This particular field, especially its underwater area, which is only now getting the attention it deserves, offers a wide open field to an ambitious, scientific-minded self-contained diver. If you can process a roll of film and print good photographs (or even take a good picture and have the processing done by a professional studio), you have the beginning of a photomicrography business in your grasp. However, this is a business which should not be jumped into blindly. It will require hours of patient study and experimentation.

First, what is photomicrography? It is the art of taking photographs, employing the use of a microscope. Many people confuse microphotography and photomicrography. Micrography is the product of miniature films used in extremely small cameras, such as those used by the men with the allied intelligence departments during World War II. Photomicrography is the photographing of objects through a microscope.

Secondly, what is the market for photomicrographs? There are thousands of secondary schools that cannot afford 50 or 100 prepared microscopic slides of the same specimen. A diver in the photomicrography business has but to prepare one good slide, photograph it and, from the negatives, print thousands of pictures or 35 mm. projection slides. One good photograph which can be shown in full by an opaque projector or a 35 mm. transparency shown on a screen is worth far more than the old glass microscopic slides. Photographs and film slides can withstand many years of handling; glass slides are easily chipped and broken.

A group of interested divers can collect the materials, prepare the slides, photograph them, process the film, print the pictures, and sell them. Sounds like work? It is. Photomicrography may require the divers to maintain fresh water and marine aquariums to keep living specimens on hand for immediate use. In aquariums, the minute microscopic animals and creatures can be cultured. Under the microscope, these specimens may be photographed alive and in action through a process known as cinephotomicrography. Complete films can be made of the eternal struggles and life cycles of microscopic animals.

Many camera manufacturers supply microscopic attachments for their cameras. The attachments are, for the most part, inexpensively priced. Most of these attachments are for cameras with removable lenses. However, with patience and experiment, photomicrography is possible with cameras which have fixed lenses.

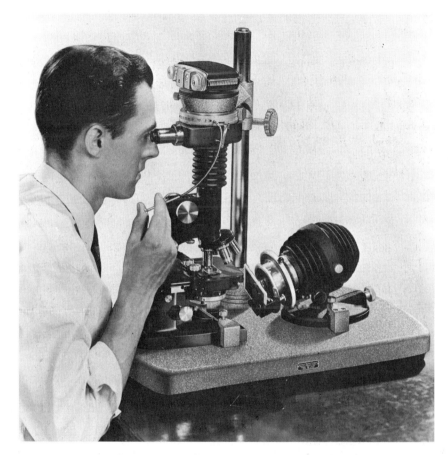

Fig. 75.   Vertical photomicrography setup featuring American Optical Company, Instrument Division, products. (American Optical Co.)

THE SEMI-PROFESSIONAL PROCEDURE

Photomicrography involves the magnification of objects in low, medium and high ranges from 10x to 2,500x diameters. In the semi-professional procedure that will now be outlined, the Kodak Master View Camera, 4 x 5, will be used.*

* The procedures of photomicrography described in this chapter are based on the Eastman Kodak publication, *Photography Through the Microscope*.

The most important factor is aligning the lamp, microscope, and camera on the optical axis of the microscope. Filters, polarizers, etc., will not be taken into consideration during this discusson—only the simplest equipment will be examined.

Step 1. Locate the microscope at the approximate middle of a 30″ x 30″ table. Tip the microscope at the joint (a) so that the microscope tube is parallel to the table top. Remove the substage mirror from the microscope.

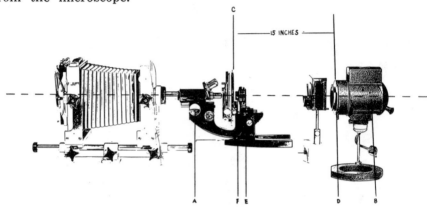

Fig. 76.   Schematic drawing of photomicrographic setup. (Eastman Kodak Co.)

Step 2. Set up the lamp house (b) at about 15 inches from the microscope stage (c), with the lamp-house condenser diaphragm (d) open. This permits a beam of light from the lamp to reach the microscope and allows a rough positioning of the lamp with respect to the axis of the microscope.

The bulb should be positioned in the lamp house so that the filament of the lamp is on the axis of the lamphouse condenser lens. Otherwise, it may be difficult to obtain correct illumination of the specimen.

A water cell must be placed between the lamp-house condenser and the substage condenser to absorb heat from the lamp so that the specimen will not be damaged.

Step 3. Measure the distances from the bench to the center of the lamp-house condenser, to the center of the substage-condenser diaphragm, and to the center of the ocular. Make any adjustments necessary to make these three distances equal.

Step 4. Close the substage-condenser diaphragm (e). Adjust the lamp-house condenser until a sharply focused image of the lamp filament is observed on the closed substage-condenser diaphragm (e).

Step 5. Open the substage-condenser diaphragm (e). Preferably under subdued light conditions, place a white card about 12 inches from the ocular so that subsequent adjustments can be carried out easily by observing the image projected onto the white card. Center the specimen on the microscope stage and focus it on the white card, using a low-power objective and ocular. A special slide containing mounted cross hairs is helpful for this operation. Alignment is obtained more readily with low power.

Step 6. Close the lamp-house condenser diaphragm (d) to a small opening.

Step 7. Rock the substage condenser (f) back and forth until a sharp image of the lamp-house condenser diaphragm (e) is observed on the white card. This should be a very intense bright spot approximately in the center of the field of view as seen on the white card.

Should the whole field of view be difficult to see, open the lamp-house condenser diaphragm until it can be determined whether or not its image is centered in the field of view.

Step 8. If the image is not in the center of the field, adjust the position of the lamp house to center the image.

Step 9. Open the lamp-house condenser diaphragm (d) until its edges coincide with the field of view and are concentric with it. A minor adjustment can be made with the substage-condenser centering screws.

Should it be impossible to illuminate the circular field completely when (d) is fully opened, it is usually an indication that the substage condenser does not have the correct focal length for the objective in use.

Basically, for best resolution, it is necessary to use a substage condenser which has a numerical aperture large enough to fill the back element of the objective with light.

With most condensers, it is possible to remove one or more of the individual optical elements in order to increase the focal length, though on some instruments no mechanical support is provided for the lower lens. Use of the bottom element alone provides the longest possible focal length for a given substage condenser as indicated in Table 14. When removal of the optical elements, one after another, does not permit complete illumination of the circular field, or if the condenser is not divisible, then a condenser of different focal length is needed.

Note: Sometimes, when a burned-out lamp is replaced, the circular field may not be uniformly illuminated. Check the position of the lamp filament to make sure that it is properly centered with respect to the axis of the lamp-house condenser.

Step 10. When a substage condenser of different focal length is installed, Steps 1 to 9 should be rechecked to assure alignment.

At this point, the equipment (except the camera) is in alignment, the object is in focus, and the back element of the objective is filled completely with light.

Step 11. Remove the eyepiece from the microscope and look down the tube at the back element of the objective. Use a neutral density filter (about 2.0) or a piece of heavily smoked glass to protect the eyes from the intense light, or else reduce the intensity of the lamp by means of a suitable rheostat. The back element of the objective should appear filled with light. An image of the lamp filament may also be seen, but it can be disregarded.

Step 12. Close the diaphragm of the substage condenser slowly until the illuminated area of the back lens of the objective (the bright area) is reduced approximately one-third. In other words, about two-thirds of the back lens of the objective is retained.

The chief function of the substage-condenser diaphragm is to limit the angle of the cone of illumination—as it is closed, the angle is decreased; as it is opened, the angle is increased. When it is adjusted so that the objective is about two-thirds filled with light, the effects of light reflections within the objective are minimized and the image contrast is improved, while the resolution is very little affected.

Step 13. Replace the eyepiece, increase the light intensity to normal (that is, to the intensity previous to Step 11), and check the focus of the microscope. Remove the white card.

Step 14. Place the part of the light-tight adapter for the microscope over the microscope tube. Mount the other half of the adapter on a lens board and attach it to the camera.

Step 15. Position the camera so that the center of the light-tight adapter is at the same height as the center of the eyepiece. Move the camera close to the microscope, centering it so that the two parts of the adapter overlap but do not touch. Some slight adjustment of the camera position may be needed to center the image on the ground glass which, for normal use, should be 10 inches from the ocular.

Step 16. Use the fine adjustment on the microscope to bring the image into sharp focus on the ground glass. The image should be examined with a good magnifier to obtain the sharpest image.

Step 17. Exposure must be carefully controlled for best results and for future duplication of results.

Cocking the shutter, manipulating the microscope, or drawing a dark slide from the film holder or plateholder can cause vibration. After any of these operations, it is advisable to wait for a few seconds before making the actual exposure. A cable release should be used to operate a mechanical shutter.

USING A SIMPLE HAND CAMERA

The technique using a simple hand camera has fewer complex steps to follow, but the final product is not so good as with the better cameras.

As in the case of the semi-professional process just outlined, the alignment of the instruments (lamp, microscope, and camera) is of major importance. All of the steps from 1 to 13 are followed, as in the semi-professional process. Of course, rather than using a horizontal setup, a vertical one may be employed. Here, too, the same principles are used in setting up the microscope and lamp to transmit light by the substage mirror. The ease of handling makes the vertical photomicrography setup one of the simplest.

PARTS LIST FOR THE VERTICAL SETUP

A base plate for a 19 mm. rod
A 19 mm. round support rod, 60 cm. long
A right-angle clamp with V and round holes
A right-angle clamp with 2 V grooves
Round rods (unthreaded), 12 mm. in diameter and 15 cm. long
An extension ring, 7 in. in diameter
A 7½" x 7¼" x ⅜" board

If this equipment is set up on a beach, the base can be omitted for the base plate holder, for the 19 mm. rod can be placed into the bench top. Nevertheless, stops are made for the correct relocation of the microscope. Item (7) is fastened to the extension ring after an opening has been made for the camera.

The procedure following Step 13 is as follows:

Step 14. Determine the eyepoint of the microscope. The eyepoint is the point at which an image of the objective is formed by the eyepiece. Its position is determined by moving a thin piece of paper above the microscope and finding the distance from the eyepiece where the spot of light on the paper is smallest.

Step 15. Focus the camera at 25 feet or some other predetermined distance. A focus at 25 feet is satisfactory for the majority of workers. Fixed-focus cameras, such as the Brownie, are satisfactory. The best focal distance can be determined by examining a series of photomicrographic negatives made at different camera-footage settings.

Step 16. Adjust the camera support so that the front surface of the lens will coincide with the eyepoint (Step 14).

The best definition is obtained under these conditions. Definition decreases as the camera lens is located on either side of the eyepoint. It is satisfactory for a slight distance below it. The simple thin meniscus lens of an inexpensive camera is preferred to an anastigmat, although the latter does produce satisfactory results. As stated before, there are fewer inter-reflections in a simple lens.

In practice, high-power eyepieces are more satisfactory than those of 10 power or lower. Low-power eyepieces reduce the apparent magnification observed visually in the microscope. Those of 25 power or higher minimize this effect.

Step 17. Tighten a second clamp just below the clamp holding the extension ring and camera. This allows the camera to be swung out and then returned to the same position.

Fig. 77. The Histoslide camera is a 35 mm. photomicrography instrument with attachments to be used on either monocular or binocular microscopes, capable of producing black and white and color photographs. (Histoslide Co.)

Step 18. Align the camera lens with the eyepiece.

The middle of the visual field should be in the middle of the photograph, with the edges of the photographic field symmetrically placed.

The camera lens diaphragm should be wide open. If possible, the back of the camera should be opened and the position of the field observed on a ground glass or waxed paper placed in the film plane.

A round rod can be locked in the lower clamp on the stand to act as a stop for automatic centering in subsequent operations. If the camera back is not opened, a spirit level should be used to insure that there is no tilt to the camera.

Step 19. Attach a light-tight adapter.

Infinity Focus of the Camera. Infinity focus can be used if the microscope is focused visually through a telescope with reticle. Focus a standard simple telescope visually at infinity and lock it in this position, if possible. Then focus the microscope through the telescope. An alternative method is to place a piece of ground glass in the film plane of the camera and focus the microscope to produce a sharp image on the glass.

The few disadvantages in using this method do not outweigh resorting to it if necessary. Practice will produce better photographs each time the equipment is used. It must be remembered also that the camera lens and the lenses of the microscope should be cleaned to keep dust and marks on the lenses from casting weird shadows on the negative.

There will be times when the negatives will show a flare spot. This is caused by the bright back lens of the 'scope objective being formed too near to the film surface. If you use a Brownie Kodak for any of your photomicrography operations, this effect will be greatly reduced; coated lenses will also reduce this glare spot of increased density.

This same simple setup can also be used in the horizontal position, such as the semi-professional one. Herein are described the simple steps to follow in the horizontal procedure.

The microscope is laid horizontally. Next, align the camera and the microscope. The camera's lens should be centered perfectly with the microscope's ocular. On leaving the microscope, the rays of light which are reflected by the mirror through the iris diaphragm, condenser, objective, barrel and eyepiece, converge to a focus point above the ocular. This converging point is known as the Ramsden disc.

The camera's back is removed and the camera is again aligned with the ocular. With the shutter of the camera closed, the focus point is brought to its smallest circle on the front of the lens. A piece of tissue paper can be used to determine the smallest point of focus (Ramsden disc). Move the paper slowly back and forth to find this point. The shutter is then opened, the lens is set at infinity and a plate of ground glass is used to further bring the image into focus. The camera is now loaded and photomicrography operations are about to commence. But first, there must be a light-tight connection between the camera lens and the microscope's ocular. A cardboard mailing tube, cut to the proper length, will suffice for the final operating step.

Other than just black-and-white shots, color film can be used, but the practice here is again at painstaking expense to the photomicrographer.

CINEPHOTOMICROGRAPHY

What is cinephotomicrography (other than a big word containing 20 letters)? Cinephotomicrography is the art of taking photographs through the microscope, employing the use of a movie camera.

Regardless of the speed of the specimen being photographed, all motion can be recorded by the camera. Complete life cycles or cycles of behavior can be printed on film and speeded up or slowed down, such as, in five minutes, viewing picture sequences of the creation of the egg and hatching of a chicken. At any time during the process of photographing creatures under the microscope, the film speed may be increased to deliver slow motion when reviewed by the human eye or the film can be slowed down to produce a rapid motion effect.

When setting up for cinephotomicrography, the microscopic equipment, aligning and equipment arrangement are almost the same as in the setup used for taking still pictures. The film speed (i.e., the rate the film travels) and the shutter opening of the camera control the exposure time. Normally, a 750-watt projection lamp is used as the light source.

An observation eyepiece, or beamsplitter, is a piece of equipment used in cinephotomicrography. This instrument assists in permitting the accurate framing and focusing of the specimen throughout the entire filming operation. The observation eyepiece, or beamsplitter, is located at the ocular position. It is supported by the camera and acts as the light-tight connection between the beamsplitter and the microscope, although it does not come in contact with either.

The beamsplitter has a prism which allows approximately 90% of the light transmitted through the microscope to reach the film, the remaining 10% is reflected to allow the photomicrographer to view the subject being photographed at all times throughout the process. However, the beamsplitter is only useful on cameras having detachable lenses.

Equipment. Cameras used in cinephotomicrography should be equipped with a single-frame release and powered by an electrical motor or a spring with sufficient tension to allow for a long run of film. Interchangeable magazine features are another important point. A camera having these features makes reloading a speedy task, which also allows for continuance of the action being recorded without too much delay. A camera which has the "fades" or "dissolves" features and a variable shutter is also good in this type of work. A camera with a detachable lens system can readily be adapted to the beamsplitter.

Any of the Cine-Kodak Special Cameras are satisfactory for cine-photomicrography. The Cine-Kodak Royal Magazine Camera has a detachable lens and focusing eyepiece, which can be used rather than the beamsplitter to observe the specimen.

Films recommended for cinephotomicrography are Super-X, Super-XX, and Kodachrome, Type A. They are available in 50-foot or 100-foot rolls and in 50-foot magazines.

SALE OF FILMS

Unlike most of the products of business open to self-contained divers, the photomicrography business has very few outlets. However, there are enough outlets and the prices of the products are high enough so that the photomicrographer will be sufficiently rewarded for his efforts if he persists.

For the most part, high schools, colleges, universities, and other educational institutions will be the best market. Research organizations, biological supply houses, and scientific groups are other possible outlets for your merchandise. Then there are film booking agents, libraries, museums, and television studios. In short, all the persons and organizations listed in the preceding chapter are prospective customers.

Chapter XII

BIOLOGICAL SUPPLY

Biological supply has, without doubt, the best business possibilities for the individual diver or for a group partnership. There are thousands of high schools, junior colleges, colleges and universities throughout the United States and Canada that have no access to the sea. Less than half of the 50 American states have access to the blue kingdom, and only three of Canada's twelve provinces and territories can obtain gratis the necessary biological specimens which are needed for the classroom.

Biological supplies from established biological supply houses are expensive because of the high overhead and high salaries paid the technical staff which prepares the merchandise. A diver can collect and prepare specimens to supply his immediate area at a lower cost, and a group of Scuba divers working together can supply a much wider area.

Basically, there are two types of specimens used in courses in biology, zoology, ichthyology, botany, and other natural sciences. These are: Dry specimens, such as starfish, sea urchins, sponges, etc., and liquid specimens, such as sea anemones and other soft-bodied animals, which must be preserved in liquid.

PREPARING SPECIMENS

The Dry Specimen. The dry specimen, for the most part, is the easiest to prepare; the only requirement is a thorough drying. A low temperature oven or several infrared lamps will speed the drying process tremendously, if desired. Of course, specimens that are partially dried should never be mounted or stored in airtight containers.

There are times when some marine specimens will retain an unpleasant odor even after the drying process. Specimen odor can be prevented by soaking the specimen in 70% alcohol or 10% formalin for 24 hours prior to the drying period. After the soaking period, the specimens are removed from the alcohol or formalin, rinsed in fresh water, and thoroughly dried.

Some specimens are subject to total destruction by insects; for example, starfish and sea urchins. If the creatures are soaked in a saturated borax solution before drying, they will be protected against insect destruction.

208

Fig. 78. (Top) A dry collection of marine specimens for a biology or zoology classroom. Included in the group: sand dollars, sea urchins, turtle shells, brain coral, staghorn coral, finger sponge, sea fans, and a king (horseshoe) crab. (Bottom) An interesting collection of large seashells, some with the rough outer coatings polished off. (Bangor High School, Me.)

Crustaceans (animals having a hard outer protective coating, such as crabs, lobster, and crayfish) are preserved by a 24-hour soaking in a saturated solution of borax and water. Openings are made in the joint membranes to allow the borax solution to penetrate fully. After the soaking period, the specimens are rinsed in fresh water and set to dry. Remember to arrange the specimen in the desired shape, because, once it has dried, as in the case of the starfish, the legs or body parts cannot be moved to different positions. Set the specimen before the drying period begins.

Sheets of balsa wood, purchased at any hobby shop, or sheets of cork, obtainable at department stores in the form of table hot mats, can be used to set and pin wet specimens for drying. Once the borax specimens are thoroughly dry, they are odorless and will remain perfect for many years. Unfortunately, the original, natural colors of the specimen *cannot* be preserved. A coat of varnish can be applied to the dry specimen, then an application of oil paints to tint in the original color will help restore the natural beauty. But, for the most part, dry specimens should be left in their natural state and condition.

However, a thin coat of white varnish or colorless lacquer will not only heighten the colors of some shells, but also will serve as a preservative. Lacquer, as thin as water, can be brush-painted (or better, sprayed) on skeletal specimens after they have been degreased and bleached.

Degreasing bones, after the meat has been cleaned off, is performed by a carbon tetrachloride treatment. The bones are placed in carbon tetrachloride for several hours, removed, rinsed in hot water, and set to dry. Bleaching bones is performed by placing them in a solution of hydrogen peroxide.

Dry specimens are usually mounted in display cases or display jars. The cases can be constructed of any light wood or heavy cardboard. They may have any number of small compartments or be left plain for large flat specimens. Some of the smaller fragile specimens can be mounted on boards or colored glass, labeled, and kept in glass display jars.

The Liquid Specimen. There are many specimens, such as sea anemones, soft-bodied animals and fleshy plants, which are best displayed in the liquid form. Many dissections are well worth keeping and these must be mounted in a liquid preservative.

Living specimens, of course, must be killed (methods for killing are described on Page 212). Once the specimen is dead, it should be set in position and pinned. This is done in a deep wax-lined tray. Any local metal shop can make a 10″ x 16″ x 6″ tray, and canning wax or bee's wax can be used to give it a 1″ bottom lining. Once the specimen is arranged, the preservative is poured in, covering it completely. In the case of larger aquatic animals, such as fish, turtles, frogs, etc., the preservative should be injected into the larger muscles and body cavity. Colored latex, a rubbery compound, is often used when a dissected specimen is to be mounted in the display jar. Blue latex is injected into the veins, and red latex into the arteries. Preserving these larger specimens usually requires several days soaking in the appropriate solution. After the preservation period, they are ready for mounting in a glass jar of the correct size and shape.

The display jars should be made of clear glass. Once the proper size jar has been selected, a rectangular glass, labeled and mounted plate should be cut to fit as snugly as possible. The mounting plates are of three types: (1) Plain window glass, (2) opaque white glass, and (3) opaque black glass. The color of the specimen will determine the color of the mounting glass.

A needle threaded with black or white heavy cotton or linen thread is used to attach the specimen to the mounting glass. The thread is passed through the specimen and is tied at the back of the plate. To complete the mounting, a water and alcohol-proof label is marked and attached to the plate. When this is accomplished, the plate is placed in the jar, and preservative is poured in.

Most of the smaller animals are preserved in alcohol or formalin. Formalin is 40% formaldehyde, or, technically, a 40% (saturated) solution of formaldehyde gas in water. Nevertheless, formalin is considered on the 100% basis and most formulae work from this assumption.

Pure ethyl alcohol is unobtainable except by certain institutions and special government permit holders. Denatured alcohol (the automotive type) is impure and, therefore, worthless for preserving specimens. "Rubbing" alcohol, which varies in strength from 50% to 75%, can be used as a general preservative, although it is not considered satisfactory.

Iso-propanol is a new alcohol, mixes easily with water, and does not have any disagreeable odors. Isopropanol, anhydrous grade, costs slightly over a half dollar a pint.

Other than the alcohol and formalin solutions of varying strengths, there are a number of different formulae which are used in preserving specimens.

    1.   Zenker's Solution: (preservation of small animals)

Water	100 cc.
Glacial Acetic Acid	5 cc.
Potassium Bichromate	2-1/2 gms.
Corrosive Sublimate	5 gms.
Sodium Sulphate	1 gm.

2. Formal-Acetic-Alcohol: (preservation of plant life)
    Alcohol, 50% solution   100 cc.
    Commercial Formalin   6-1/2 cc.
    Glacial Acetic Acid   2-1/2 cc.

3. Gilson's Fluid: (used in delicate fixation)
    Water   880 cc.
    Alcohol, 60% solution   100 cc.
    Corrosive Sublimate   20 gms.
    Nitric Acid   15 cc.
    Glacial Acetic Acid   4 cc.

4. Boulin's Fluid: (preservation of embryos and histological
             material
    Glacial Acetic Acid   5 cc.
    Commercial Formalin   20 cc.
    Picric Acid, saturated   75 cc.

Most of the specimens in your work will come from the sea, although there are a few fresh water forms which are valuable.

Killing. The large specimens are killed by drowning or gas. Formalin, approximately 8% strength, is injected into the large muscles and body cavity. Then, the specimen is preserved in a formalin solution of the same strength.

Aquatic reptiles, such as turtles, water snakes, crocodiles, etc., are captured by nets and killed by drowning in 70% alcohol or by injecting ether into the body cavity. Fishes are taken with hook and line, seines and nets, and killed by dropping them into formalin, full strength. Ten percent formalin is injected into the body cavity to serve as an internal preservative, and 8% formalin is used as the final preservative. Fresh and salt water clams can be obtained by using a clam hoe. These specimens are killed by placing wooden pegs between the shell halves and soaking them in 10% formalin. Eight percent strength formalin is the preservative. Fresh and salt water snails are anesthetized in warm water by adding sulphate magnesium, causing the snail to expand in its shell and drop out. The body is fixed in 10% formalin and preserved in 8%.

Sponges are strange creatures to preserve. They are killed in 70% alcohol, fixed by the same amount, and preserved in a 70% alcohol solution. But, the preservation must be changed because specimens of sponge discolor the alcohol after a period of time.

Botanical Specimens. Another method of making money from the sea's vast storehouse of wealth is derived from the thousands of marine plant specimens which the self-contained diver can secure on every trip below. The use of marine botanical specimens in junior college, college, and university botany classrooms and laboratories has increased greatly since the end of World War II.

Botany specimens are preserved for three specific purposes: laboratory study, microscopic examination, and herbarium and display purposes. The preservation of botanical specimens is much easier than that of the zoological ones.

The majority of marine botany specimens are used in laboratory study. For general preservation, 4% to 6% formalin is used. In this solution, the specimens will keep indefinitely. But, as in the case of certain zoological specimens, the formalin properties cause certain plants to lose their color.

Plants having green leaves are discolored by a 4% formalin solution. The chlorophyll, or green matter, becomes yellowish or whitish; alcohol has the same effect on the chlorophyll in leaves. The natural green color in plants can be preserved by dropping them into the following formula:

Glycerine, Sp. Gr. 1.25	40	gms.
Phenol, C. P.	20	"
Lactic Acid, Sp. Gr. 1.21	20	"
Cupric Chloride	0.2	"
Cupric Acetate	0.2	"
Distilled H_2O	20	cc.

When using this formula to preserve the chlorophyll in green leaf plants, complete preservation takes place in five to ten days.

Marine algae of the fleshier type are preserved by soaking the specimen in glycerine. After the soaking period, the specimen is thoroughly dried. Thus, it is used as a herbarium specimen.

Preserving botanical specimens for study under the microscope is done with considerable care. The specimens must be sectioned (cut thinly), stained, and then preserved. Unfortunately, very little work has been done on the preservation of marine botanical specimens. There is a great need for much experimentation to determine the proper formulae to use for various specimens.

A solution which is accepted for general preservation is Turtox F.A.A.

Formalin, 40% strength	6-1/2 cc.
Alcohol, 50%	100 cc.
Acid, Glacial Acetic	2-1/2 cc.

Microscopic plant tissues can be preserved in this solution indefinitely.

Preserving common forms of green algae so they will not plasmolyse (lose their natural green color) is accomplished by using the following solution:

Water	500 cc.
Formalin, 40% strength	5 cc.
Potassium Chrome Alum	10 gms.

This solution will maintain the specimens and keep them in good condition until needed for actual viewing under the microscope.

Marine botanical specimens can be used in the various herbarium collections for schools and colleges. However, a greater part of the fine-leaved specimens must be handled with great care to prevent their destruction. These specimens are usually mounted on standard size (11½" x 16½") herbarium mounting paper. Specimens are glued or taped to the sheets and then covered with cellophane. This protects them from unnecessary abuse. Some are pressed on wax paper. This also serves to prevent their destruction. Many of the flowering species are pressed in this manner. The wax on the paper helps to hold the specimen in place.

Specimens for Dissection. Underwater creatures are used in the classrooms for laboratory dissection. The body cavity of most of these specimens are injected with various colored compounds so that the students, when they are dissecting them, will be able to make quick, correct identification of the numerous parts. In order to display liver or heart, veins or arteries, or any part of the inner body, these colored solutions are injected separately into the veins, arteries, and heart.

There are three types of solutions used in this work: starch, gelatin, and latex. The starch formula is:

Cornstarch	1 lb.
Water	500 cc.
Glycerine	100 cc.
Formalin (full strength)	100 cc.

The cornstarch is first mixed with the glycerine, then add the formalin, and finally the water. The preparation must be stirred until it is free from lumps. Carmine (red), Berlin blue (insoluble), or chrome yellow is added in the amount desired for the proper shade. This mixture yields about 1¼ pints of injection fluid. Unless there is a great deal of injecting to be done with one color, this 1¼ pints of compound can be divided evenly to make all three colors.

Each separate solution is strained through a double thickness of cheesecloth. But, before the actual injection, the compound must be stirred and strained again if it has set for any length of time. During the second straining, consistency must be closely checked. The compound must be thin enough to flow freely into each of the body capillaries and heavy enough in texture to set. The starch compound which is not thick enough to jell when injected into a blood vessel will run out when cut during a dissection and discolor other tissues. Keep a constant check on the starch solution.

The gelatin injection fluid is easy to mix, gives good results, but requires more patience and checking to use successfully. The formula follow:

Commercial Gelatin (bulk)	1 part
Water (cold)	4 parts

After the solution is thoroughly mixed, it is heated. The colors are added in the same manner as prescribed for the starch compound. The gelatin also is strained through a double thickness of cheesecloth. A precaution to be observed when using the gelatin solution is to be sure that both the needle and syringe are kept as warm as the compound during the injection process. The needle and syringe are heated to insure free flowage of the fluid. Remember, gelatin hardens quickly.

Latex, the ready-mixed commercial compound, is available in various colors. It does not require any additional mixing or preparation. Once the circulatory system (veins and arteries) have been injected with latex, the specimen is then preserved in this acid-formalin solution:

| Formalin Solution | 5% or 10% |
| Acetic Acid | 1/2% or 1% |

The acid helps to harden the latex when it is in this preservative.

Latex can be purchased at a number of biological supply houses and scientific companies. Only the finest of dissections and displays need the latex injection. For classroom work, specimens can be injected with either the starch or gelatin compounds.

Skeletons. Skeletons of specimens that can be obtained in the sea or fresh water are widely used for instructional purposes.

Skeletons are prepared by fleshing, maceration, bleaching, and mounting.

The Squalus (Dogfish), a member of the shark family, has a cartilaginous skeleton, which means that it is not true, hard bone. Biological supply houses gather many of these specimens off the coast of Maine every summer. Preparing this type of skeleton does not require much skill. But the work is smelly and messy and requires much time and patience. The equipment and supplies needed are: an earthenware container (large enough to hold a few specimens), commercial hydrochloric acid, special denatured alcohol (Formula 30), formalin, and water.

First, the head is severed from the body, leaving the gills intact. The specimen is cut from the dorsal side around to the fifth gill cleft carefully to avoid cutting the fifth gill cleft cartilages or the pectoral girdle cartilages. Dissecting the pectoral girdle and fins from the body wall is the next step, followed by the dissection of the pelvic fins. Using the finger to trace the cartilages of the pelvic fins, cut around them. Next, the intestines and flanks are cut away carefully to avoid cutting too high and severing a vertebra or rib cartilage.

Fleshing. Fleshing the body is the next step, but don't flesh it too thoroughly, as the maceration process will eliminate a good part of this. Do not flesh the head and gill arches.

Maceration. Scoring the animal's skin with a fine-point scalpel will allow the acid solution to get under the skin and soften it, thus making removal easy. With this accomplished, the dogfish parts are ready to be placed in this acid solution for maceration:

Distilled Water   40 parts
Commercial Hydrochloric Acid   1 part

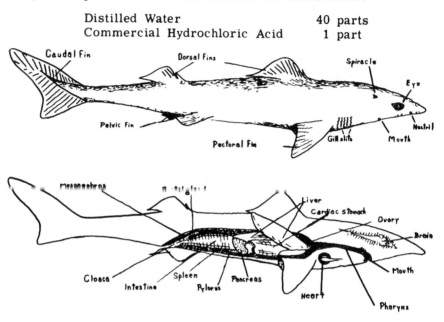

Fig. 79. Dogfish shark (Squalus) (Class *Chondrichthyes*). (Top) External features. (Bottom) Lateral view of a dissection in which the relative positions of the organs are shown (one liver lobe has been moved to expose certain organs normally concealed by it).

The specimen should be completely covered with the acid solution when it is placed in the earthenware container, and the container should be large enough to avoid bending the specimen in any way. Allow it to remain in this maceration solution for a period of 12 hours.

After the 12-hour maceration period, the flesh should rub off easily. Rubbing the finger over a soft part of the body will determine the completion of the soaking time. Remove the specimen from the solution and wash it gently in plain water for 2 or 3 minutes. The parts are then submerged in an ammonia bath composed of 1 gallon of water and 2 ounces of ammonia (liquid).

This solution serves to stop the maceration process and neutralize the acid. Thirty minutes is long enough for the sections to remain in this bath. After removing the sections, the remainder of the surplus flesh is carefully worked off. The cartilages are extremely soft and easily broken away. As the cleaning progresses and the arches, skull, and vertebrae outlines are visible, work ceases. The sections are gently washed in plain water, thus readying the parts for hardening.

Six alcohol baths are prepared in the following percentages: 10%, 20%, 35%, 60%, 85%, and 95%. Denatured ethyl alcohol (Formula 30) is used to mix this formula. The skeleton is then submerged in the baths for the following time periods:

10% solution	20 mins.	60% solution	45 mins.
20% "	20 "	85% "	45 "
35% "	20 "	95% "	4 to 6 days

At the completion of the 6-day setting period, the final cleaning and setting is completed. The skeleton is taken from the 95% alcohol solution and washed gently under plain water for 60 minutes. With a blunt scalpel or similar instrument, the remainder of the flesh is scraped away. Forceps come in handy on this operation. Place the specimen in a shallow pan of water and use a toothbrush to brush completely over the skeleton. During this process, the water is changed when necessary.

Bleaching. If the skeleton is stained or discolored, it can be whitened in a 10% hydrogen peroxide solution. The specimens remain in the cleansing bath long enough for the stains to disappear. The skeleton is then removed, washed in plain water and submerged in a 5% solution of formalin to harden.

Mounting. Formalin is the best preservative for a permanent skeleton mounting, but will make the cartilaginous skeleton brittle. However, this so-called "wet" type skeleton can be embedded in a clear plastic mold, thus preserving it forever. In a plastic coat, the skeleton may be handled as roughly as possible without causing damage.

Embedding in Plastic. Embedding specimens in plastic is an interesting process in the biological supply business.

Today, on the American market, there are a number of casting materials produced in which biological, botanical, and zoological specimens can be embedded. Resins and Polyesters, as clear as glass, are used in this embedding process rather than acrylics (plexiglass). The former have an advantage over the acrylics because, once they are cured, the casts will not soften or change shape. These materials can be purchased in the following shades: white, ivory, and clear. By adding dye to the last of these, one can achieve a variety of colors.

This form of plastic is a syrup-like liquid and keeps well below 80°F. Refrigeration is not necessary, but it is advisable to store in a cool place. Sunlight, ordinary daylight, and electric light can spoil the material. The plastics have pungent odors, but they are not toxic. However, while mixing these types of plastics, you should work in a well-ventilated room, or, as when mixing paints, take an occasional breath of fresh air.

To complete the embedding process, an accelerator (or catalyst) is added, drop by drop, to the plastic substance. These materials come separately packaged. The accelerator is added only when the plastic is ready to be poured into the mold, and the material is left to jell. Each manufacturer has a set of time-limit periods for his product, and it is advisable to follow the directions carefully.

Science specimens are usually suspended in the plastic form. To accomplish this, a layer of plastic is poured into the mold and left to thicken. Since the casting is usually poured upside down, the specimen is placed in position face down. This is done only when the bottom layer of plastic has jelled. In the jelled state, the object will easily stick to it, and then the second layer of plastic is poured in to complete the embedding process. If, before it is placed in the mold, the specimen is soaked in liquid plastic, to which hardener has been added, better results will be obtained. With leafy botanical specimens, this is advisable. The plastic will pour smoothly over the specimen and will not trap unwanted air bubbles into the cast.

Once the second layer is poured and has jelled, and the mold has had ample time to cool, the final stage to harden or cure the form begins. Curing is accomplished by heating the plastic for 30 minutes at 180°F., without removing it from the mold.

Specimens having a moisture content, delicate structure, or complex coloring patterns present a special problem and require a little more time and work to prepare them for the embedding stage. Specimens with a moisture content are packed in sand until they are thought to be perfectly dry. Others may require vacuum work or dehydrating treatments before they can be cast. The curing temperature for these specimens in plastic is lower—150°F. maximum. Special instruction sheets for this type of embedding is offered by most of the manufacturers.

SELLING SPECIMENS

Divers who wish to enter this field have their work cut out for them. As we have said from the beginning, it will require a great deal of time, study, experimentation and patience. But, in the end, your hard work will be rewarded.

The same list of institutions and firms given in Chapter X should be contacted in finding a market for your collections. In addition, write to these two firms: Turtox General Biology Supply House and Ward's Natural Science Establishment.

Chapter XIII

FIELDS OF RESEARCH

Marine research is one of the finest fields which a Scuba diver can enter. Not only is he making a wise decision regarding a career, but he is also furthering man's knowledge of the world in which he lives. This underwater field is extremely important because of the vital contributions made to science.

Marine science has many related fields and each has contributed paramount discoveries. As time progresses, scientists in many different fields are going below the water, for there lie many secrets long guarded by Mother Sea and her aquatic inhabitants.

The author and his associates feel that those of us who don flippers, mask, rubber suit, and Scuba are members of a great fraternity who stand on the threshold of a new frontier of scientific exploration and discovery. Any young person who has discovered the fascination of Scuba diving should seriously consider marine science as his lifework.

This chapter attempts to give an overall view of the opportunities in this increasingly important field of science.

The National Geographic Society's magazine, *The National Geographic*, contains many articles dealing with scientific underwater explorations, some of them made by Scuba divers. An article in the May, 1955 issue deals with the observations made by two men in a specially constructed housing beneath the waters of the Chesapeake Bay. The two men remained on the bottom of the Bay over 100 hours, filming underwater life in black-and-white and in technicolor.

In exploring the employment possibilities in the several fields of underwater research, the author corresponded with a number of officials connected with public and private research organizations. Most of the replies present a very favorable picture. Pertinent passages from two of these letters are quoted below. The following is from the U.S. Navy Hydrographic Office in Washington:

The oceanographic institutions use self-contained diving apparatus in their research work to a greater extent than Government agencies. Woods Hole Oceanographic Institute, Woods Hole, Massachusetts; Scripps Institute of Oceanography, La Jolla, California, and Chesapeake Bay Institute (Johns Hopkins University) have published reports describing the use of this technique. However, the U.S. Navy Electronics Laboratory, San Diego, California, is using self-contained diving apparatus more and more in their underwater investigations. And it is our understanding that the U.S. Navy Mine Defense Laboratory, Panama City, Florida, has trained some of their personnel in the use of self-contained diving apparatus.

From C. P. Idyll, Acting Chairman, Department of Marine Science, Marine Laboratory, University of Miami, came the following information:

At the present time, the employment opportunities for graduates in this field are excellent. Men trained in this field can secure positions with nearly all the coastal states and with several federal government agencies, as well as with Marine Laboratories. It is likely that the demand for the services of trained marine scientists will increase in the next several years.

ARCHEOLOGY

Archeology is one example of a field of science that has donned mask, flipper, and Scuba. To investigate the world's past, it has gone below the waters of the Seven Seas. France leads the world in this department, and French scientists have made some of the greatest discoveries of recent times.

Dr. Philippe Diolé, Director of Undersea Archeology Research in France, has been instrumental in raising portions of a Roman galley which sank about 100 B.C., or earlier. Dr. Diolé and his associates have brought valuable objects of art from this vessel, which is believed to have been part of the fleet of Roman vessels that took part in the pillage of Athens, Greece. Among the remains of this ancient seafaring craft were found jugs, still capped, containing wine thought to be drinkable, although it was not reported that anyone ventured to sample the contents of any of the jugs.

Off the coast of North Africa, the undersea archeology researchers found the remains of a city that went under the waves over 4,000 years ago. The work they have done provides scientists and students with valuable materials that throw light on life in ancient times.

Most of our better universities and colleges have courses in archeology and allied subjects leading to a degree in this field. Scuba divers interested in the study of the past should consider archeology as a possible career.

GEOLOGY

Geology is another field of research which has "gone below the water." Some of the country's largest organizations have employed the use of self-contained diving equipment with their geology research teams.

An excellent illustration of this development is a recent underwater research expedition in the Gulf of Mexico.

Four geologists and two geological technicians, all of them experienced divers, took part in the expedition. The scientists are members of the staff of the Field Research Laboratories of Magnolia Petroleum Co., Socony Mobil Oil Company, Inc., affiliate in the southwest, at Dallas, Texas.

Fig. 80. Geologists launch a dredge. Sediments scooped from the bottom of the Gulf of Mexico may yield clues to future oil supply. (Socony Mobil Oil Co., Inc.)

Fig. 81. From 65 feet down, geologist carrying a bag of specimens heads for surface in a cloud of bubbles. (Socony Mobil Oil Co., Inc.)

Operating from a 65-foot converted shrimp boat, chartered for the expedition, the *Cavalier*, the scientists worked in water up to 65 feet in depth and as many as 45 miles offshore south and east of Galveston, Texas.

The researchers were not hunting for offshore oil in the conventional sense. Offshore drilling locations are presently spotted by

Fig. 82. Near an offshore drilling rig, skin divers check specimens collected during underwater exploration. (Socony Mobil Oil Co., Inc.)

essentially the same geological and geophysical methods as are used on dry land. Instead, the scientists were using the Continental Shelf as a gigantic field laboratory for a sediments study.

One of the main objectives of the study is to develop techniques for predicting the presence and location of limestone reefs and sandstone bars in ancient rock formations.

The researchers think, for instance, that minute differences in the composition of the ancient sediments may provide clues that will point the way to the location of stratigraphic traps. They are seeking to test this hypothesis in their study of recent sediments.

Studying the environments in which sediments have been deposited in recent geologic times offers another key to understanding how ancient sediments were formed. To help identify these environments, the scientists collect samples of starfish, snails, shellfish, and other marine animals and plant life found on and under the ocean floor. To get the samples needed for analysis, the scientists used three principal techniques—diving, dredging, and coring.

Skin diving made it possible to extend greatly the range of underwater information the scientists could collect. They observed marine flora and fauna at first hand. They used dandelion diggers to loosen some of the specimens from the sand and coral bottom and brought them to the surface in gunny sacks. They took photographs with a camera mounted in a watertight case. They made underwater notes on their observations by writing with wax pencils on plastic slates strapped to their thighs.

Using a device called a current-meter, the divers calculated the force of the underwater currents which dump sediments into the Gulf, so that these currents could be plotted on the master chart along with other data from the survey.

The geologists hope they can eventually come up with some clues that will help locate oil-bearing stratigraphic traps. The clues will come from the answers to questions like these: Why do certain marine animals live only in mud? Why do others live in sand, and still others only in shell debris? Why is the bottom of the sea coral in one place, mud in another place, and sand only a short distance away?

OCEANOGRAPHY AND CARTOGRAPHY

Oceanography and cartography are two fields of research desperately in need of young personnel. There are less than 500 trained oceanographers in the United States today, and the country needs more to carry out the research programs scheduled, man the oceanographic equipment aboard the Navy's Hydrographic Ships, Coast and Geodetic Survey Ships, and vessels of the other Federal and private research establishments.

Cartography. Cartography includes the study of advanced surveying, astronomy, descriptive geometry, geodesy, geology, geophysics, mathematics, navigation, optics, photo-interpretation, photogrammetry, physical geography, physics, and plane surveying on the college level. High school students interested in occupations in the field of cartography should enroll in courses relating closely to those listed above. Most high schools teach geometry, physics, mathematics, and allied subjects which should give a firm background for college studies.

Duties of a Cartographer:

1. The precise measurement, evaluation, analysis, and interpretation of basic data required to determine the position, elevation, and shape of geomorphic and topographic features and phenomena and the preparation of such data for publication in a prescribed form, such as a standard topographical map.

2. The determination of physical characteristics of bodies of water needed in the various aspects of navigation. This includes measuring depths of water, locating underwater obstructions, and the determination of the nature and configuration of shorelines and all navigation aids adjacent thereto. This also includes the office compilation of photogrammetric or other methods of land forms, shoreline, and cultural information obtained from the hydrographic surveys.

3. The preparation of various types and scales of charts needed for aerial navigation over land and sea. This includes both original compilation of geographic information from sources, such as aerial photographs, and compilation from other surveys and maps previously accomplished.

4. Research in surveying and mapping techniques, methods and procedures.

The direction of such activities includes selecting the most appropriate and economical methods, planning and administering one or more phases of the technical operations involved, scheduling project priorities, assigning personnel for the performance of operations, following up assignments, training employees in techniques and procedures, and reviewing work for accuracy and good judgment, all of a high degree of complexity and responsibility.

The difficulty of the work performed, the responsibility assumed, and the extent of supervision exercised varies with the grade of the position, increasing progressively in the higher grades.

Phase 2 of the cartographer's position will, of course, be of most interest to Scuba divers who possess some degree of capabilities in drawing, mechanical designing, and art. These artistic talents, combined with education, can secure a life-long position with the United States Government for a good Scuba diver.

Oceanography. The U.S. Government Oceanographic Research Institute and private ocean-connected businesses are ready and willing to employ trained and semitrained personnel in the field of oceanography. This is truly the field for Scuba divers, for in this branch of science, the diver's talents are fully utilized.

Scuba divers, for example, were used by the Scripps Institute of Oceanography (La Jolla, California), in a project of the visual detection of temperature-density discontinuities in water. The oceanographic field has other duties for which Scuba diving is used extensively.

Oceanographers plan, direct, or assist in conducting scientific investigative or development work or fundamental research work in oceanography. This work involves the application of the exact and descriptive physical and biological sciences to the study of the oceans, their water, and plants and animals, and the media forming their boundaries, namely, the atmosphere, the sea bottom, and beaches.

The duties of the positions in various agencies of the Federal Government may include design of specialized equipment, planning tests and studies for work at sea and ashore, conducting surveys and experiments at sea and ashore, making theoretical studies, analyzing samples and data, compiling special charts and tabulations, and preparing reports and manuals.

Typical Duties of an Oceanographer:

1. Planning and conducting both broad field programs and highly specialized studies and research on the oceanographic conditions and related phenomena in different areas.

2. Using all available information, including foreign publications, to compile comprehensive data related to oceanography for selected areas and to prepare regional studies.

3. Preparing special tabulations, charts, atlases, reports and manuals on oceanography conditions and applying such information to the solution of problems of the armed forces, merchant marine, airlines, fisheries, etc.

4. Applying mathematical and statistical methods to establish and evaluate correlations between different characteristics existing within the sea, and between those of the sea and the bounding media.

5. Using established theories and empirical relationships to develop and apply techniques for forecasting either cyclic or periodic variables, such as currents, ice conditions, sea and swell, temperature, etc.

6. Conducting research and making theoretical studies of conditions in the sea involving the application of the exact and descriptive physical and natural sciences.

7. Devising improved techniques for the rapid reduction of voluminous oceanographic data to usable form, and for the graphic portrayal of oceanographic information.

8. Improving physical and chemical techniques for the analyses of sea water samples and the preparation of standards, and developing new techniques of increased accuracy and speed.

9. Developing and using model studies supplementary to field observations and theoretical considerations to aid in the interpretation of processes in the sea.

10. Designing and testing new devices and procedures for measuring currents and other physical or chemical properties of the sea, and for collecting samples of sea water, marine organisms, and sediments.

11. Assisting in the training of civilians and members of the armed forces in oceanography and its applications to the various types of problems encountered during peace and war.

Physical Oceanographers must study any combination of the following subjects: physics, engineering sciences, chemistry, physical oceanography, meteorology, and mathematics.

Geological Oceanographers study subjects, which include: physics, chemistry, oceanography, meteorology, and mathematics.

Biological Oceanographers study a combination of subjects, including: invertebrate zoology, marine biology, limnology and hydrobiology, plus 24 semester hours of the same subjects studied by Geological Oceanographers.

College students applying for Government positions, who are senior or graduate students in an accredited college or university, will be given tentative credit for all studies being pursued in the academic term during which their application is filed. Such students, who are qualified in all other respects, may receive provisional appointments before the end of the term, but may not enter on duty until they furnish proof of successful completion of either undergraduate or graduate study for which such tentative credit was given.

Agencies of the government will also give credit for all valuable experience of the type required, regardless of whether compensation was received or whether the experience was gained in a part-time or full-time occupation. Part-time or unpaid experience will be credited on the basis of time actually spent in appropriate activities. Applicants wishing to receive credit for such experience must indicate clearly the nature of their duties and responsibilities in each position and the number of hours a week spent in such employment.

The University of Miami, Coral Gables, Florida, offers a full program of study in marine sciences. Any high school graduate who has an interest in the sea and its life, would do well to drop a line to the director of admissions at the University of Miami and request all the information available on their courses in this area.

EDUCATION AND TRAINING OF OCEANOGRAPHERS*

by

Vern O. Knudsen, Alfred C. Redfield, Roger Revelle, and Robert R. Shrock
University of California, Los Angeles; Woods Hole Oceanographic Institution, Woods Hole, Massachusetts; Scripps Institution of Oceanography of the University of California, La Jolla; and Massachusetts Institute of Technology, Cambridge.

The shortage of scientists is general. Two circumstances combine, however, to exaggerate the present need for men trained in oceanography. Revolutionary developments in the military techniques of the late war created an unprecedented demand for knowledge of the sea and trained oceanographers. Knowledge of the sea can contribute to the solution of peacetime as well as military problems. Thus, the state of the postwar world makes it only too clear that the food resources of the sea must be exploited to the utmost. Oceanographers are needed to lay foundations for technological advances in military techniques, in transportation and communication across the sea, and in the expansion of sea fisheries. Yet no increase of effort in the investigation of the sea is possible, since all trained oceanographers are now employed.

Three factors must be considered in connection with oceanographic training: (a) What positions may students look forward to after receiving their oceanographic training (b) What distinguishes oceanography as a separate scientific discipline requiring a special combinaton of skills and interests? (c) How can such skills be obtained within the usual academic pattern, or what special modifications and additions does this pattern require?

Opportunities for employment in oceanography exist primarily in the federal government and in university or associated research laboratories. Within the federal government, the Hydrographic Office, the Coast Guard, the Geological Survey, the Coast and Geodetic Survey, the Office of Naval Research (including

* Reprinted from *Science* (June 23, 1950, III, No. 2895), pp. 700–703.

the Naval Research Laboratory), the Bureau of Ships (including the Navy Electronics Laboratory and the U. S. Navy Underwater Sound Laboratory), the Naval Ordnance Laboratory, the U.S. Engineers, and the Beach Erosion Board, are the principal agencies interested in physical oceanography. The Fish and Wildlife Service of the Department of the Interior, the conservation agencies of many maritime states, and various international fisheries commissions are interested in oceanography from the biological standpoint. Private interests in oceanography include the oil companies now engaged in an extensive search for new oil reserves under continental shelves.

Two well-established oceanographic laboratories are maintained by universities: the Scripps Institution of Oceanography of the University of California (including the Marine Physical Laboratory) and the Oceanographic Laboratories of the University of Washington. A third laboratory, the Chesapeake Bay Institute, has been established recently at the Johns Hopkins University. The Woods Hole Oceanographic Institution, an independent foundation, provides facilities for investigators from other institutions and maintains its own professional staff as well. The other institutions represented have included Harvard, Brown, Yale, Columbia, Rutgers, Princeton, New York and Queens Universities, the Massachusetts Institute of Technology, the Universities of Chicago and of Maine, and Amherst, Wellesley, Barnard, and Rhode Island State Colleges.

Marine research involving oceanography is conducted by the Bingham Oceanographic Foundation at Yale, the Department of Engineering of the University of California at Berkeley, the Department of Geology at Columbia, the University of Southern California, Harvard University, New York University, the University of Miami Marine Laboratory, and other biological laboratories. Research closely akin to oceanography is being done on the Great Lakes and on smaller lakes throughout the country, most notably at the Universities of Wisconsin, Michigan, and Chicago and at Ohio State and Northwestern Universities.

Although these lists suggest a rather extensive interest in oceanography on the part of government and educational institutions, the number of persons in the profession is small. A recent survey of manpower available for research in oceanography lists 448 persons, and only 223 of them are reported to be doing independent research or to have done it recently. The number of graduate students now in training is about 80. There is an immediate need for 30–40 oceanographers throughout the governmental and other oceanographic institutions of the U.S., and when the present large demand levels off, it is believed that ten or more newly trained oceanographers will be required each year to take care of normal replacements and expected growth.

As in many other fields of science and engineering, needs exist for both highly trained men capable of carrying on oceanographic research independently or under very little supervision, and for men of less advanced training, for positions involving oceanographic engineering, surveying, or reducing and compiling of data. In addition, special provision should be made for the training of officers of the Department of Defense, who should profit greatly from intimate contact with the techniques of a field science such as oceanography, even though their professional responsibilities are primarily administrative.

The present professonal oceanographers in the U.S. have received their training for the most part in physics, chemistry, biology, or geology. Until recently, organized training in oceanography as such has been available only at the University of Washington and at the Scripps Institution at La Jolla. Courses in oceanography are also given as part of various curricula at Harvard, Columbia, St. Louis, Clark, Brown, Cornell, and New York Universities, at the Agricultural and Mechanical College of Texas, and at the Universities of Chicago, California (at Los Angeles), and Southern California. Amherst College has pioneered in offering instruction in oceanography as a part of the liberal arts curriculum where it shows the value of the basic sciences for interpreting the phenomena of the natural world.

Oceanography acquires its unity because it deals with everything taking place in a limited geographical sub-division of the earth—its watery envelope. Problems in oceanography fall rather definitely into two groups, those of geophysics and those of ecology. Their solutions require the various techniques of physics, chemistry, geology, and biology. It is pertinent to ask whether oceanography has its own particular disciplines or whether it is merely a collection of those parts of these other sciences which happen to deal with the phenomena of the seas.

In order to answer this question, it is necessary to consider briefly the intellectual content and methods of oceanography. Oceanography may be defined as the study of the ocean in all its aspects, including the interrelationships between marine organisms and their environment and between the ocean and its boundaries —the atmosphere, the sea bottom, and the shores. In contrast to the exact sciences, it deals with the investigation of conditions and processes as they exist on a large scale in nature rather than with the conduct of controlled experiments in the laboratory. The conditions in the sea cannot be controlled; moreover, they are characterized by a high degree of complexity, great geographical diversity, and variability with time. The nature of oceanography is determined by these characteristics as well as by the large dimensions involved and by the fact that the fluid nature of the medium results in widespread interrelationships.

The oceanographer is concerned primarily with the elucidation of the individual processes in the sea which together produce the observed conditions. In general, two or more processes oppose each other and are balanced in such a way that a state of approximate equilibrium is maintained. The principles of dynamic equilibrium may be thought of as a unifying principle of oceanography, in much the same way that the principle that the present is the key to the past underlies and unifies geology. The problems of oceanography require analysis of observed conditions that represent the integration of several processes so as to differentiate and describe the individual processes that are at work. Two methods are commonly employed for this purpose: (a) All possible parameters in a given situation are measured and processes are deduced which explain the observed relationships between these parameters in terms of physical, chemical, and biological principles; (b) Comparative studies are made of variations in certain parameters in many situations. These studies can be facilitated in some instances by model experiments in tanks, in which individual processes can be controlled. Statistical correlations are then carried out to obtain empirical relationships, or preferably, a simplified theoretical model is constructed and shown to correspond in essential features to the complex reality.

Although no individual method or principle of oceanography is unique, it is believed that the combination of principles and methods just described forms a distinct discipline which requires special training.

When the diverse quality of the disciplines on which oceanography depends is considered, together with the present limited opportunities for professional employment, it appears doubtful whether there is need for new organizations for specialized training in oceanography. What is required, rather, is the establishment of professional standards for oceanographic training. These can largely be met within the existing academic pattern of universities that recognize the special training requirements. Since oceanography comprises such a wide variety of problems, no individual can become fully competent in all its departments. Depending on his interests and aptitudes, a student must specialize in the physical, biological, geological, or chemical aspects of oceanography. It is essential, however, that each worker understand the concepts and the language of the entire subject. In a field with limited outlets for employment, it is important that the basic training be broad enough to equip students for jobs in related branches of geophysics, geology, or biology. Such breadth of training will give a wider base for the later development of a professional career and greater opportunities for intellectually satisfying research. There is need in the field sciences for research workers whose education has followed the pattern proposed herein.

With this objective in mind, we have prepared a list of subjects recommended for the basic training of a student who anticipates a professional career in oceanography. Clearly, the quality of the student's general education, and the extent to which he has been infused with scientific curiosity and the research spirit, are of primary importance in the training of special value for oceanographers.

Recommended Subjects for Oceanographic Training

Mathematics
    Algebra and trigonometry
    Analytical geometry
    Differential and integral calculus
    Differential equations
    Statistics
    Advanced mathematics, including vector analysis and Fourier integrals
Physics
    Basic physics, including mechanics, heat, sound, and light, and electricity
        and magnetism
    Wave theory and acoustics
    Electronics laboratory
    Hydrodynamics or fluid mechanics
    Advanced mechanics or theoretical physics
Chemistry
    General inorganic chemistry
    Analytical chemistry
    Organic chemistry
    Physical chemistry
    Colloid chemistry
Biology
    Elementary biology
    Invertebrate zoology
    Physiology
    Biochemistry
    Microbiology
    Ecology or limnology
    Biophysics, including applications of nuclear physics
    Summer work in marine biology
Geology
    Physical geology
    Historical geology
    Paleontology
    Introduction mineralogy and petrology
    Crystallographic and optical mineralogy
    Sedimentology or marine geology
Geophysics
    Principles of oceanography—physical, biological, chemical and geological
    Exploration geophysics—magnetic, electrical, gravity, and seismic
    Summer field course in oceanography

Physical and dynamic meteorology
Synoptic meteorology
Climatology
Advanced physical oceanography
Theoretical geophysics

These are the scientific subjects that are of direct value on oceanographic training, arranged more or less in their sequence of advancement. In Table 15, a selection is made among these subjects to indicate the relative distribution of effort considered desirable for basic training in the several fields of specialization. The programs of study outlined in Table 15 would require ordinarily about 13 course years, or about 70 to 80 semester hours. Allowing for the usual university requirements for courses in the humanities, languages, English composition, and the like, completion of one of the programs would probably require five years, particularly if the student did not start on the program at the beginning of his college career. Normally, these suggested programs would lead to the master's degree. Additional graduate courses, special seminars in oceanography, and appropriate research would be required for those who work toward the Ph.D. degree.

Table 15. Distribution of Subjects in Basic Training for Specialties in Oceanography: Course Years

	Physical	Geological	Biological	Chemical
Mathematics	3	2-1 2	2-1 2	2-1 2
Physics	3-1 2	2	2	2
Chemistry	3	3	3	4*
Geology	1	3	1	1
Biology	1	1	3	2
Oceanography	1	1	1	1
Meteorology	1 2	1	1	1
Summer field work in oceanographic lab.	x	x	x	x
Summer course in marine biology			x	

* To include biochemistry

The listed subjects are fundamental, so that, after the first two or three years of study, a student could proceed in almost any other field of science without retracing his steps. At their completion, the specialist in physical or geological oceanography would be well prepared for advanced work in any aspect of geophysics should he be unable or unwilling to continue in oceanography. The specialist in biological or chemical oceanography would have a better training than is usual among college graduates, for continued studies in ecology, limnology, physiology or biochemistry. Conversely, students thoroughly trained in geophysics may find excellent opportunities in geological oceanography, and students well trained in biochemistry may make important contributions in biological oceanography.

The programs proposed would be adequate for students contemplating an "engineering" career in oceanography and would bring the student who plans to take an advanced degree to the point where his training should become individualized. For each of the four specialties of oceanography, an advanced student should master many more of the subjects listed in Table 15, that are related to his specialty. In physical oceanography, for example, he should try to cover all courses listed in mathematics, physics and geophysics. In the end, he would be fitted for research or teaching in nearly any aspect of geophysics.

Although these basic training programs involve a minimum of specialization, they all include a year's course in the methods and principles of oceanography and a summer of work and study at one of the major oceanographic research institutions. This introduction to oceanography should be experienced as early in college as possible, in order to arouse the interest and enthusiasm of enough students to screen out those without special aptitude for a field of science, and to give concrete meaning and purpose to the other more general subjects included in the curriculum. Prerequisites for a general course in the principles of oceanography should include mathematics through differential and integral calculus, a basic course in physics, and an elementary knowledge of chemistry, biology (including taxonomy), and geology. It would therefore not be possible to take this course before the junior year. It should preferably be followed by the summer's field work in oceanography, between the junior and senior years.

A course in the principles of oceanography would be useful to biologists, geologists, and geophysicists, as well as to oceanographers. It would also have general educational value in demonstrating the application of scientific principles and methods of the phenomena of the real world—for example, in exploiting the food and mineral resources of the oceans to help solve problems created by overpopulation.

The general science courses required for basic training in the specialties of oceanography are offered in many universities—what is lacking is basic training in oceanography itself. Any university can institute a program in oceanography if it is prepared to add these introductory courses and provide for advanced study in one of the specialties. Graduate training should, of course, include some experience in research at sea, for which adequate facilities already exist at the established oceanographic institutions.

Employment Opportunities for Scientifically Trained Scuba Divers

1. The U.S. Navy Hydrographic Office
2. The Coast Guard
3. The Geological Survey
4. The Coast and Geodetic Survey
5. The Office of Naval Research
6. The Naval Research Laboratory
7. The Bureau of Ships
8. U.S. Navy Electronics Laboratory
9. U.S. Navy Underwater Sound Laboratory
10. The Naval Ordnance Laboratory
11. The U.S. Engineers
12. Beach Erosion Board
13. Fish and Wildlife Service
14. Department of the Interior
15. Private Large Oil Companies

There are additional places in need of scientifically trained personnel. Many of our coastal states employ men in the fields of marine research.

Chapter XIV

THE DIVER'S DEN

Any person who becomes a Scuba diver for either sport or business will soon feel the need of a room of his own in which he can pursue his studies. Gradually it will begin to reflect the owner's interests. Here he may keep some of his diving equipment, framed pictures of himself in diving gear and of his various operations, a growing library of books and pamphlets, large wall maps, dry and wet collections of underwater flora and fauna, and one or more aquariums.

A FRESH-WATER AQUARIUM

Maintaining a fresh-water aquarium is a fascinating hobby. A rectangular tank holding from 6 to 9 gallons of water is the best. Round aquariums are not very satisfactory; for one reason, the curved glass offers limited visibility. If you buy a new tank, wash it in running water once or twice. If you use a tank that contained fish previously, wash it thoroughly with soap and ammonia water, then rinse it with clear water three or four times.

Select some good gravel, fine, if possible, and wash this under running water from the tap. When the gravel is thoroughly clear, place it in the tank to a depth of 1½ to 2 inches, which is sufficient for the growth of the plants.

Clear pond water should be used in the fresh-water aquarium; city water is likely to be loaded with harmful chemicals. If pond water is unavailable, rain water is the next best. But if you must use tap water, set it in open containers and let it stand for a day or so. To avoid stirring up the bottom, place a sheet of typing paper on the sand and start pouring the water in slowly, hitting the paper directly in the center. Fill the tank to within about 6 or 7 inches of the top.

Many who keep aquariums set them in the front window so they can receive the full benefits of the sun's rays. For an hour or so each day, this is all right, but the aquarium should be placed where it will be exposed to a strong diffused light. A North or East exposure is considered good.

Plant only a few specimens at the beginning, for if there are too many plants, they will die and decay and cause the water to become foul. It is advisable to buy tank-grown plants for your aquarium until you can grow your own.

A few of the rooted plants should be placed in the tank first. Spread the roots and cover them with sand up to the crowns. Then, after the rooted plants are secured, add several non-rooted plants. Tie a small stone to the plant at the lower end and place it in the tank. Be sure to remove all dead or broken leaves and stalks. When the planting is finished, fill the tank to within 1 inch of the top. Under normal conditions, the plants will begin to grow in approximately two weeks, and the water will clear in a couple of days.

If the water does not clear in this period, there are some dead and decaying plants or organic matter still in the tank. If this is the case, remove the plants very carefully, empty the water, and start again. This time, allow the aquarium to set for a few days until the water is clear of cloudiness.

When the plants have begun to grow in about two weeks, it is time to add the first animals. Snails are good to begin with, for they keep the tank clean and require very little of the oxygen given off by the plants. In a 6 gallon tank, six to a dozen snails are the limit. There should be one or two viviparous (live-bearing) species and various types of pond snails (egg layers), and, possibly, one or two red snails. Newts are very active and interesting; one or two of these animals may be kept in the aquarium. A 1- or 2-inch freshwater clam may be put on the bottom, but a constant watch must be kept to see that he remains alive.

Turtox General Biological Supply House of Chicago, Illinois, recommends one 1-inch fish for one gallon of water. Thus, in a 6-gallon tank, you can maintain six 1-inch fish or three 2-inch fish. However, the number of fish also depends upon the amount of other animals which you stock. Several small fish are much better than one large one. Minnow, dace, bullhead, and sunfish are far more interesting than the dime store goldfish.

Aquarium Plants. Elodea; Cabomba; Myriophyllum; Nitella; Vallisneria; Sagittaria; Water Poppy; Ludwigia.

Feeding Snails. These animals are hearty eaters and they live on the algae which grows on the plants. A little lettuce or spinach once a week will keep the snails from eating the leaves of the aquarium plants. These little housed animals also eat shredded shrimp and other fish food, and will gather up the remains of the fishes' extra food.

If white spots develop on the snail's shell, it is a sign that there is too much acid accumulating in the water. This condition can be remedied by placing a small piece of Plaster of Paris in the tank.

Feeding Fish. Fish eat very little and they enjoy bread crumbs, egg yolk, oatmeal, and shredded shrimp. Prepared fish food can be fed also, but only a very little at a time. The uneaten food decays and fouls up the aquarium. Chopped lobsters, clams, and shredded beef can be used to give the fish a change of diet.

Feeding Newts. Commonly called salamanders, newts eat raw meat for their diet. When feeding these animals, it is best to transfer them to a small shallow pan of water and feed them in it, then wash them off and replace them in the aquarium. They are quite friendly when you feed them chopped earthworms, liver, or lean beef. Both the liver and beef should be well ground.

Cold-blooded animals, such as fish, newts, snails, etc., can survive for extended periods without food. Small quantities of food should be fed the aquarium animals at frequent times rather than a great amount at longer feeding intervals. Never overfeed.

Patience and gentle handling is all that is required to maintain a successful home aquarium. A diver will find the aquarium grows more and more interesting week after week, and, as his interest grows, so does his aquarium.

Dip-net. A dip-net, which is an essential item in maintaining an aquarium, can be made with a 12-inch dowel, a length of wire (heavy gauge), and a piece of cheesecloth. Drill a 2-inch hole in one end of the dowel, just large enough to hold both strands of wire. Shape the wire in a round or rectangular form, leaving a 2-inch end on each piece and cutting them off square. Using double-ply cheesecloth, fit it to the wire so as to have a 2-inch dip to the net. Cut away all the unnecessary material and sew it to the wire with double-ply thread. Take the dowel and fill the hole with a good glue, then insert the two wire ends and let it dry.

The fish can be removed with this dip-net when the water is changed.

If the aquarium is properly stocked and the animals keep it fairly clean, a water change is needed only about once a year. The water is dipped out by a cup and the fresh water is replaced very slowly so as not to cause the gravel to cloud the water; then the fish are returned after a soft rinse under clean water.

An aquarium is a good hobby for a scientifically-minded diver. Try one and see.

MAPS

Aside from maintaining a fresh-water aquarium, the skin diver and the self-contained diver can add beauty and interest to his den by wall maps on which can be marked the spots where treasure-laden ships went to the bottom.

The International Map Company and the Hammond Map Company will be glad to supply a diver with sectional maps of any part of the world he may desire. Then, purchase or borrow from the local library, Lieutenant H. E. Rieseberg's book, *I Dive for Treasure*. Lieutenant Rieseberg has included a long list of sunken ships which have gone below the waters carrying vast sums of money aboard.

A good map to start with is one depicting the Florida and the West Indies area. For over four hundred years, ships from many nations have gone down in this territory. With a little study and research, your map will have plenty of "X-marks-the-spots" on it. After you have graduated from Florida, try our Great Lakes or the Pacific Coast. A great deal of Alaskan gold has been lost along that rugged coastline.

COLLECTIONS

Divers who use their equipment in salt water, pass over thousands of interesting objects and specimens on each dive into the blue kingdom. In the author's personal den, there are collections of various types of coral displayed in an open case with numerous sections. Each specimen has been classified and properly named. Beside that collection case is one containing many colorful sea shells. There is one plain case, without sections, which displays various types of dried starfish, sand dollars, sea urchins, and sea fans.

Some of the specimens will have to be kept in liquid (*see* Chapter XII). Sea anemones, newts, octopi, squid, and other small animals, plants, and sea life may make up but a very little part of this liquid collection. A diver can add to his own private collection each time he goes below, for the sea has almost unlimited treasure to offer those who choose to study her habits and abundant animal and plant life.

EPILOGUE

Below the waters of the seven seas lies life in such abundance that throughout the life span of this writer not so much as one-hundredth of the sea's great mysteries will ever be known to him or to the inhabitants of this earth-world.

Sitting here thinking about what I have seen of that world below the sea over the short span of fifteen years of diving, and of the primitive equipment I used on those first journeys, our world has progressed almost beyond the scope of man's dreams. Since Captain Cousteau and his friend, Emile Gagnan, gave the world the key which opened the door to another world, thousands of humans have invaded this new world, and hundreds have revealed her long-guarded secrets.

APPENDIX

APPENDIX

Check List of Manufacturers of Diving and Related Products

The firms manufacturing or selling material of interest are listed in the following manner:

Name
Address
City
Code No.

	Code No.
Self-contained Diving Lungs (Compressed Air Scuba);	
Accessories	1
Electronics Equipment	1a
Rubber Frogman Suits	2
Swim Fins, Face Masks, etc.	3
Compressors	4
Welding and Cutting Torches	5
Electrodes	6
Surplus Bomb Hoists	7
Lifting Bags	8
Gaff Hooks, Ropes and Chain	9
Small Rafts and Boats	10
Hand Pumps and Hoses	11
Photographic Equipment	12
Photomicrography Equipment	13
Biological Supplies	14
Pipe Manufacturers	15
Pipe Accessories	15a
Foreign Manufacturers and Dealers	16

All of the firms listed are primarily manufacturers or wholesale suppliers. They will gladly send catalogs to those who are interested. Some firms have a small service charge for their catalogs. The products of the listed firms are available from dealers throughout the world.

Airco Corp.
60 E. 42nd St.
New York, N. Y.   5

Alfa American Corp.
303 West 42nd St.
New York 36, N. Y.   12

American Marietta Co.
Concrete Pipe Div.
101 E. Ontario St.
Chicago 11, Ill.   15

American Optical Co.
Instrument Division
Buffalo, N. Y.   13

American Pipe & Construction Co.
4635 Firestone Blvd.
South Gate, Calif.
    Bulletin #2   15

American Vitrified Products Co.
Pipe Division
Cleveland, Ohio   15

Andrews & Dalton
126 Hanworth Road
Hounslow, Middlesex
England   16

ANSCO
Binghamton, New York   12

Aqua Instrument Co., Inc.
105 S. Townsend St.
Syracuse, New York   1a

Aqua Products Inc.
P. O. Box 384
Toledo, Ohio   4

Aquavision
    (Prescriptions, Lens, Masks)
Coeur d'Alene, Idaho   3

Atlas Equipment and Salvage Co.
229 Southwest Blvd.
Kansas City 8, Mo.   4

Auxima
62 Avenue Emile-Duray
Brussels, Belgium   16

Balcom Trading Co.
Central P.O. 176
Tokyo, Japan   16

Bamboo Reef
584 4th St.
San Francisco, Calif.   12

Bauer-Kompressoren
8 Munich 25
Wolfratshauser Str. 34
West Germany   4

Bausch & Lomb Optical Co.
Rochester, N. Y.   13

Bayley Suit Co.
2408 Meadow Lane
Eureka, Calif.   2

Beaufort Equipment, Ltd.
Beaufort Road
Birkenhead, England   16

Bendix Corp., Marine Div.
8211 Linkershin Blvd.
N. Hollywood, Calif.   1a

Bethlehem Steel Co.
Steel Pipe Div.
Bethlehem, Pa.   15

Bioengionics Co.
8677 Wilshire Blvd.
Beverly Hill, Calif.   3

Bludworth Marine Co.
92 Gold St.
New York 38, N. Y.   12

Brunner Manufacturing Co.
Utica, N. Y.   4

Burleigh Brooks, Inc.
10 West 46th St.
New York 36, N. Y.   12

Buttons, Ltd.
Portland St.
Birmingham, England   16

C. & H. Sales Co.
2176 E. Colorado St.
Pasadena 8, Calif.   4

Canterline Corp.
140 Cedar St.
New York 6, N. Y.   15a

Carbonnel Gimeno S. A.
Dos de Mayo 236
Barcelona, Spain   16

Castello Lopes
Praca Marquez de Pombal 6-1º
Lisbon, Portugal   16

Cast Iron Pipe Research Assn.
122 So. Michigan Ave.
Chicago 3, Ill   15

Celestronics, Inc.
24216 Crenshaw Blvd.
Torrance, Calif.   1a

Central Scientific Company
1700 Erving Park Rd.
Chicago 13, Ill.   13, 14

Century Engineers, Inc.
2741 N. Naomi Street
Burbank, Calif.   12

Chemical Rubber Company
2310 Superior Avenue
Cleveland 14, Ohio   14

James B. Clow & Sons
210-299 N. Talman Ave.
Chicago 80, Ill.   15

Coe-Palm Biological Supply House
1126 Milwaukee Avenue
Chicago 22, Ill.   14

Cogswell & Harrison, Ltd.
167 Piccadilly
London W. 1, England   16

Craftsweld Equipment Corp.
2626 Jackson Ave.
Long Island City 1, N. Y.   5

Dacor Corp.
P. O. Box 551
Evanston, Ill.   1

Dart Aircraft, Ltd.
Market Place
Chalfont St.
Peter, Bucks.,
England   12

Diving Equip. Supply Co.
234 N. Broadway
Milwaukee 2, Wisc.   1

Dresser Manufacturing Div.
319 Fisher Ave.
Bradford, Pa.
   Re: Penstock Pipe   15

Dunlop Sports Co., Ltd.
136-142 Victoria St.
London S. W. 1, England   16

Eddy Valve Co.
Waterford, N. Y.   15a

Ellicott Machine Corp.
1603 Bush St.
Baltimore 30, Md.
   Bulletin - 826   15a

Ellis & Ford Mfg. Co.
Ferndale 20, Mich.
   Re: Pipe Cutters u/w Circul.
   No. 35 - AC   15a

Establissements Meyer Freres
Rue de la Republique
Port-of-France, Martinique   16

F. Paschek Marlier
Casilla 944
Valparaiso, Chile   16

Fenjohn Underwater Photo &
   Equipment Co.
90 Cricket Ave.
Ardmore, Pa.   2, 12

R. Y. Ferner Co.
(Cooke Ltd.)
110 Pleasant St.
Boston 48, Mass.   13

Firma Nimrod
Radio Division
Hollandia Haven, New Guinea   16

Gamma Instrument Co.
Great Neck, N. Y.   13

General Electric Co.
Apparatus Sales Div
1 River Road
Schenectady, N. Y.   6

General Tire & Rubber Co.
Pennsylvania Athletic Products
   Div.
Box 951
Akron, Ohio   3

Golden Anderson Valve
   Specialty Co.
1208 Ridge Ave.
Pittsburgh 33, Pa.
   Bulletin # W-7   15a

Grands Magasins Innovation
Lausanne, Switzerland   16

Gray's of Cambridge
Cambridge, England   16

Carl A. Grutter
Kaiser Wilhelm Strasse 89
Hamburg, Germany   16

Healthways of Los Angeles
3669 - 7th Ave.
Los Angeles 18, Calif.   1, 2, 3, 12

C. E. Heinke & Co., Ltd.
87 Grange Road-Bermondsey
London S. E. 1, England   16

High-Pressure Engr. Co.
P. O. Box 3747
Oklahoma City, Okla.   12

Histoslide Co., Inc.
1133 E. 63rd St.
Chicago 37, Ill.   13

George W. Hoffman Co.
Vibrapipe Div.
Box 452
Sioux City, Iowa   15

Hypro-Dive Equip. Co.
Allston, Massachusetts   8

Ikelite
3361 N. Illinois St.
Indianapolis 8, Ind.   1a

Imagineered Products Corp.
3737 N. 35th St.
Milwaukee, Wisc.   1a

Importex Tahiti
Papeete, Tahiti   16

Ingersoll-Rand Co.
285 Columbia Ave.
Boston 16, Mass.   4

International Undersea Services
Eastern Division
43-45 Maple Street   1, 2, 3, 4,
Brewer, Maine 04412   5, 8, 14

Janus Company
210 Michael Drive
Syosset, Long Island, N. Y.   1a

Johns-Mansville
Transite Pipe Div.
Box 60
New York 16, N. Y.   15

John W. Stang Corp.
Wellpoint Pipe Div.
8221 Atlantic Ave.
Bell, Calif.
  Booklet: Stang Wellpoint System   15

K-G Equipment Co.
Allentown, Pa.   5

Karske OY
Hameenitie 70
Helsinki, Finland   16

Kennedy Valve Mfg. Co.
Elmira, N. Y.
  Bulletin 106   15a

Koppers Co., Inc.
Tar Products Div.
1222-T
Pittsburgh 19, Pa.   15a

La Spirotechnique
27, Rue Trebois
Levallois (Seine), France   16

The Leadite Co.
Girard Trust Co. Bldg.
Philadelphia 2, Pa.   15a

L'Equipment Sous-Marine
47 Rue Georges Rayemaeckers
Brussels, Belgium   16

Leco Engineering Co.
P. O. Box 908
Lincoln, Neb.   4

E. Leitz, Inc.
486 Fourth Ave.
New York 16, N. Y.   13

Guy Lepinay
4 bis, Rue la Victoire
Saint-Denis, France
  (Le Reunion)   16

Lillywhites
Piccadilly Circus
London S. W. 1, England   16

Lincoln Electric Co.
22777 St. Claire Ave.
Cleveland 17, Ohio   6

Lock Joint Pipe Co.
East Orange, N. J.   15

M. & E. Marine Supply Co.
P. O. Box 601
Camden 1, N. J.   9, 10, 11

M & H Valve & Fittings Co.
Anniston, Ala.   15a

Mako Products Inc.
2931 N. E. 2nd Ave.
Miami 37, Florida   4, 12

McWhorter Engineering Co.
1053 Gadsden Rd.
Birmingham, Ala.   12

Mécaniques Reunies
Immeuble Comaty
Rue Nahr
Beyrouth, Lebanon   16

Mesbla, S. A.
Rue de Passeio 42/56
Rio De Janeiro, Brazil   16

Metal & Thermit Corp.
102 East 42nd St.
New York, N. Y.   6

Millard Brothers, Ltd.
Carfin, Lanarkshire
Scotland   16

Mine Safety Appliance Co.
Pittsburgh 8, Pa.   3

Morse Diving Equipment Co.
470 Atlantic Ave.
Boston 10, Mass.   4, 9

Mueller Co.
Tapping Sleeves & Valve Div.
Decatur, Ill.
     Bulletin W-96   15a

National Cylinder Gas Co.
840 N. Michigan Ave.
Chicago, Ill.   5

New England Divers, Inc.
42 Water St.
Beverly, Mass.   1

Normalair Company, Ltd.
Underwater Division
Yeoville, England   1

Och Sport
Behnhofstrasse 56
Zurich, Switzerland   16

Opplem Co., Inc.
352 - 4th Ave.
New York 10, N. Y.   13

Pacific Moulded Products Co.
905 East 59th St.
Los Angeles 1, Calif.   3

Pacific States Cast Iron Pipe Co.
Provo, Utah   15

Palley Supply Co.
2236 E. Vernon Ave
Los Angeles 58, Calif.   7

Parkway Fabricators,
348 Bordentown Ave.
So. Amboy, New Jersey   2

Pennsylvania Athletic Co.
Jeannette, Pa.   2, 3

E. E. Peterson Co.
7055 Eastondale Ave.
Long Beach 5, Calif.   12

Pipe Linings, Inc.
2414 East 223rd St.
Wilmington, Calif.   15a

Precision Optical Co.
4379 Sunset Blvd.
Los Angeles 27, Calif.   13

The Rix Co.
528 Sixth St.
San Francisco 3, Calif.   4

Robinson Clay Products Co.
65 W. State. St.
Akron, Ohio   15a

W. S. Rockwell Co.
2706 Eliot St.
Fairfield, Conn.   15a

Rodolfo Berger
Apartado Postal 2522
Mexico I.D.F., Mexico   16

L. Rondon & Co., Ltd.
French Bank Bldg.
5, Queens Road
Hong Kong, B.C.C.   16

Rose Aviation, Inc.
Aurora, Ohio   1

Sampson-Hall Company
1604 Newport Blvd.
Costa Mesa, Calif.   12

Scubapro Co.
17000 So. Broadway
Gardena, Calif.   1

Scopicon, Inc.
215 E. 149th St.
New York 51, N. Y.   13

Sea-All Corp.
P.O. Box 524
Billerica, Mass.   3

Seahawk Products
P.O. Box 1157
Miami, Fla.   12

Siebe Gorman and Co., Ltd.
Neptune Works-Davis Road
Chessington, Surrey, England   16

Silge & Kuhne Co.
153 Kearney St.
San Francisco 8, Calif.   13

Simplex Valve & Meter Co.
7 E. Orange St.
Lancaster, Pa.
   Bulletin 1202-1200
   Booklet: Prevent Pipe Line
          Rupture   15a

E. T. Skinner & Co. , Ltd.
2 Lochaline St.
London W. 6, England   16

M. B. Skinner Co.
South Bend 21, Ind.
   Cat. GW   15a

A. O. Smith Co.
2619 - 4th St., S.E.
Minneapolis, Minn.   6

Smith Welding Co.
2633-4th St. , S. E.
Minneapolis 14, Minn.   5

Société Air Liquide
1 Rue de Lyon
Algiers, Algeria   16

Société l'Oxygene
10, Rue Sina
Athens, Greece   16

Société Pesche-Sport
Marseilles, France   16

So-Lo Marx Rubber Co.
Loveland, Ohio   2

Sportsways Inc.
7701 E. Compton Blvd.
Paramount, Calif.   1

Stewart Warner Corp.
Cornelius Compressor Division
Indianapolis 7, Ind.   4

Th. Brenni & Co. , Ltd.
Grev. Wedelspi
Oslo, Norway   16

Thompson Engineering Co. (TECO)
Torrance, Calif.   10

Turtox General Biological
   Supply House
8200 South Hoyne Ave.
Chicago 20, Ill.   14

Underwater Photo Service, Inc.
Marathon, Florida   12

Underwater Products
P. O. Box 45903
Westchester, Calif.   2

Underwater Sports, Inc.
2219 Biscayne Blvd.
Miami 37, Fla.   12

Union Liquid Air Company
185 Jeppe St.
Johannesburg, South Africa   16

United Scientific Co.
200 N. Jefferson St.
Chicago 6, Ill.   14

U.S. Concrete Pipe Co.
1500 Union Commerce Bldg.
Cleveland 14, Ohio   15

U. S. Divers Corp.
3323 West Warner Ave.   1, 1a, 2,
Santa Ana, Calif.   3, 12

U.S. Pipe and Foundry Co.
Birmingham 2, Ala.   15

Universal Development Co.
P. O. Box 2195
Newport Beach, Calif.   1a

Victor Equipment Co.
850 Folsom St.
San Francisco, Calif.   5

J. J. Vosatka Assoc.
6115 S. Richmond St.
Chicago, Ill.   1a

The E. H. Wachs Co.
1525 N. Dayton St.
Chicago 22, Ill.
   Re: Pipe Cutters   15a

Ward's Natural Science
   Establishment
3000 River Ridge Rd.
Rochester, N. Y.   14

Warren Foundry & Pipe Co.
55 Liberty St.
New York 5, N. Y.
   Booklet: Warren-Spun Mechanical
   Joint and Pipe Fittings.   15

Watersports
268 Avenue de la Californie
Nice, France   16

Weldit, Inc.
999 Oakman Blvd.
Detroit, Mich.   5

Wellworth Trading Co.
1831 S. State St.
Chicago 16, Ill.   4

Welshes Scientific Co.
1515 Sedgwick St.
Chicago 10, Ill.   14

Westinghouse Electric Co.
Electrodes Div.
P. O. Box 868
Pittsburgh, Pa.   5

Wollman Schmidt Undersea Camera
   & Equipment Co., Inc.
352 Seventh Ave.
New York 1, N. Y.   12

Y-Square Marine Inc.
2001 S. Eastwood St.
Santa Ana, Calif.   1a

Carl Zeiss, Inc.
458 - 5th Ave.
New York, N. Y.   13

Location of Recompression Chambers Under Control of U. S. Navy

East Coast and Atlantic

Boston Naval Shipyard*	Charlestown, Mass.
Charleston Naval Shipyard*	Charleston, S. C.
Deep Sea Diving School (Naval Gun Factory)**	Washington, D. C.
Escape Training Tank (Submarine Base)**	New London, Conn.
Mine Disposal Unit TWO*	Charleston, S. C.
Naval Operating Base*	Trinidad, B. W. I.
Naval Ordnance Station**	Newport, R. I.
Naval Powder Factory**	Indian Head, Md.
Naval School (Ship Salvage)**	Bayonne, N. J.
Naval Station*	Rodman, Canal Zone
Naval Station*	Guantanamo, Cuba
Old Dominion Research & Development Co. *	Erica, Va.
Pier 88, Portsmouth Naval Shipyard*	Kittery, Me.
Submarine Force Vessels (if present) Conway and Escort Piers	Norfolk, Va.
Submarine Force Vessels (if present) Submarine Base or State Pier	New London, Conn.
Submarine Force Vessels (if present) Naval Station	Key West, Fla.
Transport School, Fort Eustis**	near Yorktown, Va.
Underwater Swimmer's School, Naval Station	Key West, Fla.
N. Y. City Health Dept. Metropolitan Hospital	Welfare I., N. Y.
U. D. T. Unit TWO, U. S. N. A. B.	Little Creek, Va.

West Coast and Pacific

Escape Training Tank**	Pearl Harbor, Hawaii
ESSM Pool*	Yokosuka, Japan
Explosive Ordnance Disposal Unit 1*	Pearl Harbor, Hawaii
Fleet Activities*	Sasebo, Japan
Long Beach Naval Shipyard*	Long Beach, Cal.
Mare Island Naval Shipyard*	Vallejo, Cal.
Morris Dam Torpedo Range* Naval Ordnance Test Station	Inyokern, China Lake, Cal.
Naval Air Station (North Island)*	Coronado, Cal.
Naval Operating Base	Adak, Alaska
Naval Station*	San Francisco, Cal.
Naval Station*	Guam
Naval Torpedo Station**	Kayport, Wash.
Puget Sound Naval Shipyard*	Bremerton, Wash.
San Francisco Naval Shipyard (Hunter's Point)*	San Francisco, Cal.
Submarine Force Vessels (if present)	Coronado, Cal.

U. D. T. Unit ONE, Amphibious Base   Coronado, Cal.
Mr. E. R. Cross, 1468 Bay View Avenue,   Wilmington, Cal.
Holmes & Narver Construction Co.,   Eniwetok, S. Pac.
Siebe, Gorman & Co., Ltd.   London, England

U. S. Naval Ships

All commissioned: Auxiliary Rescue and Salvage (ARS)

All commissioned: Auxiliary Submarine Repair (AS)

The above ships are generally located in:

New London, Conn.
New York Area
San Francisco, Cal.
Honolulu, Hawaii
San Diego, Cal.
Norfolk, Va.
Coco Solo, Canal Zone
Seattle, Wash.
Manila, P. I.

* Indicates a chamber having only one compartment and a small medical lock. Once inside, there is no opportunity to come and go. Attendant must remain with the diver for entire decompression.
** Indicates a chamber having two compartments and a small medical lock. It is possible to come and go.
Recompression chambers are found on several types of vessels, such as AS (Submarine Tenders). ASR (Submarine Rescue Vessels), ARS (Repair Ships) and AN (Net Tenders). Security regulations prohibit giving exact locations of ships beyond a Fleet Post Office number. However, it is presumed anyone interested in this subject can learn whether such a vessel is in port if help is needed.

Bibliography

OCEANS - MARINE GEOLOGY AND BIOLOGY - MARINE LIFE

ABBOTT, T., American Sea Shells. Princeton, N. J.; D. Van Nostrand Co., Inc., 1955.

BARNES, H., Oceanography and Marine Biology. New York, N. Y.; The Macmillan Co., 1958.

BUZZATI-TRAVERSE, A. A., Perspectives in Marine Biology. Berkeley, California; University of California Press, 1958.

GUILCHER, A., Coastal and Submarine Morphology. New York, N. Y.; John Wiley and Sons, Inc., 1958.

KEEN, M. A., Sea Shells of Tropical West America. Palo Alto, California; Stanford University Press, 1958.

KUENEN, P. H. Marine Geology. New York, N. Y.; John Wiley and Sons, Inc., 1950.

KUENEN, P. H., Realms of Water: Some Aspects of its Cycle in Nature. New York, N. Y.; John Wiley and Sons, Inc., 1956.

MACGINITIE, G. A., and N., Natural History of Marine Animals. New York, N. Y. McGraw-Hill Book Co., Inc., 1949.

MOORE, H. B., Marine Ecology. New York, N. Y.; John Wiley and Sons, Inc., 1958.

PENCK, W., Morphological Analysis. New York, N. Y.; St. Martin's Press.

RUSSELL, R. C. H., and MACMILLAN, D. H., Waves and Tides. New York, N. Y.; Frederick Warne & Co.

SHEPARD, F. P., Submarine Geology. New York, N. Y.; Harper and Bros., 1948.

SVERDRUP, H. U., and others, The Oceans: Their Physics, Chemistry and General Biology. Englewood Cliffs, N. J., Prentice-Hall, 1942.

TRESSLER, D. K., and LEMON, J. M., Marine Products of Commerce. New York, N. Y.; Reinhold Publishing Corp., 1951.

WALFORD, L. A., Living Resources of the Sea. New York, N. Y.; Ronald Press, 1958.

UNDERWATER PHOTOGRAPHY

CROSS, E. R., Underwater Photography and Television. New York, N. Y.; Exposition Press, 1955.

REBIKOFF, D., and CHERNEY, P., A Guide to Underwater Photography. New York, N. Y.; Greenberg, Publisher., 1955.

SCHENCK, H., and KENDALL, H., Underwater Photography. Cambridge, Maryland; Cornell Maritime Press, 1957. (The finest book covering underwater photography.)

PHOTOMICROGRAPHY

BEISER, A., A Guide to the Microscope. New York, N. Y.; E. P. Dutton and Co., Inc., 1957.

GAGE, S. H., Microscope - 17th Ed. Ithaca, N. Y.; Comstock Publishing Co.

SHILLABER, C. P., Photomicrography in Theory and Practice. New York, N. Y.; John Wiley and Sons, Inc., 1944.

SHIP SALVAGE

BRADY, E. M., Marine Salvage Operations. Cambridge, Maryland; Cornell Maritime Press, October 1959.

WHEELER, G. J., Ship Salvage. New York, N. Y.; Edward W. Sweetman & Co., 1958.

DIVING

BROOKES, G. F. , and BROADHURST, A. , Underwater Diving Manual.
Newton Centre, Massachusetts; Chas. T. Branford Co. , 1961.

CARRIER, R. and B. , Dive: Complete Book of Skin Diving. New York, N. Y. ;
Wilfred Funk, Inc. , 1955.

CAYFORD, J. E. , Skin & Scuba Diving. New York, N. Y. ; Fawcett Inc. , 1963.

CAYFORD, J. E. , and SCOTT, R. E. , Underwater Logging. Cambridge, Md. ;
Cornell Maritime Press, Inc. , 1965.

Conference for National Co-operation in Aquatics, Science of Skin and Scuba
Diving. New York, N. Y. ; Association Press, 1957.

DAVIS, R. H. , Deep Diving and Submarine Operations: A Manual for Compressed
Air Workers and Deep Sea Divers. London (Distributed in the U. S. A. by U. S.
Diver's Corp. , Los Angeles, California), 1955.

LONSDALE A. , and KAPLAN, H. , A Guide To Sunken Ships In American Waters.
Arlington, Va. ; Compass Publications, Inc. , 1965.

OWEN, D. , Manual for Free Divers Using Compressed Air. New York, N. Y. ;
Pergamon Press, Inc. , 1955.

ROBERTS, F. , Basic Scuba. Princeton, N. J. ; Van Nostrand, 1960.

SCHENCK, H. , and KENDALL, H. , Shallow Water Diving and Spearfishing,
2nd Edition. Cambridge, Maryland; Cornell Maritime Press, 1954.

U. S. NAVY, Diving Manual. Washington, D. C. ; Superintendent of Documents,
U. S. Government Printing Office, 1959.

TAILLIEZ, P. , Complete Manual of Free Diving. New York, N. Y. ; G. P.
Putnam's Sons, 1957.

UNDERWATER CUTTING AND WELDING

THOMPSON, F. A. , Diving Cutting and Welding in Underwater Salvage Operations.
Cambridge, Maryland; Cornell Maritime Press, 1944 (Out of Print). An excellent book that may be located through second-hand book dealers.

U. S. NAVY, Underwater Cutting Manual. Washington, D. C. ; Supt. of Documents,
U. S. Government Printing Office, 1958.

In addition, the following books contain information on this subject:

SCHENCK and KENDALL, Shallow Water Diving and Spearfishing.

DAVIS, Deep Diving and Submarine Operations.

BRADY, Marine Salvage Operations.

The following government bureaus are a source of valuable bulletins.

Office of Naval Research
Washington 25, D. C.

United States Beach Erosion Board
Washington 25, D. C.

U. S. Coast and Geodetic Survey
Washington 25, D. C.

United States Corps. of Engineers
Map Division (Cartography)
Washington 25, D. C.

U. S. Fish and Wildlife Service
Dept. of the Interior
Washington 25, D. C.

U. S. Geological Survey
Washington 25, D. C.

U. S. Hydrographic Office
Washington 25, D. C.

U. S. N. Underwater Sound Laboratory
Washington 25, D. C.

Naval Research Laboratory
Potomac River Naval Command
Washington 25, D. C.

INDEX